The
Corrupt Kingdom

THE RISE AND FALL
OF THE UNITED MINE WORKERS

JOSEPH E. FINLEY

SIMON AND SCHUSTER · NEW YORK

SBN 671-21375-X
LIBRARY OF CONGRESS CATALOG CARD NUMBER: 72-83928
DESIGNED BY EVE METZ
MANUFACTURED IN THE UNITED STATES OF AMERICA
BY THE BOOK PRESS, BRATTLEBORO, VT.

FOR
SCOTT AND SONIA AND JOANNE
GREAT TEACHERS ALL

Contents

Foreword

Labor and workers and CIO were words that inspired many young men and women in the Roosevelt era and through World War II days. Unions were the hope of those years for a progressive, democratic America. Many young idealists, intellectuals and lawyers committed their talents to a cause they considered just, much in the same manner that later generations worked for racial equality and the eradication of poverty.

The union that won the respect, admiration, and even awe of all of us was the United Mine Workers of America. The achievements of John L. Lewis in organizing the CIO and industrial America were not greatly dimmed by his political aberration in 1940 of opposing our other hero, Franklin D. Roosevelt. When Lewis and the UMW fought stubbornly for economic justice after World War II was ended, most of us applauded. When the Mine Workers created their magnificent Welfare and Retirement Fund to heal the bodies of men who went underground, we believed indeed that our faith had been justified.

Then came the quiet years. There were no more strikes, no more turbulence, no more of the brilliant phrasemaking of John L. Lewis. We did begin to hear that Lewis was the savior of the coal industry, that he had become a "labor statesman," a troubling label indeed for any man who seeks to maintain the welfare of his constituents.

Doubt and dismay were soon to follow. As a lawyer, I read the court decisions telling of vast damage verdicts in Tennessee and Kentucky against the UMW, which raised serious and troubling questions about the bloody violence there and what it meant. Not until the 1969 campaign of Jock Yablonski against incumbent UMW president Tony Boyle was there much national interest paid to what had once been proclaimed as America's greatest labor union.

Then Yablonski was murdered. The brutality of it, the senseless slaying of his wife and daughter, the immediate awareness that it had to be linked to his campaign for the presidency of the UMW—all helped to shatter the last illusions. Then, a personal note entered. Murder suspects out of Cleveland, Ohio, were soon apprehended. The federal prosecutor in charge of the investigation was my recent law partner, Robert B. Krupansky, now a federal district judge. Our family housekeeper's son, who had played with my oldest boy on occasion, had lived as a tenant in the home of Paul and Annette Gilly, prime suspects in the murder. One of my old legal adversaries and a good friend, Robert J. Rotatori, was associated with the defense of the Gillys. Another old and admired friend in Washington, Joseph L. Rauh, Jr., had represented and fought for the murdered Jock Yablonski. All of these factors made an inquiry into the UMW a matter of intense concern, personally, professionally, historically. What had caused this once great union, which so many of us had admired, to descend to its apparent level of utter corruption and murder?

Then the work began. There was a search into old archives which uncovered the inspiring story of Daniel Weaver, the first leader of coal miners in America. After a time there came the days of Lewis, both disappointing and great, raising new questions about the character of leadership in organizations that men create. The law was a useful compendium too, extremely helpful in unraveling what had happened both to the union and to its once revered Welfare and Retirement Fund. The Boyle-Yablonski campaign, the murder and its aftermath, and the rise of the rebel movement inside the UMW—all combined to make what appeared to be a classic story of man's conduct.

It goes far beyond labor unions, even though it comprehends the UMW. It is more realistically a study of how men behave inside their own organizations when powerful leaders assume command and deify themselves through strength and accomplishment. Its parallels are everywhere in all of man's political, social and economic institutions.

The tragedies of the United Mine Workers are not those of most of America's unions, who still fulfill their function of representing their membership as a part of our self-interest society. They must have their advocates, upholding and maintaining their positions, as full partners in our adversary system. While much of the bloom of early idealism may have dissipated, as is the case in all of mankind's crusading ventures, the other unions go on, standing for their constituents with their own particular strengths and human weaknesses.

There are always the appreciations: to Joe Rauh and Chip Yablonski for their assistance and information, to Congressman Ken Hechler for his helpfulness, to men like Dr. Donald Rasmussen, Bill Savitsky, and the late Gus Scholle for their willingness to give valuable time, and to my wife, Joanne, for her constant encouragement. Many, many others helped along the way, some of them not aware of their contributions. Writing this book was a labor of love and learning; may it leave some insights into what men may predictably do when restraints and rules are obliterated.

JOSEPH E. FINLEY

1. Politics and Poetry

THE ARCH IS FORMED

It was a time of turmoil that seemed to affect the entire nation. A new man from Illinois had been elected to the Presidency. South Carolina had withdrawn from the Union. The country's confidence in money was evaporating. The economists could call it by any name, but dollars were scarce and tight, and with all the uncertainty, there seemed to be a rush everywhere to retrench.

And, as always, men were hurt. Industry had spread westward to the gateway city of St. Louis. There were mills and factories and foundries to compete with the interests of the traders and trappers and Forty-Niners who embarked for the mountains and plains and the lure of gold. The manufacturers of St. Louis had found coal, the new fuel of their time, and it worked well in the furnaces they stoked.

There was a great abundance of it across the river to the east, in Illinois. Men who knew coal started hacking it from outcroppings in Illinois hillsides before 1840, when there was little need for it in the West. Ten years later, there were coal mines functioning in the state. There was more and more of it than the imagination could conceive. As the coal burners used more, the mines grew. As the mines multiplied and more coal went across the Mississippi, new entrepreneurs were encouraged to use the new fuel that was already supplying the Eastern factories from the Pennsylvania fields and spurring industry in the Middle West from the vast deposits in Ohio and the western parts of Pennsylvania.

There had to be men to do the mining. English coal diggers, tired of the conditions that depressed their lives, had joined the masses of immigrants who were coming to the United States. Many of them went to the new anthracite fields in Pennsylvania; and others, along with the Welsh and the Scottish diggers, went westward to the Alleghenies and across into Ohio. There was an awareness of the deposits under Illinois, too, and it attracted another host of men, who behaved like thousands of immigrants before and after by seeking out the same work they had hoped to escape.

By 1860, there were seventy-three mines in Illinois, many of them rudimentary diggings near the surface. The census figures of those days reported that 1,430 men were working at this new trade. In St. Clair County, across from St. Louis, the largest and most successful mines worked for the Missouri market. The economic slump after the election of Lincoln slowed the pace of general production in St. Louis and made its impact on the mine operators in the St. Clair fields. State banks in Illinois were selling their dollar notes for eighty cents, and others were passing their paper for a half dollar.

There was for the miners in late 1860 a standard pay rate of 2½ cents for each bushel they could pry loose from the earth. This was the measurement of the day; eighty pounds to the bushel and twenty-five bushels to the ton—if a man could get a fair weight. A fast man with a pick was supposed to do a hundred bushels, said the operators. The miners argued that the output was far less than that, and when they paid for their tools and their powder, and lost arguments on the weights, they had so little left for the long hours in the shafts that it meant hard times for them.

The downturn hit harder with the new year and wound up with the dubious label of "secession depression." The coal operators told the men before Christmas that their rate would be cut to 2¼ cents per bushel. There was grumbling in every pit, but no action. The operators then took stock again, and in early January, 1861, they made another announcement. The new rate was now down to an even two pennies.

In the sixteen coal mines in St. Clair County, men simply stopped working. Where it began and who sounded the first call are unknown to the searchers of history. Like a different movement a hundred years later in Alabama, where Rosa Parks was "too tired" to move to the back of the bus, men apparently had run out of subservience. The two weekly newspapers of Belleville, the county seat, told of fist fights in two of the mines, as tempers, passions and words began to move coal miners.

In a few days, there was not a bushel moving. Every mine in St. Clair County was down, as the word went from pit to pit. There was need for a leader, as in every movement when people begin to act together for a common purpose. Every eruption in events seems to produce one, as if by mystical planting, and the miners found an eloquence they never knew existed in their corner of Illinois.

Daniel Weaver had come from Staffordshire in England and had followed the paths of the miners in his new country. He brought a wife and two children with him, sometime in the 1840's, stopping first in the anthracite fields in Pottsville, Pennsylvania. He moved to the Mahoning Valley in Ohio, among the Welsh miners, and then picked up again for Illinois. He taught himself, and everywhere he read voraciously. Weaver talked with miners as he moved westward, and after he had been in Illinois long enough to be called an "old-time resident," he was known as the most learned man in the mines.

Weaver and others called meetings in Belleville, and the miners gathered. He stood before them, neatly dressed, smooth-shaven down to the chin whiskers that were so common in those years. Weaver had a finely chiseled face and the perceptive stare of a professor, with alert, lively eyes. He had prepared a document for the miners and was ready with it when they came to the first meeting.

He started it with a poem.

It came from the Scottish poet Charles Mackay, whose works were first published in England in 1846, sometime around the years when Weaver emigrated to the United States. It was particularly appropriate for Weaver, from its title, "What Might Be Done," to the message he wished to give to the men.

What Might Be Done
What might be done if men were wise—
What glorious deeds, my suffering brother,
Would they unite,
In love and right,
And cease their scorn for one another.

Oppression's heart might be imbued
With kindling drops of loving-kindness,
And knowledge pour,

From shore to shore,
Light on the eyes of mental blindness.

All slavery, warfare, lies and wrongs,
All vice and crime might die together;
And wine and corn,
To each man born,
Be free as warmth in summer weather.

What might be done? This might be done,
And more than this, my suffering brother—
And more than the tongue
Ever said or sung,
If men were wise and loved each other.

After the poem was read, Weaver unfolded one of the most re-markable essays ever delivered to associations of men. It has been reprinted in every story of the miners' union and in many other source books of the labor movement. Its 1861 message carries the permanence of truth. No American workingman has ever chronicled the standards of union men with higher goals or nobler purposes. Its argument for a union inspired coal miners of many generations and, hopefully, will again some day.

After the Mackay poem, Weaver said that the necessity of an association of miners had been felt by "the thinking portion of the miners generally." Then he went on to say,

Union is the great fundamental principle by which every object of importance is to be accomplished. Man is a social being and, if left to himself in an isolated condition, would be one of the weakest creatures; but, associated with his kind, he works wonders. Men can do jointly what they cannot do singly; and the union of minds and hands, the concentration of their power, becomes almost omnipotent. Nor is this all; men not only accumulate power by union, but gain warmth and earnestness. There is an electric sympathy kindled, and the attractive forces inherent in human nature are called into action, and a stream of generous emotion, of friendly regard for each other, binds together and animates the whole.

Weaver pointed out that men formed societies to accomplish every purpose, from the organizing of armies to the establishing of railroads, banks and "sick societies." Then,

> Does it not behoove us, as miners, to use every means to elevate our position in society, by reformation of character, by obliterating all personal animosities and frivolous nationalities . . . and striving for the attainment of pure and high principles and generous motives, which will fit us to bear a manly, useful and honorable part in the world?

He stressed that unity was essential, and then his address concluded:

> In laying before you, therefore, the objects of this association, we desire it to be understood that our objects are not merely pecuniary, but to mutually instruct and improve each other in knowledge, which is power; to study the laws of life; the relation of Labor to Capital; politics, municipal affairs, literature, science, or any other subject relating to the general welfare of our class. Has not experience and observation taught us what one of the profoundest thinkers of the present day has said, that "all human interests, and combined human endeavors, and social growth in this world, have, at certain stages of their developments, required organizing; and Labor—the grandest of human interests—requires it now. There must be an organization of Labor; to begin with it straightway, to proceed with it, and succeed in it more and more." One of America's immortals said, "To me there is no East, no West, no North, no South," and I would say, let there be no English, no Irish, Germans, Scotch or Welsh. This is our country, and
> "All men are brethren—how the watch-words run!
> And when men act as such is justice won."
> Come, then, and rally around the standard of Union—the union of States and the unity of miners, and with honesty of purpose, zeal and watchfulness; the pledge of success—unite for the emancipation of our labor, and the regeneration and elevation physically, mentally and morally, of our species.

Weaver's words met warm response from miners who were coping with the first work crisis of their lives. A strike was a new experience.

There had been only a few in the country's short history, and this was surely the first one outside the industrial areas of the East. That January night in 1861 when Daniel Weaver read poetry and delivered words of inspiration to the strikers, the first national union of mine workers was begun.

The strike was won. An enthusiastic Weaver wrote a victory message three weeks later to the Belleville *Democrat*. It was marked with brevity and joy.

> EDITOR, DEMOCRAT—Dear Sir: I am happy to inform you that our "strike" is terminated, and the issue is successful; the Bosses have met us today, and conceded all we required, and we have agreed to resume work forthwith. Hurrah for union.
>
> D. WEAVER, *Secr'y*

Then came the work of building the union. An eloquent Irishman named Boyle was sent by Weaver and his companions to visit other Illinois mines. They called him a "lecturer," and he told the miners to form lodges and join the union. By late March, Boyle's "lectures" were so successful that Weaver reported "upwards of five hundred members," including German immigrants along with the *émigrés* from the British Isles.

But it was Weaver who kept the goals of knowledge and unity alive. He wrote regularly to the two Belleville newspapers, whose apparent sympathies with the strikers made them the channels of communication in the area. He wrote weekly, like an earlier-day Publius, both reporting on events and setting forth his concepts of trade-unionism. He cautioned against excessive use of strikes. He acknowledged the rights of the employers. With an evangelistic fervor, he appealed for unity and justice.

He made a reference to heroes and issues from Washington to Confucius to the Dred Scott decision and then wrote, "No one, I think, who has been enraptured with the beauties of an Irving, a Bryant, a Willis, a Whittier, a Taylor, a Poe, to say nothing of the heroes and demigods of the Old World, can ever waste his time in low and degrading pursuits." He preached knowledge as power and urged the miners to read and learn.

The Miners Association spread into northern Illinois and into

Ohio and western Pennsylvania. Weaver withdrew to start his own mine, but continued to give advice and assistance to the leaders who came after him. A weekly newspaper was begun in 1863, and it became a prosperous and influential journal under a talented editor named Hinchcliffe, who was also an Illinois lawyer. Hinchcliffe announced its publication by stating:

> It will be devoted to Family Literature, Agriculture, Social Science, General Knowledge, and the Current News of the day. It will contain full reports of the state of the Markets and Commerce generally. As an advertising Medium it will possess peculiar advantages, circulating as it must, among a class of consumers who are cash customers. It will be the advocate of no partisan schemes, but will fearlessly expose wrongs, no matter by whom they are perpetrated, while the Right will be upheld and defended, irrespective of partisanship, at all hazard.

As the new organization grew in size and influence, the expected counterattack from the employers began. Another successful strike in the Belleville fields in early 1863 brought the operators together in a Chicago meeting. They unfolded a resolution, too. While less poetic than Weaver's manifesto, it set forth a blunt employer position that became familiar in American industry for nearly a century and still finds fashion in some parts of the country today. The "conspiracy" of the miners could lead only to their "impoverishment." "The coal operators will not acknowledge or deal with any association of miners whatsoever, but will hire and discharge individuals, as the exigencies of the business and the conduct of those individuals may compel them to do."

In addition to a notice that wages would be paid as the market would "authorize," there was a further resolution that in every contract with an individual miner, there would be a clause forbidding him to be a member of any "Association of Miners." This was one of the first recorded versions of what later became notorious in labor history as the "yellow-dog" contract.

With a scarcity of miner manpower due to the Civil War, the Association continued to score. By 1864, another of its frequent conventions turned to the serious business of adopting a new and permanent constitution to supplant the general rules brought over from

English society. The cover page, printed by the *Weekly Miner,* paid
its tribute to the absent Daniel Weaver by inscribing the slogan,
"Union is Strength—Knowledge is Power."

Then, another poem familiar to the miners was inscribed in the
center of the cover of the constitution for all to see:

Step by step, the longest march
    Can be won, can be won;
Single stones will form an arch,
    One by one, one by one.
And, by union, what we will
Can be all accomplished still.
Drop of water turn a mill,
Singly none, singly none.

When the war ended in 1865, the operators were able to give full
attention to the doctrines of their Chicago resolution, adopted two
years earlier. A company town in Pennsylvania was the first testimonial to the power of the employers. The union was told to get out,
and four thousand men, women and children were summarily evicted
from the company houses in an announced effort to smash the Association and eliminate every person who had been a member. After a
five-month lockout, the union was finished in Pennsylvania.

It began to lose in other areas too, as the pressure and power of
the employers reached into every part of mining-town society. A
wage cut in the Mahoning Valley in the summer of 1865 brought a
strike that turned into another disaster. When the men went back to
the pits, they not only worked at the lower rate but were compelled
to give up their union as a necessary condition. By 1868, the American Miners Association, the first national union in the coal fields, was
almost totally destroyed. Remnants survived in the Belleville area,
and scattered local unions in other parts of the United States kept a
dormant existence, sustained by the dreams of Weaver and the memories of wartime successes.

Another miner of vision and determination rose to pick up the
pieces. In the anthracite fields of northeast Pennsylvania, John Siney,
like Weaver, wrote letters to newspapers, defending the goals of the
local unions he was organizing. In 1869, he too built upon a success-

ful strike to weld a struggling organization together. In 1873, Siney called for a convention in Youngstown, Ohio, to form another national union. He started his call with a quest often used by a prominent leader of our time, who, unfortunately, was never able to make it work as well as it sounded.

"Come and reason together," Siney wrote. "Form an organization in which brother will be pledged to brother, an organization which will form a bulwark alike in the day of prosperity and adversity. Will you do so, or do you prefer to occupy your present unenviable position? The answer and the issue are in your hands."

Siney, whose learning and aspirations approached those of Daniel Weaver, became a tireless advocate of the new union, which was called the Miners National Association of the United States. He was its only president. At its second convention in 1874, he faced the results of the depression of 1873, which had caused wage cuts and layoffs throughout the coal fields. Mineowners were compelling workmen to put their signatures on yellow-dog contracts if they wanted to keep working. "Sign them," said Siney. "Sign them on the same grounds Galileo took before the Inquisition, exclaiming, 'But it does move after all!' "

As Siney struggled to hold his new union together, the operators turned to the law to try to eliminate him. He and one of his organizers, Xingo Parks, were indicted by a western Pennsylvania grand jury for violation of the criminal-conspiracy law of the Commonwealth. The charge was founded upon an ancient legalism transported from English common law that combination of men in a union to raise wages was unlawful. The only evidence at the trial consisted of speeches, printed documents, and the constitution of the union.

Two of the country's most renowned lawyers came to Siney's defense. Matthew Carpenter of Wisconsin and Benjamin Butler of Massachusetts traveled to the courtroom in Clearfield, Pennsylvania, for the trial. The coal operators responded by bringing in United States Senator William A. Wallace of Pennsylvania to head the prosecution team. It became a slightly more civilized version of the Scopes trial in Tennessee half a century later. Great crowds filled the courthouse area, and the thundering orations of the legal gladiators were spread across the country by newspaper report.

The passionate defense plea to the jury was to attack the ancient conspiracy law that had long since been repealed in England. The argument closed with these words: "If you convict John Siney and Xingo Parks under this law, will it be, in the minds of a reading and intelligent public, John Siney or Xingo Parks, or the county of Clearfield and the State of Pennsylvania that is disgraced? This I leave to you, gentlemen of the jury, by your verdict to decide."

The prosecution knew its grounds, too. Senator Wallace met the defense attack head on and closed his final summation:

> Shall this court and this jury fear to punish these men for a criminal violation of our law because the counsel for the defense says our law is old? Setting aside the provision which makes it a crime to combine for the purpose stated, if that could be done, and it cannot be done, every state in the Union has a conspiracy law, also a law which makes riot a crime. By the testimony those men, John Siney and Xingo Parks, did assist, in this combination of miners, for the purpose of raising wages, and it is your bounden duty under the provision of the law to bring in a verdict of guilty.

Law and order of a century ago hewed reasonably close to the issues. The timeless conflict of man's quest for freedom of expression was committed against society's desire for order, and in this case, it was the order of the operators who were seeking to stamp out the dissent of the men who worked for them. The jury came back with a verdict of not guilty for Siney, but found against Parks on one count of inciting to riot. Cheering miners carried Siney on their shoulders into the streets of Clearfield.

But the depression and the ceaseless war of the operators wrecked Siney's union. He closed the national office in Cleveland in 1876, refusing to accept contributions to pay for the past salary that was owed him. One of his last efforts was to go to Tennessee to try to buy coal lands to start a cooperative mine where blacklisted union leaders could come and work their own pits. Siney, like Weaver, remains one of the most heroic figures in the story of man's struggle in America to create and build organizations of people to work together for their own advancement.

But there were still miners' unions in existence in local areas. New leaders arose constantly. New assemblies under the Knights of Labor were formed. Ohio miners tried to put together another national union in 1883. There was steady progress, even among rival factions, and another national convention was called for Columbus, Ohio, in 1890. Strong men had emerged again, and the cry was "Unity!" Rivals shook hands, pounded one another on the back, agreed upon a constitution, and swore allegiance to a new organization, put together out of the original pieces started by Daniel Weaver and John Siney.

They called it the United Mine Workers of America. The arch was formed.

The first constitution was an emergence of practicality over poetry. Brotherhood was relegated to a lesser role than that of economics. Proper earnings were placed first among the objects of the new organization. A second goal was safety—"To reduce to the lowest possible minimum the awful catastrophes which have been sweeping our fellow craftsmen to untimely graves by the thousands." There was a demand for an eight-hour day, and a plea for laws to prevent children under fourteen from working in the mines. This was phrased in terms of providing for their proper education rather than the sheer inhumanity of working children underground. There was a final aim of labor peace by arbitration and conciliation, "that strikes may become unnecessary."

Yet the new union flourished on the spirit of Weaver and Siney. Siney's story, of more recent origin, was particularly impressed upon some of the men who participated in the founding convention at Columbus and who later wrote the early histories of the United Mine Workers of America. Chris Evans, who wrote an "official" two-volume story of the union in World War I days, had worked with Siney, and he wrote of him in ecstatic terms. Evans also wrote of Weaver's efforts with the same impressions.

One of the principal architects of the Columbus unification was John McBride, who later became the only man to defeat Samuel Gompers in a contest for the presidency of the American Federation of Labor. McBride was the consummate politician who wooed the rival factions into agreement. He was one of the chief draftsmen of the document of practicality, but it was Weaver's inspiration that moved him. In published works in 1888, even before he could visualize the Columbus merger, it was McBride who put into print the story of Weaver and the American Miners Association. His proudest quotations were from Weaver's January 28, 1861, address to the Belleville strikers. In the preamble to the 1890 constitution, McBride's influence contributed to these opening words:

> There is no fact more generally known, nor more widely believed, than that without coal there would not have been any such grand achievements, privileges and blessings as those which characterize the nineteenth-century civilization, and believing as we do, that those whose lot it is to daily toil in the recesses of the earth, mining and putting out this coal which makes these blessings possible, are entitled to a fair and equitable share of the same.

The practical political workmen like John McBride and John B. Rae, a heavily bearded, somber Scotsman from the Knights of Labor, who became the union's first president, were shortly succeeded by another young idealist under whose leadership the union emerged into a significant force in America's economic life. John Mitchell, at the age of twenty-nine, was elected the union's president in 1899. He too was more poet than politician, but his idealism, combined with driving energy, caught the imagination of both the miners and the nation.

Mitchell moved quickly into a major strike in the anthracite fields in Pennsylvania, where the union was struggling to stay alive. He walked among the Pennsylvania miners preaching the brotherhood of Daniel Weaver. "The coal you dig isn't Slavish or Polish or Irish coal. It's just coal." He turned to the British-born miners and their American descendants to warn them against slurs about "hunks" and "dagoes." He went into Scranton and Wilkes-Barre and talked to Hungarians and Italians, supported by Bishop Hoban of Scranton and Father Curran of Wilkes-Barre, early leaders of the Catholic clergy in labor's fights to organize.

Mitchell told them of the early origins of the union in Illinois and of the concepts of Weaver that there were no English or Irish or German miners, but that all men were indeed "brethren." His fight to stamp out divisiveness and hostility among miners was a vital prelude to winning against the operators. The Italian miners quickly adopted as their slogan, "Johnny da Mitch will win."

He marshaled the nation's intellectuals to fight in his behalf. He talked to liberals in the cities and sought out newspaper editors to tell them the miners' story. He had men like Robert Ingersoll, Henry Demarest Lloyd and John Graham Brooks lending their talents and influence to the cause, somewhat like the latter-day Cesar Chavez enlisting the aid of a national conscience to support California grape pickers. He brought lawyer Clarence Darrow into the defense of the union and wooed President Theodore Roosevelt into forcing the coal operators into the nation's first great arbitration before the Anthracite Coal Commission in 1903.

Mitchell and Darrow worked as a team in the long hearings before the Commission. When George Baer, the most lordly of the operators, denounced the union, there was Darrow to respond. "The unions," said Baer, "are corrupting the children of America by letting them join their illegal organizations." Said Darrow, "If the children had not been at work in the mines they could not have joined the union."

Mitchell was the witness and Darrow the advocate. The fight for better working conditions and shorter hours brought out a final plea from Darrow that blended the aspirations of Weaver, Siney, and Mitchell into a moving statement of the miners' cause. "The laborer who asks for shorter hours, asks for a breath of life; he asks for a chance to develop the best that is in him. It is no answer to say, 'If you give him shorter hours he will not use them wisely.' Our country, our civilization, our race is based upon the belief that for all his weaknesses there is still in man that divine spark that will make him reach upward for something higher and better than anything he has known."

By 1903, the union had attained a membership of 175,000, and a treasury of a million dollars. When Mitchell was forced out five years later, membership had reached 263,000, far more than fill the rolls in 1972. But Mitchell's triumphs were assailed from his own ranks as not enough. The growth of the union brought factionalism and personal rivalries that mark man's social behavior in every scene, and pressures and enemies taxed the young man's health. There was a gentle softness about John Mitchell, with few of the attributes of the iron will of some of the men who came after him. He was the compromiser, he studied all sides, he even admonished Darrow not to make "Socialist speeches."

Mitchell, in poor physical condition, resigned under fire at the

1908 convention. He poured his vision into a farewell speech that brought tears to the delegates. He told stories of the suffering of children in the mines and begged the men to fight for a sixteen-year minimum-age law. He talked about what machinery would do to men in the years ahead, and talked about the laws that were necessary to safeguard lives. His farewell became so emotional that even Big Bill Haywood, himself a fiery delegate, and a scornful foe of Mitchell's moderate policies, came forward to grasp his hand. He left the hall with the miners chanting, "God bless you, John."

The United Mine Workers of America, created out of a combination of the poetic aspirations of men like Weaver, Siney and Mitchell, and the political practicalities of men like John McBride, John B. Rae, and others less well known, became one of the most remarkable institutions of men in American history. Its creation and initial growth was similar to that of the young country in its maturing and conflicts. Both union and nation emerged out of intolerable conditions. Both battled established rulers. There was a dream and a vision in the founding of both. The union had Weaver's knowledge, brotherhood, and belief in the betterment of the soul; the nation had the unalienable rights of Jefferson and the analytic discourses of a Madison. Even the ultimate unifications were comparable, from the scattered union localities to the separate conflicting colonies. Weaver himself drew the parallel over a hundred years ago when he exhorted the miners to, "Come, then, and rally around the standard of union—the union of states and the unity of miners."

It established its own government, a kingdom within a kingdom. It exerted a compelling influence over the lives of the men who joined it, and its power in later years was enough to force a confrontation with the country. It produced estimable leaders, of whom the redoubtable John L. Lewis will always stand foremost. One of its early founders, William B. Wallace, became the first Secretary of Labor of the United States, in Woodrow Wilson's cabinet. It spawned the presidents of labor federations like William Green and Philip Murray. Some of its men were elected to high offices in state governments, and others filled the legislatures. These were men who came out of the pits, as did John Mitchell and John L. Lewis, both of whom worked as children in Midwestern coal mines.

The United Mine Workers of America, led by Lewis, and with its

money, power and influence, remade the American labor movement
in the 1930's. Its lieutenants formed the cadres that created the Congress of Industrial Organizations, built the United Automobile Workers and started the United Steelworkers, two of the most powerful
industrial unions of today. Its achievement in creating a health and
welfare fund was the beginning of the restructuring of American social security, as health care, hospitalization, medical benefits, and
pensions were brought to workingmen everywhere as a result of the
examples set by the United Mine Workers.

In the strikes of World War II it produced a unity of human beings
that has hardly been equaled in any story of people. Despite the fury
of a nation at war, coal miners followed the leadership word of
John L. Lewis to a man. It was not at all the dictatorial power of a
single leader in that instance that dominated, as so many mistakenly
tried to portray, but a unification of thousands of men into one. The
pressures of a Franklin D. Roosevelt, who was both loved and admired by the miners despite the antagonisms of Lewis, the condemnation of all the opinion makers, the angers of a citizen army—none
could move the solidarity of these men who believed their economic
cause was just.

One of the few similar examples that come to mind is the behavior
of the British people during the bombing raids over London in the
same wartime years. The English psychiatrist Anthony Storr wrote
of that experience:

> Faced with a common enemy, whether this be flood or fire or a
> human opponent, we become brothers in a way which never obtains
> in ordinary life. Londoners who are old enough to recall 1940 will
> remember the increased warmth they both showed towards, and
> received from, their fellow-men after exposure to a night's bombing;
> and there are many who look back to the days of the blitz with
> nostalgia, as is evidenced by the eagerness with which, even after a
> quarter of a century, they are prepared to recall those sleepless
> nights and smoking dawns.

What could produce this kind of unity among coal miners? How
was it that they among few American workingmen caught the spirit
of Weaver, Siney and Mitchell, and created a union of men at a time
when law gave their antagonistic employers an open hunting season
on their aspirations, when any man could be fired for even thinking

union? Without a special skill to sell, like the carpenter or bricklayer, a surviving union of workingmen was a near-impossibility for so many struggling groups. Yet this one of all others became the premier of trade-unions.

Coal—dirty, dusty black rocks of the earth—and the way it was taken from the ground, surely provided part of the answer. The dangers every man faced moved him nearer to brotherhood, as Storr's analysis of the British bombing experience suggests. There was in the pits a special kind of gloom that produced the need of one man to "sense" another, and perhaps accounted for the spontaneity of the 1861 Belleville strike that started a union and brought forth a Daniel Weaver.

But there were also drabness and desolation in the shabby mining towns where the people lived. The atmosphere was stultifying enough to stamp out any creative instinct, but perhaps it played a dual, sometimes conflicting, function in their lives. While it produced despair on the one hand, it brought resolution for improvement on the other. Both emotions, combined with the unity of peril, stoked with politics and poetry, were powerful ingredients in the success of the United Mine Workers of America. And when there were men who cared—like Johnny da Mitch, and even the rumbling giant of a Lewis in his own way—who could touch the spirit of men in the mines, then there was something for which to live.

Coal, and the way it has been mined in later years, also may have made its contribution to developments that have made this organization something far different from the visions of the dreamers who started it. Automation came into the mines a long time ago, but became a dominant force only in the present generation. The pick miner and his mule have been replaced by monstrous machines.

There is a contraption of man that stands three stories high, weighs more than a million and a half pounds, and is called Push-Button Miner. Three men can operate it by remote control from a panel outside the mine shaft, never requiring their presence underground. This mechanical giant can rip and pull 266 tons of coal an hour from the earth, without drilling or blasting. The men who push the buttons can even sit in an air-conditioned cab and do it.

There is another machine, which does go underground, called a twin-borer continuous miner; it can pass out coal to a conveyor at the rate of eight tons a minute. It moves relentlessly on caterpillar tracks, needs but one man to guide it and, like the surface Push-Button Miner, has made this occupation an impersonal, mechanical work, instead of the rugged man's work that it once was. It has brought with it enormous productive capacities, far fewer men in the colleries, and its own contribution to the miseries of American mining towns.

Those who run the machines are the members of the United Mine Workers of America now. The strip mines, with their bulldozers and cat drivers and truck drivers who haul the coal away, provide another segment of the membership. And there are some who remain from the more traditional ways of bringing coal from the earth, who still face the perils of the past, breathing dust that destroys their lungs and fearing explosions of methane gas.

As darkness and danger shaped men's actions in the days of birth and growth of their organization, so has automation had its influence on the modern members. The evidence of the past is that there was a reciprocity of concern—men for their leaders and leaders for their men. Could the push-button man and the bulldozer driver, whose daily response was a reaction to machinery, know or care or feel or even think about what occurred within the organization to which he paid his monthly requirement? How would the chieftains, who sat in a headquarters building in a city remote and removed, react to this different kind of membership?

Along with the inevitable changes in the methods of mining, imprinting its influences on the men who made up the organization, there were also, in the higher echelons of the union, events that made a new history. There was political despotism, nurtured by a strong man whose ultimate triumphs made it seem unnecessary. There was violence, more of it than an unaware public could ever imagine. There was entrepreneurism, virulent and power-controlled, an uneasy contrast to the fellowship aspirations of a Daniel Weaver.

The arch that was formed by single stones a century ago was now perhaps more an amalgamation of concrete, de-personalized and modernized. The transition, dominated as it was by the three forces of political despotism, violence and entrepreneurism, raises the question of how an association of truly free men can survive—or, better, how it can live. And within this awareness and this inquiry, there is always a revival of the haunting question of the poem that Weaver read, "What Might Be Done?"

2. The Defendants

For a century or more, the miners of America and their organization were brought into courts of law by their natural antagonists. Cases against them now are being brought by their brothers.

This litigation and its source reveals what is happening in this body of people more than almost any other series of events. It portrays their existence, it tells of their troubles, it tests their level of involvement in the world in which they live. Lawsuits are often barometers of the difficulties, as well as the accomplishments, of any organization. The kind of opposition one faces, what it seeks, what results may emerge, all require tests of effectiveness, gauges of purpose.

There is a severity about litigation that makes this so. Cases result in orders of judges, and those orders must be carried out. The power of the law is put behind the search for facts, when documents otherwise private must be opened for inspection, when people must testify to sworn truth, when they must submit to the most searching questions their opposition can muster. There is no other test like it in American life. The political debater or the pundit can ignore facts, questions and issues, can evade the unpleasant counterrealities, and can pour out irrelevancies with squidlike obliteration. These tactics are tried in courtrooms too, because they are human characteristics. But in the law rooms there are rules which seek both to prevent these diversions and to allow the opponent to keep to the essentials.

When coal miners saw the state, in league with the operators, put John Siney and Xingo Parks on trial a century ago for conspiracy to raise wages, they knew what the opposing forces sought. As the decades passed, there were hundreds of injunctions and court orders that forbade striking and picketing, all brought by the antagonists outside, seeking to counter and check the progress of the mine workers. The use of the sheriff's writ to eject mining families from company houses was likewise under the ruling law of the times, brought in an effort to break the union. The enemies on the outside were relentless in their use of the law against the union. They won their occasional days, but the Mine Workers grew and prospered, because as a body of men it met the basic needs of American miners. The organization survived the use of the Sherman Anti-Trust Act, employed by the operators in another effort to destroy the union. They fought great legal battles to the United States Supreme Court in the 1920's, when the wealth and prestige of the union was able to bring America's most distinguished lawyer, Charles Evans Hughes, former Supreme Court justice, almost-President, and later Chief Justice of the United States, to argue their cause to the high bench.

Then the miners fought the most formidable legal antagonist of all, the United States. When the government took over the mines in World War II and extended this beyond the end of the fighting, there was a court order obtained against a nationwide strike. The miners refused to work, and perhaps the most momentous contempt-of-court case in our legal history was brought against the union and John L. Lewis. Fines were assessed that challenged the imagination, and even though their final figures were reduced when the case itself was finally lost in the Supreme Court, their impact was enormous.

These contests brought some victories that were enjoyed and many defeats that were endured. All of them represented struggle and conflict in the thrust for advancement of the lives of coal miners. Even when not victorious, the association of these workingmen was standing for miner welfare, resisting opposing forces whose aims were to use the law to frustrate and defeat the union. This was the economic struggle of contending factions in the industrial market place extended to the courtroom.

Almost always, the defendants were the United Mine Workers of America. Among them, there was a proud unity. Miners rallied behind Lewis as he defied the sovereign, because his stand was for them. Cheering men carried John Siney on their shoulders into the street when a jury found him not guilty, because he represented their aspirations. Verdicts from hostile judges and biased juries could be tolerated because the miners believed, as their leaders taught them, that their organization fought for them against the natural enemy, always resisting.

The litigation of today comes from a quite different source. There is now a civil war of lawsuits, as old miners, young miners, widows of miners, and miners fearful and distrusting have turned to the courts for relief against the men who hold the chairs designed to protect them. Just as the hundred years of cases brought by enemies on the outside told the story of Mine Worker activity, force and progress, so now the cases brought by those who hold union cards adequately portray what is central to the life of this body of workingmen.

For our present purposes, it may not matter which side wins or loses, although about each there is a desperation of desire to win. But these are exposure cases, morality cases, political cases, almost, to re-use a familiar phrase in an entirely new context, "soul" cases. They are no longer interested in the gloss history of the union; they now search the real history. What has this institution of men done to its own?

There had been a quiet secrecy about the conduct of the United Mine Workers after the upheavals of the World War II strikes and the turmoil of the years shortly thereafter. While the country was coping with McCarthy (Joseph) and resting somnolently under Eisenhower, the names of John L. Lewis and the Mine Workers lapsed far into the background of the nation's problems. Lewis was hailed as a labor statesman, and in 1960, after forty years as the union's president, he retired.

The successors were quiet, too. Lewis passed the presidency to an aging lieutenant, Thomas Kennedy, who died within three years, long before the elderly Lewis was to succumb. Then came Tony Boyle, who had served under Lewis as an administrative assistant, claiming to be the anointed heir of the old lion. Boyle was in office through two conventions and one election before the unraveling of old complaints, new rivalries, and accumulated miseries brought questions that had never been asked before.

The union's headquarters in an imposing old building in downtown Washington became an isolated fortress in those years, inaccessible and silent. The McClellan Committee investigations in the late 1950's that brought the enactment of the Labor-Management Reporting and Disclosure Act of 1959, popularly known as the Landrum-Griffin Act, never noticed the Mine Workers, and at that time, probably had no reason to do so. Labor's bad boys in those days were Jimmy Hoffa and the Teamsters. The Mine Workers had long ago resigned from the American Federation of Labor, took no part in the merger with the Congress of Industrial Organizations, and was generally left alone as it dealt with a coal industry that no longer aroused the nation.

The fortress was impenetrable. There were complaints and questions here and there, and an occasional newspaper report that was usually lost among the occurrences of tomorrow's headlines. The union of John L. Lewis was so highly regarded that no one paid serious attention to the rising murmurs. The miners in West Virginia and in Pennsylvania and in the old battlegrounds of Ohio and Illinois were far away from the awesome old structure on Fifteenth Street in Washington. Occasional jibes of discontent were usually dismissed, therefore, as the routine bits of discord that are found in every assembly of men.

An explosion was the catalyst of the massive inquiry that was soon to come. A highly inflammable gas known as methane had been causing the deaths of coal miners from the time men made deep caverns underground. In late November, 1968, a blast in Farmington, West Virginia, at the Consol No. 9 mine of the Mountaineer Coal Company, buried seventy-eight men forever. President Tony Boyle came to the scene and expressed his grief for the dead miners. He also made the unfortunate comment that this was "one of the better companies to work with as far as cooperation and safety are concerned."

A wiry, hard-working Congressman from West Virginia named Ken Hechler began to ask questions. Why had so many good West Virginia men died in the mine? Why had there been explosions of methane decade after decade? Why was coal mining in the late 1960's an occupation that was perhaps the country's busiest killer of men? Most important, what was the union doing about all this, other than regretting that it had happened in one of the "better companies"? Hechler became an aroused watchman, and he would not be ignored. In a short period of time, his incessant probing became an anathema to the leadership of the UMW.

Then, there came another critic, who soon surpassed Congressman Hechler. Ralph Nader, a new public ombudsman, who had humbled General Motors, frightened administrative bureaucrats in Washington, stood up for the consumer and the hapless citizen, had made the union one of his targets. He drafted his own personal indictment and sent it to the Senate of the United States, asking for an investigation of both the union and its renowned Welfare and Retirement Fund. Some of his charges later found their way into the litigation that is occupying the union at present. By this time, most of the Eastern information centers had begun to pay attention.

In 1969, President Boyle had to stand for re-election. One of the union's executive-board members, Joseph A. "Jock" Yablonski, heeded the call and challenged Boyle for the leadership job. It was the first serious election in the union since the early days of Lewis. There were charges and countercharges, and Boyle won a disputed count for another term. At the end of 1969, after the votes were counted, Yablonski and his wife and daughter were found murdered in their Pennsylvania home.

The bloody brutality of the crime aroused the nation. Yablonski's wife and daughter were total innocents, slain in their beds by gunmen who broke into their home. Yablonski had lost the election; the question arose as to why he should lose his life as well. The inquiries concerning the United Mine Workers in 1969 during the election campaign were intensified. The killers clumsily left a series of clues that led to the arrest of three men within weeks after the discovery of the slaying. As the investigation progressed, two more were apprehended, the wife of one of the original trio arrested, and her father. The father was the president of a local union of the United Mine Workers of America.

The institution immediately responded with indignation. Its officers deplored the killings; reward money was offered for information leading to arrest and conviction. The charges against it were false; its election had been fair, its conduct reasonable, its stewardship faithful to its trust.

After the trials of the accused started, the confessions and signed statements began to come. Annette Gilly, the wife of the convicted leader of the actual slayers, said that her father had worked with William J. Prater, a prominent international representative of the UMW, to arrange the details of the killing. Then it was her father's turn. Silous Huddleston said, in a signed statement read in open court, that his orders had come from Albert Pass, secretary-treasurer of District 19 in Middlesboro, Kentucky.

Albert Pass was a member of the executive board of the United Mine Workers of America, the highest office in the institution below the three positions of president, vice-president, and secretary-treasurer.

Pass and Prater, who worked directly under Pass in District 19, were indicted for the federal crime of interfering with the trade-union rights of Yablonski. Both of them were indicted for murder in Pennsylvania. There was a brooding uneasiness over the UMWA in the summer of 1972—when and where might the next blow fall?

Even before the unraveling of the Yablonski murder trials, the institution had suffered a series of legal defeats that revealed another side of its story. Throughout the decade of the 1960's, judgments had been emerging from United States courts in Kentucky and Tennessee, most of them little known outside the legal community. They were of two kinds, both devastating in their significance. One group was made up of cases of violence, claims for recovery of damages inflicted by dynamite, murder, mass terrorism. The other involved a new use of the Sherman Anti-Trust Act, alleging conspiracies between the union and big coal operators to wipe out owners of small coal mines.

The violence cases produced verdict after verdict against the United Mine Workers of America, awarding vast sums in damages, all to be paid from the union treasury. The antitrust cases, more complex and more difficult to assess, involved great legal issues that found their way to the United States Supreme Court. But findings of guilt had been made, and money judgments in the millions were emerging.

These verdicts sounded their warnings. No other labor organization in America had ever been found liable in so many trials for violent conduct. No other institution, corporate or labor or other, had been involved in so many defenses under the Sherman Act, all in such a short period of time. They were deeply unsettling, a foreboding that something unusual had been happening in that particular body of men.

The new cases came out of the internal war they had begun even before Jock Yablonski offered his candidacy and gave his life. The first had its beginnings among elderly miners and widows in West Virginia who had become disenchanted with the performance of the

Welfare and Retirement Fund, the proudest creation of John L. Lewis and the union. They had complained about the loss of benefits, about rules and red tape that deprived men of their rights, of a callousness of the staff representatives who rejected them instead of assisting them. With help from sympathetic lawyers, they formed their own nonprofit corporation, began to collect their own dues money, and prepared to file one of the most massive lawsuits in American legal history.

They brought it to Washington, and through a young lawyer from the firm of Arnold and Porter (from which Abe Fortas had previously gone on to the Supreme Court) it was entered in the United States District Court for the District of Columbia. The primary defendant was their union and the officers who had managed their affairs.

The action also named all the trustees of the Welfare Fund and the National Bank of Washington, a banking corporation owned by the UMW.

It charged a breach of fiduciary duty, a failure to act in good faith toward coal miners and their widows, a wasting of their money, and a grave misuse of the funds that were available.

That case went to trial in 1971. Judge Gerhard Gesell found the union guilty of a breach of trust; the trustees had likewise violated their duties; the plaintiffs were entitled to judgment. An order was issued to pay 11.5 million dollars back into the Fund and to the individuals who had brought the case. Its holding quickly became a classic in the law; its consequences a determination of unfaithfulness by those who were charged with the responsibility of working on behalf of coal miners.

The Welfare Fund case was an enigma; the public appeared to recognize only that the union was hit with another verdict of 11.5 million dollars. But the National Bank of Washington was ordered to share in the burden, too, and Josephine Roche, an elderly lady who had served as the neutral trustee of the Fund for most of its history, was found personally liable, along with a man named Barnum L. Colton, who was president of the bank. These intricacies of high finance may have been incomprehensible to coal miners and editorial writers alike, but the question occurred as to how and why it had happened. Was this another piece of decay of the union itself? Was there in actuality a conspiracy to deprive workingmen of the benefits that were rightfully theirs?

The challenger Yablonski saturated the courts with cases in 1969 shortly after he declared his candidacy. He was compelled to bring four suits to seek to preserve his status, to even keep alive his efforts to compete for the union's top office. He sued to force the union to mail his campaign literature; he acted to enjoin the use of the union's newspaper, the *United Mine Workers Journal,* as a campaign sheet for the incumbent; he was compelled to sue to be reinstated in his job, from which he had been fired after he announced his candidacy; he brought an action to protect his right to have observers at the polls at voting time.

These cases might have been dismissed as a litigation ploy during an internal fight, except for one salient fact. Yablonski's lawyer was victorious in every one of them. Each time the United Mine Workers was found to be in violation of federal law.

There was also a charge that the union had ignored basic democratic practices. The government had sued more than five years previously to seek to enjoin the UMW from continuing an old practice of filling second-echelon positions by appointment instead of by election, as the law required. This was a blow against an organization that had regularly boasted that it was more democratic in its government than the Congress of the United States.

Shortly before the election Yablonski brought another legal action, far more serious and more searching than the quick thrusts to protect his campaign. In a long, carefully drawn and carefully prepared complaint, he charged massive mismanagement of the union by its incumbent officers. It alleged misappropriation, nepotism, high living, personal glorification of officers, waste of union money to preserve the political status of Boyle, and unlawful use of union money in the election campaign itself. It asked for the repayment of millions of dollars back into the union treasury by Boyle and other officers. Its goal was the reformation of the union itself. It challenged some practices of a half century; it raised fundamental inquiries about what was faithful performance of duty by those elected to offices in labor unions.

Throughout the 1969 election campaign, Yablonski's lawyer, Joseph L. Rauh, Jr., charged that the UMW was violating federal law concerning the coming referendum. He pleaded for an investigation by the Secretary of Labor. After the votes were counted, Yablonski filed an official protest, as he was required to do under law, seeking to invalidate the triumph of Boyle and have a new poll conducted under government supervision. His complaint was pending when he was slain. The Secretary of Labor, who had been unwilling to act before that time, promptly filed suit in Washington, D.C., to declare the election of Boyle unlawful. The government alleged that the United Mine Workers had failed to conduct a secret-ballot election, had improperly campaigned at the polls, had refused Yablonski the right to have election observers, had denied some union members the right to vote, and had unlawfully used union money to promote the election of Tony Boyle. This case came to trial in Washington before Federal Judge William B. Bryant in late 1971 and spilled over into early 1972. On May 1, 1972, Judge Bryant ruled that the Mine Workers had violated federal law over and over again. A new election must be held. Government agents would conduct it this time, not UMW district and local officials.

The union was subjected to one of the most searching investigations ever performed on any organization in American society. Its officers and representatives were questioned by federal agents. Its books and records were studied. Another lawsuit was filed by the government, alleging that the UMW had failed to keep the records that the law required. This too brought a judgment against the union. Once more, the law had affixed blame for wrongdoing. Evidence was submitted to federal grand juries, and criminal indictments followed.

In western Pennsylvania, Michael Budzanoski and John Seddon, UMW officials who worked for the re-election of Boyle, were indicted for misusing union money in the 1969 campaign. A Pittsburgh federal jury found them guilty on all counts. A Virginia official named Ray Thornbury, who had received his union position by appointment from Boyle, was named in another charge for criminal handling of union money during the election. Thornbury too was found guilty as charged.

Then, the most damaging criminal accusation of all was made against Tony Boyle himself. On March 1, 1971, he was indicted, along with Secretary-Treasurer John Owens and James Kmetz, director of Labor's Non-Partisan League, for embezzling union money to use in the 1968 Presidential campaign in support of Hubert H. Humphrey and other candidates. The union's attorney, Edward L. Carey, was outraged when the indictment was issued. He pointed out that the Federal Corrupt Practices Act made the receiver of the money equally guilty with the person who paid, yet only Boyle and union officials were indicted. "We are sick and tired of being made the whipping boys of the Department of Labor and the Department of Justice," said Carey. "We will fight this all the way."

Carey's brave words were for naught. On March 31, 1972, a federal-court jury in Washington found Boyle guilty on all thirteen counts under which he had been charged. There were one count of conspiracy, eleven counts on specific contributions in violation of the Corrupt Practices Act and one count of illegal conversion of union funds in violation of the Landrum-Griffin Act. John Owens and James Kmetz were found not guilty because the primary responsibility for the handling of the money resided with Tony Boyle himself.

This blow would disqualify Boyle from holding any union office for five years unless he could reverse the verdict on appeal. Until higher-court review resolved the issue, he could retain his presidency. More important to his staggering regime, he could even run again in the new government-supervised election as long as his appeal was still pending. Final action in the United States Supreme Court, where Boyle could try to obtain a hearing if he lost his case in the United States Court of Appeals, could delay his disqualification day until at least late 1973 or early 1974.

More cases continued to pour into the courts, one after another. Yablonski supporters filed new actions against the Budzanoski management of the union's District 5 in Pittsburgh. They brought suit to enjoin the UMW from imposing discipline upon them. They entered new trusteeship cases to try to win the right to have elections in the district offices of the union. They even brought suit to enjoin the union's new password in 1971, "Loyal to Boyle." This was one of their easier successes.

What had happened inside this body of men, who had united together so many years in the past, to cause it to be assailed in the courts by its own members and by the government on behalf of those who were enrolled within it? Had it committed the massive wrongs charged against it, or were there sound, rational defenses for every action it had taken? Were the findings of violations and guilt in the cases that had been resolved no more than aberrations in a successful, functioning organization? Or, was there intrinsic rot and decay, making necessary a reformation inside?

There were deeper questions going to America's labor unions themselves. Institutions of workingmen had become so important in the United States that the Congress had been concerned with legislation concerning them for many sessions over the decades. The federal and state courts were annually filled with litigation to resolve controversies concerning unions and their activities. The Supreme Court of the United States accepted each term large numbers of labor cases because of their legal and industrial importance to the nation. Some of the statutes that dealt with their affairs, from the Wagner Act to the Taft-Hartley Act to the Landrum-Griffin Act, along with scores of other significant laws, were among the most compelling in the chronicles of the Republic. Unions had become as important a part of the nation as the corporation; they had developed into major institutions, with millions of dollars of funds, with impressive headquarters buildings, with large staffs of trained professional people, with members throughout every segment of American life.

Were the travails of the United Mine Workers of America symptomatic of illnesses that pervaded other labor organizations? Was there something intrinsic in their structure that led to the claims of unfaithfulness, of fraud, of despotism? Or, was there some massive frailty in the human beings that made up their membership that led to the strife that absorbed the Mine Workers? Were the dreams of Weaver ever capable of fulfillment?

Did these men who dug coal out of the earth act any differently in their struggle from other human beings in similar periods of stress? Was their chronicle indeed a "people" story rather than a union story?

In all the inquiries that may be raised, there was yet another element to it. It was the dominance of a single man, John L. Lewis, who influenced a nation and directly affected the lives of hundreds of thousands of workingmen. When the great mass of litigation put the union to test, John L. Lewis was dead. Some of those who were present raised as defenses that they were doing no more than following the policies of the man often considered as the greatest labor leader in America's history. But he was no longer there to justify, to persuade, to defend, to attack, as he had done so many times in the years of the union's glory.

But his deeds, poignant, irrepressible, flamboyant, not always understandable, became an integral part of the inquiry into the events of a body of men founded on dreams of achievement and later mired into a litigation of inner destructiveness. For he too was a defendant.

3. Leaders of Men

IRON JOHN AND GENTLE JOHN

Every organization, every institution, every establishment that has made an impact on the world around it, and this includes nations as well, has exerted its influence through a man, a leader. Mine unionism began with leadership, fueled by the inspirational dreams of Daniel Weaver, which sustained it until the actual founding of the United Mine Workers in 1890. Its next period of growth and influence came under John Mitchell, who gave it a strength and impact upon society that made the union the most prominent labor force in America before World War I.

But it was John L. Lewis who gave it a different kind of leadership, who dominated the United Mine Workers for half the union's life, who led it to its greatest glories, and who laid the foundations for a painful disintegration that has come afterward—which raises a question worth the deepest of inquiries as to whether despotic leadership inevitably, or almost always, leads to a decay that obliterates man's highest values; and which may transform King Louis XV's famed statement *"Après moi, le déluge"* from arrogance to philosophy.

Lewis ruled the union through a period of vicious internal warfare, at a time when it declined year after year, lost membership, lost contracts and recognition, saw its treasury nearly disappear, and itself fought for existence. But Lewis established his dominance, destroyed his enemies, and exercised his authority to end democratic participation by those who made up the institution. And after all this, Lewis took the union to its greatest influence and accomplishment.

While Lewis had many rivals, one stands out among all the others. A gentle Irish miner out of western Pennsylvania, from a tiny coal town named Nanty Glo, became the very antithesis of John L. Lewis. He was John Brophy, the idealist, the dreamer, who could never be crushed by Lewis, but ended working with him. The battles of Brophy against Lewis run through the middle years of the union, one man grossly outmatched by the other, one the conscience and one the power. Their contrasting styles of leadership are common in the affairs of men, as their prototypes pervade so many of the associations of society. When there is a contest between these kinds of personality, the outcome is almost always a certainty. In these arenas of practicality, there are no Davids to overcome the Goliaths. These triumphs of inevitability have their hazards and leave us their destructiveness.

1·

When, before the end of the last century, the Scottish theorist and historian Thomas Carlyle wrote about leaders and heroes, he was almost drafting a design for a future John Llewellyn Lewis. Carlyle argued that a country should find its ablest man, raise him to the supreme place, loyally revere him, and then there would be a perfect government for that nation. The indispensable force was the hero, the one man against whom the many are powerless, but with whom they are powerful. Carlyle believed that leadership rested upon intuitive insight into reality, a trait that Lewis was able to exhibit time after time with a remarkable capacity in his many struggles.

The concept that only through power can there be achievement has beguiled both thinkers and activists for centuries. Whether it be from Carlyle or from Machiavelli, there has always been the argument that power is a virtue in the sense that no organization can achieve great and lasting things, including its noblest ideals, unless one individual is able to rise to the top, dominate the group, and exercise his great authority. The thesis is that the hero, or leader, when he settles the struggle for power, can then prepare the organization for a singular devotion to its purposes. This too is a part of the story of Lewis.

Labor unions have been particularly adapted to this kind of leadership. Many of them have been involved in intense inner rivalries, where strong and powerful men have emerged to impose a long-lived autocracy. Examples come to mind quickly: Big Bill Hutcheson ruled the International Brotherhood of Carpenters for decades with such kingly domain that he was able to pass his succession as president to his son Maurice; the dominance of Dave Beck and then Jimmy Hoffa over the Teamsters is of more recent awareness; many lesser-known leaders have ruled their organizations with the same severity. Even such benign leaders as Hillman, Dubinsky and Reuther kept tight hands over the organizations which they headed. Those who look upon unions as armies girded for battle against enemies who are both powerful and cunning proclaim the need for strong leadership at the top and unquestioning discipline below.

Unions, of course, are not alone in their experience of personal-power syndromes. Other organizations and institutions, from nations to corporations to symphony orchestras to sports teams, have been dominated by strong leaders. Historians tell of Caesars and Cromwells. Our country has had strong Presidents from Jackson to the two Roosevelts, and its tycoons of industry from Gould to Ford. The late George Szell, whose leadership made the Cleveland Symphony Orchestra one of the world's best, was called autocrat, tyrant, inhuman, merciless, arrogant. Some of his musicians who said they hated him would admit in their next sentences that he was a genius. Older baseball fans recall the tyrannical leadership of John McGraw of the New York Giants and younger football fans extol the successes of the late Vince Lombardi, whose penchant for authority became as well known as his victories. Internal organizations of government such as the Federal Bureau of Investigation have their autocracies, too, as the relentless hold of J. Edgar Hoover for a half century demonstrates.

In each instance, a powerful case can be made for achievement. The strength of the man at the top accounts for the accomplishment, as the theories of Carlyle are examined in the world of reality. Even leaders with conscientious awareness of the democratic rights of others yearn for the authority to put their programs into effect. Then, there are history's classic examples of the perils of autocratic brinkmanship—Bonaparte, Mussolini, Hitler. Nonetheless, the achiever, the man of authority, the dominant ruler, emerges in every institution in society, and it is indeed his resolute strength that often accounts for what his group does.

It is difficult to conceive of a more fascinating example of all these traits than John L. Lewis. Many who studied him during his days of authority wrote of him with awe. C. L. Sulzberger, in a passion of eloquence over Lewis, described his physique in terms of a mythical hero. "His arms are short and powerful . . . His hands are heavy but quick, with gnarled, strong fingers. His legs are squat, supple. He is remarkably light on his feet, walks with the speed and agility of a cat." Stories were told of his shaggy eyebrows, his courage, his voice. Sulzberger said: "He can use his voice like a policeman's billy or like a monk at prisons. He can talk an assemblage into a state of eruption. He can translate a group of people into a pageant of misery, and back again."

One of his principal biographers, the astute Saul Alinsky, turned the story of Lewis into a paean of admiration. Lewis was "something of a man." There were legendary stories told of how he killed with one blow the vicious mule, Spanish Pete, during his youthful days in the mine; of how, with no more than his bare hands, he threatened men with guns in their pockets; of how he intimidated men with a stare. The hero has become a Bunyanesque legend.

Then there are those of us who admired his eloquence most of all. One of his finest hours came in a 1946 negotiating session with the coal operators when he was bargaining for creation of the welfare fund that was to remake American industrial life. After a period of disgust with the positions of the operators, Lewis wrote on a yellow legal pad and then arose to read to the representatives of management.

> For four weeks we have sat with you; we have attended when you fixed the hour; we departed when weariness affected your pleasure.
>
> Our effort to resolve mutual questions has been vain; you have been intolerant of suggestions and impatient of analysis.
>
> When we sought surcease from bloodletting, you professed indifference. When we cried aloud for the safety of our numbers, you answered—be content—'twas always thus!
>
> When we urged that you abate stench you averred that your nostrils were not offended.
>
> When we emphasized the importance of life, you pleaded the priority of profit; when we spoke of little children in unkempt surroundings, you said—look to the state.
>
> You aver that you own the mines; we suggest that, as yet, you do not own the people.

You profess annoyance at our temerity; we condemn your imbecility.

You are smug in your complacency; we are abashed by your shamelessness; you prate your respectability; we are shocked at your lack of public morality.

You scorn the toils, the abstinence and the perils of the miner; we withhold approval of your luxurious mode of life and the nights you spend in merriment.

You invert the natural order of things and charge to the public the pleasures of your own indolence; we denounce the senseless cupidity that withholds from the miner the rewards of honorable and perilous exertion.

To cavil further is futile. We trust that time, as it shrinks your purse, may modify your niggardly and antisocial propensities.

This was Shakespearean. It was defiance of the enemy, it was a confrontation of equity. It was an exposition of brilliance from a man whose formal schooling stopped at the eighth grade, but whose knowledge of power and people and the language transcended that of most men of his time. This was more real than the slaying of Spanish Pete, because the words have been preserved, while the tale is perhaps apocryphal.

Lewis rose to his original seat of power in typical American success-story fashion, combining aggressiveness, ambition and intelligence with—in the words of the popular song—"a little bit of bloomin' luck." He was first of all a coal miner, as he often liked to remind people. "Think of me as a coal miner, and you will make no mistake," he said. But this was only a fanciful image of his own, for the mines were quickly left far behind for the more fascinating field of union politics.

His father was a Welsh miner, who was fired from colliery after colliery because he fought for the union cause in the pits of Wales. Tom Lewis came to America, had many sons, and pursued his natural instincts for organizing the workingmen. In nineteenth-century America, mine bosses in Iowa, where the family settled, were as quick to discharge the union agitator as those in Britain, and life was never easy for the Lewis family. Young John, like the sons of other miners, went to work in the pits as a boy, and then left to travel the West. He later returned to his home area of Lucas, Iowa, and married a schoolteacher named Myrta Bell, who is usually credited with shaping and developing his education. Iowa was not prime mining country, and the restless young Lewis and his bride moved to southern Illinois, not far from the collieries where Daniel Weaver and his supporters founded the first union.

Five other sons of Tom Lewis left Iowa to join brother John in Illinois. With this kind of solidarity, a political machine of Lewis boys quickly made John L. the president of their small local union in Panama, Illinois. It required only another ten years for him to become president of the largest and most powerful labor organization in America.

His next step was to go to Springfield like a young Lincoln, not as a member of the legislature, but as a lobbyist, to plead the miners' cause. Because Illinois was a prominent mining state, and in those days before federal power became so predominant, lobbying work at the state level was of major importance to all labor unions. Lewis had learned to use words, and with his impressive physique and quickness of mind it was easy enough for higher lords in the movement to recognize his ability. After a year, he received an appointment from Samuel Gompers to serve as legislative representative for the American Federation of Labor, to work throughout the United States.

Lewis learned about American industry in his new job, about the organization of unions, the process of making law, and above all, who commanded power and why. It was only natural for Lewis to keep close ties with the Mine Workers, not only because this was perhaps the most important American union, but because he was a miner himself. In 1916, he was asked to return to his own union, on the headquarters staff in Indianapolis as statistician. This is when he began to learn of the economics of the coal industry and further build his political strength inside the UMW. By 1918, when John P. White, the UMW president, resigned to take a federal post, he was fully aware of the leadership potentiality of Lewis. An alcoholic vice-president named Frank Hayes succeeded White, who used his influence to cause Hayes to appoint Lewis to the newly vacated vice-presidential office. While most labor unions usually have as many vice-presidents as their corporate counterparts, the UMW has always had but one who has been truly second in command and usually has been groomed to succeed to the highest post when it should become vacant.

Hayes was not up to the demands of the job, and in 1919 the higher echelons of union leadership forced his resignation. The vice-president was named by the executive board to take over, and John L. Lewis became president without the casting of an electoral ballot. He ran for election in 1920, winning a full term only by a narrow margin. The closeness of a presidential election result was never to happen again in the United Mine Workers.

John L. Lewis, at thirty-nine years of age, was president of the largest, the richest, and by far the most powerful union in America. He was in the prime of life, with blooming physical power, conveying the impression of a giant with his 230 pounds filling out a broad and thick frame, even though his height did not exceed six feet. He was ready to attack his enemies with his fists or his wit. He was filled with ambition and a sense of both power and destiny. The great promise he had shown at that time as a young leader of labor, however, was headed for years of turmoil, internal conflict, near-destruction of the union, and an eventual impotence on the public scene that reduced both him and his union to a struggle for nothing more than simple survival.

2·

While John L. Lewis paid attention to power, John Brophy paid attention to policy. Three years younger than Lewis, Brophy rose to prominence in the United Mine Workers at about the same time. Like Lewis, he came from a family of miners and was taken into the mines as a boy by his father. Brophy was a small man, sleek and handsome, with a cheerful, clean-cut boyish appearance he carried with him until the graying and balding of his later years made him a more serious version of a beneficent leprechaun.

Brophy was born in England, where his Irish father had moved to follow miner's work. Several of the Brophys had emigrated to America at about the time the father of John L. Lewis came, as masses of mine workers left the British Isles to dig coal in the United States. Brophy was brought by his father to west-central Pennsylvania in

1892, when the boy was nine years of age. Patrick Brophy and one of
his brothers were leaders in an 1894 strike in the collieries, and were
honored by the operators with an attack as "part of a foreign conspiracy" seeking to destroy the American way of life. Since most of
the miners had originally come from Great Britain, the "foreign conspiracy" was obviously an outgrowth of the evils of George IV, according to the propaganda line of the day.

With less than three years of formal schooling, young John was
taken into the mine at the age of twelve to begin his lifework. Brophy
cheerfully told of his start: "The boss, a good-hearted man, gave me
a new mine cap and an oil lamp. I got a dinner bucket with a short-
enough handle so it wouldn't trail on the ground, a small shovel
which had been worn thin by the trackmen, a small pick, my first
long pants, and I was equipped to go to work. I was small even for
my age—I couldn't have weighed over seventy-five pounds—so for a
while I was the subject of good-natured teasing by the other miners."

Young Brophy first joined the United Mine Workers when he was
fifteen years old, standing alongside his father to take the oath of
obligation. It was an impressive ceremony to the youngster, especially one part which he never forgot: ". . . to defend freedom of
thought whether expressed by tongue or pen." Despite his lack of
familiarity with the inside of a schoolroom, Brophy burned with that
same intensity of desire to learn about the world that moved so many
young men in the late nineteenth century. Miners passed old copies
of newspapers from hand to hand until holes and tears destroyed
them. As a member of the union, he began to receive the *United
Mine Workers Journal*. It carried advertisements for pamphlets and
publications sponsored by the American Federation of Labor, and
Brophy sent for every one of them. He borrowed every book he
could find. As his miner's wages increased, he ordered books by
mail and took correspondence courses in English and mathematics.

Brophy held his first union office at the age of twenty, in Greenwich, Pennsylvania, a town that disappeared many years ago when
its sole livelihood, the mine, was worked out. The company owned
the entire village, and every possession in it. The miners bought a
corner of a farm on the edge of the settlement. Miners became
woodsmen in their few daylight hours out of the pit, and cleared
timber from the land. A crude log assembly hall was built large

enough to hold the union's membership. It became the center of community life, the only place in the village where there was a freedom from the pervasive atmosphere of company dominance. The union, with Brophy as secretary, record keeper and friendly spirit, became the guardian and sustenance of the people, akin to the role visualized by Weaver, but long forgotten in the later diversification of industrial life.

After a lost strike at Greenwich, Brophy moved to Nanty Glo, another nearby mining town, where he resumed his activities in the union. He was a delegate from the Nanty Glo local to the 1908 UMW convention at Indianapolis, even before Lewis had begun his movement to the top of the union rolls. Then, as now, the second echelon of UMW government was in the districts, and Brophy later led a rebel movement against the incumbent officers of District 2. He was deeply dissatisfied with their policies and performance, and by 1917 he had been elected to the presidency of the district, a position of considerable prominence and power in the international union. At that time, Lewis had not yet left the AFL payroll, and he exerted no visible influence in the Mine Workers.

Brophy first met "Jack" Lewis, as he was called then, at a Washington wage conference when Lewis was still working under Samuel Gompers. When Lewis received his appointment as vice-president of the Mine Workers, he began to work with Brophy on various internal union matters. Their first visible conflict arose in 1918, when Lewis came into Pennsylvania to lead a campaign to try to defeat the incumbent president of the Pennsylvania State Federation of Labor, James H. Maurer, who had been critical of our involvement in World War I. Lewis wanted Brophy to swing the UMW districts, which were a powerful contingent in the state body, against Maurer, whom Brophy had come to admire. Brophy held firm, rejected Lewis's attempts, supported Maurer, and was instrumental in his re-election. Lewis displayed to Brophy both his coolness and his charm, one to be turned on and the other discarded as the politics of the moment demanded. Brophy never forgot this incident; he later told of it in this way: "Lewis was concerned solely with his own political ambitions. He wanted to be kingmaker and to have the state president under obligation to him. Ethical and human considerations were brushed aside if they interfered with his ambition. On many union matters I agreed with him and would willingly have worked with him, yet again and again the ruthlessness and extreme egotism of the man drove us apart." This lack of empathy, political, emotional and deeply personal, was to dominate their relationship all the rest of their lives, even when the moving developments of New Deal days brought them together again. Brophy, never too deeply involved in political machinations, watched Lewis take over the UMW presidency with the sad thought that he had done it without being elected, a strange precedent for the democratically inclined Mine Workers.

By 1923, Lewis was consistently attacking Brophy and his views inside the union. The two men moved farther apart in the Presidential election of 1924, when Lewis loudly proclaimed his support for Calvin Coolidge. Brophy and many other labor leaders swung their support to Senator Robert M. La Follette that year. Again, the practical man "triumphed" over the idealists.

The different worlds of Lewis and Brophy and the forces they represented were revealed in another of the noble experiments of the 1920's that failed. Brophy's self-education expanded rapidly after he became president of District 2. His friendship with the like-minded James Maurer of the Pennsylvania Federation, especially after the unsuccessful effort of Lewis to defeat Maurer, brought Brophy into the Workers' Education Bureau, of which Maurer was chairman. Some of the thoughtful trade-unionists, along with socially directed intellectuals, were searching for expansion of a program of classes, pamphlets, and additional schooling for workingmen. Maurer, Brophy, and a few others went to Samuel Gompers to seek support from the AFL, without which the Bureau could not succeed. With the endorsement of Gompers, the Bureau expanded, and out of this grew the first school for labor.

Brookwood Labor College was started in Westchester County, New York, in 1921, by many of the movers in the Worker's Education Bureau. Gifts from some of the early foundations, primitive fund raising, and scholarships given by more than a dozen unions kept the institution going. A two-year course was offered to approximately fifty trade-unionists, to educate them in economics, government, political science and the labor movement. Brophy, of course, was an enthusiastic participant, but it was his association with Brookwood that later led to its death. Lewis, if he even knew of Brookwood's existence, despite the many miners who attended its classes, scarcely cared to recognize it.

When the rivalry between Lewis and Brophy culminated in the 1926 UMW election with Brophy challenging Lewis for the presidency, a cadre of Brookwood graduates and organizers went into the field to form the nucleus of the Brophy organization. When Lewis rose at the AFL convention in October of that year to denounce the election campaign against him as part of a Bolshevik plot to take over American labor, Brookwood College was on its way to extinction. While the reflection of almost a half century may cause the "Bolshevik plot" routine to sound simply ridiculous, it was an extremely effective maneuver by John L. Lewis at that time.

A few radical instructors at Brookwood, some questioning of the sacred positions taken by high leaders of the Federation, and the support of Brophy were enough. Matthew Woll, whose hostility to any idea was notorious, was commissioned to investigate Brookwood. His report that Brookwood College was "propagandistic" and "communistic," as well as a threat to the principles of the American Federation of Labor, was received with solemn gratification. The "principles" so threatened were those against "dual-unionism," primarily because of the support of Brophy. Lewis—who was to hear much of the charge of dual-unionism in less than another ten years—cheerfully joined the unanimous condemnation with its order to all affiliates of the AFL to withdraw their support from Brookwood. When the 1928 AFL convention, after some debate, approved the Woll report and the action of the Executive Council, Brookwood was finished. Brophy, whose devotion to learning had earlier led him to start classes in District 2 in labor history, public speaking, parliamentary law and economics of the coal industry, saw another dream destroyed. The practical mind of John L. Lewis had no interest in this aspect of miner life, or any similar ethereal approaches to human betterment, during those years of his political ascendancy.

Yet Brophy stood always as the antithesis of John L. Lewis. His presence was a gnawing integrity, his vision an irritant among matters of practicality. When Lewis fought his personal battles with the bulls of the UMW, he knew how to defeat them, because he understood them. Never understanding Brophy, he undertook to simply demolish him. But one of the strengths of the vast and mysterious man that was John L. Lewis was that his perception of the mettle of men was so great that he could call back a John Brophy to use him when the need was overwhelming. And it was one of the strengths of John Brophy that he would come and serve.

3.

As soon as Lewis had his appointment as president, he began to move to fortify his position. He appointed his own vice-president, Philip Murray, whose years of service were never marred by disloyalty to Lewis. William Green was then secretary-treasurer of the UMW, before Lewis ultimately made him president of the American Federation of Labor. Green's timidity, vacillation and willingness to compromise made him no threat to the new president. But enemies there were, able, ambitious, and with some of the same sense of power that pervaded Lewis. In Illinois, where District 12 supplied more money and manpower than any other portion of the union, there was Frank Farrington, an even brawnier man than Lewis, intensely disappointed that Lewis had surpassed him in the union's ranks. Illinois also had John H. Walker, who became president of the State Federation and was acknowledged widely as one of the ablest men in American labor in those years. In the Kansas District 14, the president was Alexander Howat, whose battles with Lewis make colorful, interesting stories in the union's history. John Brophy was not considered a threat to John L. Lewis in the early 1920's, as Brophy's interests in educating miners in District 2, representing the men in their grievances, launching Brookwood College, and learning about social forces kept him more aloof from the earlier political struggles around Lewis.

Lewis faced his first election in 1920. A western miner from Washington, Robert J. Harlin, president of District 10 in Seattle, was well known throughout the union and had been prominent in its affairs long enough to entitle him to the first chance to defeat Lewis. Howat and Farrington were strongly behind Harlin, but Lewis campaigned vigorously, used his selected headquarters men wisely, and won over Harlin by 173,064 votes to 106,132, in what was very likely the last free and open election held by the United Mine Workers to this day.

Then the warfare with Howat and Farrington began. Young Lewis was confident enough of his powers in 1921 to throw a direct challenge even at Samuel Gompers. The elderly cigar maker had been president of the AFL since 1881, except for the one year that John McBride of the UMW had defeated him. Lewis went to the AFL convention in Denver to run against Gompers for president. Since the UMW was the largest and strongest union in the Federation, Lewis apparently believed he could use this bloc of votes along with the alliances with other unions he had made as a traveling representative for Gompers to carry him past the old master. But Harlin, Alex Howat and Frank Farrington were all UMW delegates. Their votes went to Gompers and against their own young president—which was the primary factor in the defeat of Lewis, whose case was almost destroyed when he could not even obtain the support of the best-known delegates from his own union. "It is indeed a sad commentary upon the intelligence of our representatives," wrote Lewis, "when we cannot reconcile our own differences to a degree where we would be able to extend a complimentary vote to the President of the organization in his candidacy against the present incumbent of the American Federation of Labor."

The excesses of Howat on the Kansas front made him one of Lewis's most memorable victims. Howat, rough, impetuous, always aggressive, was involved in a continual series of strikes. The niceties of either the law of Kansas or the rules of the UMW were never observed too carefully in his fights against the bosses, the newspapers, the politicians, and anyone else who stood in his way. Always a constitutionalist, Lewis had what he needed under UMW law to suppress Howat.

The Mine Worker constitution, in Article III, Section 2, had a provision that was enacted before John L. Lewis became president. "Charters of Districts, Sub-Districts and Local Unions may be revoked by the International President, who shall have authority to create a provisional government for the subordinate branch whose charter has been revoked." That was all there was to it. No reason need be given. No charges had to be specified. No trial was required. There was not a word in the governing document to define what conduct would sustain the unusual powers of the president.

This unusual authority has survived to this day. One could perhaps make an inexact comparison of districts, which are geographical segments of the UMW across the country, with states of the Union, and subdistricts and local unions could even be analogized to counties and cities. Even though the centralized authority of a labor organization is far greater than we have seen fit to bestow upon political organs of government, it would be unthinkable for the President of the United States to suspend a government of a state or any county or any city with a wayward leader. This is to say nothing of the complete absence of such established rights as being informed of what one is supposed to have done, and the opportunity to present a defense. The fact is that such a provision is patently illegal today under federal law, and was found to be so forty years ago when it came under litigation in court. But what is remarkable is that it was used so many times thereafter by Lewis with so little objection by those victimized by it.

Lewis unfolded Article III, Section 2, and suspended District 14, Alexander Howat, and all those who worked under him. The union's constitution did provide for a review of the president's authority by the executive board, but again there were no standards of any kind for guidance. Howat had little chance there. There was the additional right of appeal to the convention, where Howat and his supporters could expect to roll up considerable support. They did. But Lewis took the floor, defended his actions with some of his finest oratory, and by a narrow vote he was upheld.

This was almost literally the end of responsible second-echelon government in the United Mine Workers of America. By 1948, out of the thirty-one districts of the union, some twenty-one had been suspended by Lewis and "provisionals" appointed. When a district was suspended, there were no further elections; only those men sent in by John L. Lewis could act. This ancient authority too fell before court edict in 1972. Two federal judges in Washington and Pittsburgh ruled that such prolonged supervision of the districts violated federal law.

Under directions from the top, Alex Howat was expelled from membership in the UMW. He returned to convention after convention to fight for his restoration. He obtained a membership card from his old Kansas local union, had himself chosen as a delegate, and went to the convention in 1927 to try once again. The first effort was with the credentials committee, appointed by the president. Rejection there was a certainty. The next move was an appeal to the floor when the credentials committee gave its report.

An Illinois delegate named Hindmarsh, a convention gadfly for many seasons, rose to ask the credentials committee why Howat was not seated. Lewis had no intention of even allowing the credentials committee to engage in a debate on the subject. From the chair, he boomed out the answer.

"The credentials of Alexander Howat have not been reported to this convention because the International President returned his credentials to the local union in Kansas which gave them to him. That action was taken because he is not a member of the United Mine Workers of America."

Hindmarsh struggled for the floor, asking for permission to read a letter from William Green, who was by then president of the American Federation of Labor, in an effort to prove that Howat was indeed a member. Lewis denied permission.

A delegate named Stevenson then challenged Lewis, asking why Howat's dues were accepted by the local union in Kansas. Lewis said he knew neither why nor even that it happened. Stevenson started again: "I think everybody in this convention—"

"It does not make any difference what you think," roared Lewis. "The chair has ruled."

The report of the credentials committee, rejecting Howat's bid, was then accepted. Howat, who was present to argue his cause, stood and asked, "May I be given an opportunity to explain to the delegates why I should have a seat?"

"You will not, and you will sit down. Sit down now. The chair is talking to you."

Chairman John L. had spoken. Delegates began to shout and stamp; there was hissing and booing of Lewis; curses and threats were commonplace. There were roars and counterroars; then Lewis spoke again. "May the Chair state that you may shout until you meet each other in hell and he will not change his ruling."

Howat was swept out with wives, children, and other onlookers. His fights in the UMW convention to regain his place in the union were finished. By this time, the strength and skill of Lewis at dominating a convention were apparent to every delegate. Even when resolutions not acceptable to Lewis were passed, there was little hope for them. On one such occasion, after the body had acted contrary to the word that had been passed down, Lewis, before calling the next order of business, bluntly told those assembled what would happen.

"It is deplorable," he said, "that so much of the valuable time of this convention has been devoted to the discussion and passage of this resolution. All of your energies and all of your passions have been a tragic waste, for I tell you that this resolution is going where all resolutions go!"

By the time Lewis had finally disposed of Howat as an internal force, he had won other convention fights which added to his authority year after year. The president of the UMW, as is the case in practically all large unions, had the power for many years to appoint organizers and representatives. This is as widely accepted today as the right of General Motors to hire its representatives in all aspects of corporate life, but to trade-unionists in the 1920's, it was a serious issue fundamental to how unions should be operated. Many in the Mine Workers, seeded by shades of socialist intellectuals among descendants of European workers, were unsettled by the growing authority of John L. Lewis. There was genuine hostility among them against concentrations of power, no matter whether king, tsar, governor, or president of their own union. A movement to amend the constitution to elect organizers and representatives spread quickly in the early Lewis years. It reached its peak at the 1924 convention, and became the critical issue at that gathering.

Delegate Hindmarsh of Illinois, as on later occasions in taking a position opposite to that of Lewis, was one of the principal speakers supporting the election effort. But when he rose to speak, he was already under the spell of John L. Lewis. As he argued his cause, he stopped to pay tribute to Lewis, almost with an apology for the position he espoused. "I don't mean by anything I have said to detract from President Lewis. I give him credit for whipping into line, through the machine that he has, every rebel in the form of an officer that he had a short time ago. That has been possible because of the fact that he handles machines."

Hindmarsh paused. He reflected before he went to the basic issue. "Maybe it is a good thing for the organization. I say maybe it is, but even at that, the whole thing simmers down and resolves itself to the question: Are we to have an organization of democracy or are we to have an organization with a dictator at the head of it?"

Good miner Hindmarsh was asking a question that has been raised a thousand times through the centuries. The delegates gave him his answer. There was a roll-call vote, one of the closest Lewis ever faced. By a margin of 2,261 to 2,103, Lewis kept his control. The opponents never made a serious threat on this issue again.

The man most like Lewis in the union was Frank Farrington, president of District 12 in Illinois. He was considered a tough negotiator with the coal companies, after winning contract gains that surpassed those achieved by anyone else in the UMW. He carried his hefty presence with the same kind of majestic sweep as did Lewis. He authorized and supported one of the most remarkable labor publications ever to exist in the country, *The Illinois Miner,* edited by Oscar Ameringer. Ameringer's column under the pseudonym of Adam Coaldigger, impishly pronounced a-DAM coal digger, was widely read both by miners and intellectuals. Its barbs were hardly friendly to John L. Lewis.

Farrington shrewdly used his power base to attack the union's president. "It is my intent and purpose to destroy John L. Lewis." Farrington said this publicly in a union speech in Oklahoma, and he set about to do it. His refusal to back Lewis for the presidency of the AFL in 1921 was just the beginning. As a member of the UMW executive board, he opposed Lewis on point after point. He maintained a distant independence in District 12, and was the core of the opposition to Lewis throughout the UMW after the downfall of Howat and before the direct election challenge of John Brophy.

But it was Farrington who was destroyed by Lewis.

In 1926, Farrington had apparently signed a secret contract with the Peabody Coal Company in Illinois to serve as a labor consultant at $25,000 a year if he ever left the union ranks. While Farrington was absent in Europe as a fraternal delegate to the British Trades Union Congress, Lewis made the dramatic announcement that he had discovered the unknown contract. He immediately suspended the absent Farrington from his position as president of District 12. When Farrington finally returned to find his power shorn, it was too late. His attempts at explanation were ignored, and his usefulness in the labor movement was ended. Lewis was often asked how he came upon the document. "It is enough that I have it," he said, never revealing his source.

John Brophy had remained aloof from the warfare between Lewis and his archenemies, Howat and Farrington, although he consistently opposed the excommunication of Howat. Brophy's great interest was policies and programs. Lewis had temporarily won his political support in 1921 by endorsing government ownership of the mines as one of his planks when he challenged Samuel Gompers. But events were moving Brophy farther and farther from Lewis, and finally, the time came for Brophy to make the direct challenge himself, at great personal sacrifice. It too, like the others, was doomed to failure.

4·

The first dozen years of the reign of John L. Lewis as president of the Mine Workers was a story of disaster followed by disaster. The union he captured for himself had a half million members and a money fortress for a treasury when he took over. Union contracts dominated the industry; the daily wage of $7.50 was established. The rolls started downward year after year, and the treasury with it. By the time Lewis ended the internal warfare with his total victory, there were claims, more boastful than real, that the union still had at least 100,000 members. But other critics said there were fewer than 60,000 on the rolls. No one disputed that the mightiest union in America had fallen into weakness and ineffectiveness, existing largely because some of the mining companies declined to engage in a last campaign of total destruction. The union's inability to enforce its contracts posed so little threat to the more secure operators that they saw little point in administering the final coup.

Yet to place total responsibility upon John L. Lewis would be a selective sifting of the twenties. Almost every other union in the country fell into disarray in the same period. It was the decade of the open shop, of the American Plan, of wage cuts in a rising economy, and the outright death of many organizations of workingmen. Coal was a depressed industry, its abundance forcing prices steadily downward.

By 1926, said the Brookings Institution, the mine's capacity was at a billion tons; the need was for but half. Only a third of the men in the industry were needed full time to satisfy the demand for coal. There is no doubt that Lewis on behalf of the union resisted the trends, sometimes vigorously, whenever he could. There may be the telling charge that he never understood what was occurring; thousands of leaders of men in the same period suffered the same misfortune. There remains the even greater question of what Lewis could have done even had he possessed the wisdom of Solomon.

John Brophy too was deeply affected by what happened to coal mining and the union in the years of Harding, Coolidge and Hoover. Prices went steadily down. Railroad users had paid $4.20 a ton in 1920; and even before the crash of 1929 they were paying only $2.40. Wages were slashed relentlessly, first in the nonunion mines, and then even in those covered by contract, despite the existence of signed agreements. The eight-hour day, a rallying position for miners since the time of Daniel Weaver, likewise began to yield, as the nine-hour and ten-hour day came back into vogue. The problem of mine safety, one of the most depressing issues in industrial history, became more severe, as mine fatalities began to rise again. As work declined, youthful and vigorous men left coal mining to find other jobs, depriving the union of a vitality in its membership just as the decimation of French manhood in World War I drained the guts of the Third Republic.

Brophy, shortly after he had become president of District 2, had struggled to find a solution for the troubles he foresaw for the coal industry and the UMW. His key proposal was government ownership of the mines, a popular position among some of the older socialist miners from European backgrounds, as well as some of the more serious students of the industry among the higher echelons in the UMW. Brophy, encouraged by the support he believed Lewis was forced to give in 1921, was able to get a three-man Nationalization Research Committee established, with himself as its head. Careful plans were prepared, pamphlets were printed and distributed, and there was a kind of tireless lobbying both inside the union and outside to the public to try to win acceptance of the principles of public ownership as the way to cure a sick industry.

But as Brophy and the committee labored for wider approval, they gained less from Lewis. A gradual sniping against Brophy began to appear in the *Mine Workers Journal*. Lewis, acting with the same business outlook that pervaded his entire life, had taken a man from the Indianapolis Chamber of Commerce, Ellis Searles, and made him the *Journal*'s editor. Every printed word was the outlook of Lewis, every position taken was with the president's approval, a not unusual reflection of most union publications—and perhaps as it must be. The most that can be said against the *Journal* was that Lewis at least should have taken someone with a trade-union background, with a feeling for the men who labored in the mines, to insert an occasional worker's reflection among the edicts of the ruler. But on the other hand, an editor like Oscar Ameringer, who gave so much independence and wit and thoughtfulness to the *Illinois Miner,* could never have endured working for John L. Lewis. Ellis Searles made a perfect handmaiden.

By 1923, Lewis was ready to terminate the committee's work. His own program for the industry was simple: "Shut down 4,000 coal mines, force 200,000 miners into other industries, and the coal problem will settle itself. The public will then be assured of an adequate supply of low-priced fuel." This was the first hint of a Lewis program of a quarter century later, a program that did remake the coal industry. Even in the 1920's, Lewis was asking for more mechanization, decrying the unwillingness of the operators to modernize their methods. "We decided it is better to have a half million men working in the industry at good wages . . . than it is to have a million working in the industry in poverty."

But theories and solutions were obscured by the realities. In 1922, the union fought to hold the wage line at $7.50. In 1924, when many of the national contracts expired, union officials met in Florida with representatives of major companies in the Central Competitive Field districts. With the prospect of strong pressures for wage cuts, Lewis enlisted the aid of his friend Secretary of Commerce Herbert Hoover. Through appropriate conversations with business and industrial leaders, the companies were persuaded to extend union contracts for three more years into 1927, still holding the line on wages at the same $7.50 per day that had been in effect since World War I. The union's exultation at being able to keep the same pay scale for nine years in a row is in jarring contrast to the present patterns of wage increases in every labor contract.

But a union contract with no cut in pay became meaningless when mine after mine began to operate outside the pattern. The Southern mines had never been unionized, and by 1929, with price cutting, they had gained the market for almost half the coal mined in the country. Some of the Northern mines began to ignore the agreement, others imposed transparent dodges, and all functioned with near-immunity from the union. The largest coal company in District 2, according to Brophy, leased its mines to dummy operators, who operated without a contract and immediately cut wages 30 percent. In January, 1923, this same company paid a dividend of 103 percent.

Other operators simply ignored their contracts. Labor law was so ill-developed at that time that there was neither legal machinery to enforce the contracts nor even the knowledge of how to try it. For decades, the only methods of survival and enforcement known to unions was economic power. When muscles were weak, defeat was inevitable.

Brophy, almost alone among leaders of the UMW, tried to resist the violations. His complaints to Lewis brought a request for specific evidence almost as if Lewis had ignored the obvious. Brophy carefully compiled a list of violations by companies, covering more than a hundred mines. He returned to headquarters to confront Lewis again. John L. said he would ask the government to act, hopeful perhaps that Hoover would once more intervene. His other solution was "to tighten our belts and wait for better days."

"That's not enough," said Brophy.

Lewis testily turned to him with what Brophy called the usual "growl." "What's *your* answer?"

They had their debate, head to head, in the privacy of Lewis's office. If the government was to be asked to act, said Brophy, it should do the whole job, nationalizing the industry. Lewis's practical response was that it was impossible. Brophy pressed forward. "But we still have the duty to ask, to demand, to agitate. Pretty soon the union will be too weak to raise its voice. We can't just wait."

But waiting was all that was done. Lewis took no action, either to try to organize the nonunion mines or to stop the cuts and shutdowns throughout the Northern coal fields. Brophy was realistic enough to recognize how hard it was—his spirit was never to stop trying. He claimed that the staff organizers on the payroll were idle sycophants of Lewis, doing nothing but oiling the personal political machine of their boss. At the same time, more and more districts were suspended, some because of loss of membership and others because of incipient opposition to Lewis.

"Slowly but inexorably," said John Brophy, "I was driven to the conclusion that Lewis's power had to be challenged by a candidate for the presidency of the UMW who would offer a constructive program for rebuilding the union."

Brophy's job as president of District 2 would have to be yielded to run against Lewis. He knew the realities. "I would have to face a storm of slander. I would have to pit my puny financial resources and my tenuous links with individuals here and there against the Lewis machine, with all the funds of the international union at its disposal, with political agents masquerading as organizers spotted in every center, and with its well-oiled machinery for producing votes even where no votes existed." He could count on blocs of anti-Lewis votes in Illinois and Kansas, depend upon rank-and-filers who loyally supported him in District 2, and pick up votes of many other working miners throughout the country. Was this enough to shake the Lewis seat?

Brophy campaigned widely on the issues facing coal miners. His regular pamphlets, headed by the words, "Save the Union," pointed out the disasters. They proposed programs to deal with each item. Lewis neither talked about the issues nor even disputed the charges that Brophy made. He railed against disruption, outsiders, and Communists—a campaign litany familiar to latter-day union organizers who heard them come from half the employers in the land.

Every UMW staff man became a full-time campaign worker for John L. Lewis, with his salary paid by the union. Not many coal miners could find the time to work for John Brophy, even if they felt free enough from the imposing presence of the Lewis staff men. Old Brookwood students came to help where they could. His campaign committee was Brophy and his wife, aided by Powers Hapgood, who came to their home at night to work around the kitchen table. "I had two or three hundred dollars to spend on printing and postage, most of which went to mail out copies of my open letter," said Brophy. Fiery Alex Howat, out of his hatred for Lewis, toured coal fields to speak for Brophy, and other occasional renegades would try to get the message to the miners. Lewis, as would any incumbent concerned about his job, used the full authority of the union hierarchy to put down the last serious election challenge of his life.

The count surprised no one. In December, the tellers reported that Lewis had won by 170,000 to 60,000. The official tally was not published until May, 1927, when Brophy began to take a careful look. In the anthracite regions in District 1, where Brophy had campaigned, there was a reported membership of 9,262. Of this number, 8,466 votes were listed for Lewis; only 232 for Brophy. In District 9, Lewis was given 3,483 and Brophy only 9. In District 20, in eastern Kentucky, the union was so defunct that the entire district paid per capita tax for only one single member for the first six months of 1926, and not even that one for the last half of the year. But votes were tabulated from sixteen local unions, which listed 2,686½ members. The result: Lewis, 2,686½; Brophy, 0. Brophy wryly commented that in addition to the absolute unanimity, there was such good health and intensity of interest that not one man failed to come out and cast his ballot.

Brophy was able personally to check the votes of five local unions in District 5 to compare the results with the report of the tellers. He said the actual count was: Brophy, 635; Lewis, 487. The tellers' report showed Lewis, 1,473; Brophy, 635. Each president of each local made a sworn affidavit to the actual count, which Brophy filed with the executive board with his protest. These affidavits were ignored; the tellers' report was confirmed without comment or opinion or reason.

Brophy claimed such widespread fraud and vote stealing that he was able to maintain that he, not Lewis, had won a majority of the votes. When the executive board denied every protest, and when the outcry subsided in the *Illinois Miner* and a few other muckraking publications, Brophy knew his fight was over. John L. Lewis was still in firm command of the United Mine Workers of America.

5·

There was still one last major fight over control of the union before Lewis gained absolute, unassailable authority. John Brophy appeared at the 1927 convention, before the tellers had made their official count, and gave example after example of what he considered was the fraudulent vote. Powers Hapgood, the Harvard intellectual who had become a mine worker out of social conscience and a desire to work in the union movement, went among the delegates spreading the Brophy story wherever he could. Thereafter, during one of the convention nights, Hapgood was cornered in the hallway of his hotel floor by a team of delegates and beaten into a bloody trip to the hospital. There was no further campaigning for Brophy's lost cause that year.

Brophy's letters about the rigged results, however, kept enough of a spark alive to generate the largest anti-Lewis gathering ever held in the United Mine Workers. On April 1, 1928, a Save the Union Conference was held in Pittsburgh, attended by 1,100 men. The theme was to capture the union from "its present incompetent and greedy leadership under President John L. Lewis." Speakers denounced the record of Lewis from one debacle to another. They proposed new programs to appeal to miners. There was a singing chant throughout the meeting: "Lewis must go, Lewis must go."

While this gathering had the enthusiasm of an old-fashioned church revival meeting, it accomplished perhaps even less than emotional appeals to be saved. Men felt a common bond in their dislike and even hatred for Lewis; but no one knew how to put the bell on the cat. They were evangelists among the converted; the real power was in the hands of John L. Lewis, from the staff organizers who would execute every order down to those in the lower echelons who would have no hesitation in carrying out a suggestion to beat Powers Hapgood into bloody helplessness.

Lewis quickly struck back. In early May of 1928, the international executive board issued a decree that John Brophy was expelled from the United Mine Workers of America. There was no trial, no hearing, no statement of charges, no chance to defend. The Save the Union Committee was called a dual movement, one of the highest crimes in the labor movement, and since Brophy was its chairman, he was ordered out. His old local union in Nanty Glo was informed that he was forever barred.

The high spirits of the dissidents in April had dissipated into fragmented efforts by September. Brophy, unhappy with the negative course of the April meeting in Pittsburgh, resigned as chairman of the Save the Union Committee before the month was out, and before the UMW executive board decreed him out of the organization which had been his life to that time. Some of the delegates who were avowed Communists, along with their supporters, formed a new miners' organization and called it the National Miners' Union. One of the genuine heroes of miners' fights, Frank Keeney, went into West Virginia and organized a new West Virginia Mine Workers Union. But these efforts at opposition, with no growth or potential, were on their way to extinction when one of Lewis's major mistakes revived all their hopes.

Because of the depressing times into which the union had fallen, along with its depleted treasury and the discord and bitterness that was everywhere, Lewis simply called off the scheduled 1929 convention. Because the UMW constitution said that the organization was in existence only until its next convention, the enemies of Lewis now had a legal point which they could turn against the old constitutionalist himself. Since the union existed only until the next required convention, and since the convention had been canceled, the union itself had gone out of existence. There was no longer a United Mine Workers of America, they said.

The rebels then issued a convention call for March 10, 1930, for the Reorganized United Mine Workers of America. A man named Lewis wasn't even invited. All the energy and strength of District 12 went into hosting the new convention in Springfield. John H. Walker, who was still president of the Illinois Federation of Labor, was one of the founders, along with Alex Howat and most of the men who had fought John L. Lewis unsuccessfully since 1920. John Brophy, who was forced to earn his living as a soup salesman for the Columbia Conserve Company, a family business owned by the father of Powers Hapgood, came as a delegate, although still somewhat uneasy over the threat to the union that still meant so much to him.

The delegates exceeded the oratorical denunciations of Lewis that had colored the Pittsburgh conference in 1928. They told stories of his arrogance, his high-handedness, his neglect of the unorganized, his sympathy for the operators, the manipulation of his men through extravagance and corruption. The devil himself undoubtedly would have been embarrassed.

Lewis met the new threat with a clever ploy of his own. He called a special convention of the UMW, to meet in Indianapolis on the same day the RUMW was to convene. Both sides were serious enough about the legalities to race for the true title to the union. The Springfield convention assembled quickly, with 450 delegates, and adopted the name of the United Mine Workers of America and enough of a constitution to proclaim its existence as of 11:21 A.M. Forty minutes later, the Lewis convention at Indianapolis, as its first order of business, extended the UMW constitution. Both claimed to be the true union, like warring divisions of churches of history.

The master strategist for the Springfield convention was Oscar Ameringer. The original choice for president had been John H. Walker, but Ameringer threw his support to Howat, who was elected. The choice of the erratic and alcoholic Howat was one of the major mistakes of the rebels, since he was never able to give them real leadership. In a catharsis of democratic spirit, the delegates insisted that committees be elected rather than appointed. The salary of president was reduced from the $12,000 that Lewis received to $5,000. Two entire days were consumed in debate over whether to seat the discredited Frank Farrington as a delegate. Poor Farrington, still trying to return to the labor movement, was seated finally, and another rift was created inside the Reorganized.

The attacks upon Lewis in Springfield were equaled by the statements emanating from Indianapolis. Lewis, in opening his convention, said: "Over in Springfield there is a little band of malcontents, representing the offscourings of this organization. It is a ragtag-and-bobtail element gathered there muttering in their beards."

William Green, now thoroughly secure as president of the American Federation of Labor, with the support of Lewis, came to the aid of his old union and addressed the Indianapolis convention, giving it his blessing as the true Mine Workers Union. Green, still doing the bidding of Lewis, turned the legalities of intra-union law upon John H. Walker, who was both an old compatriot of Green in the UMW and a respected friend. Green insisted that Walker, because of his participation in the Springfield movement, resign as president of the Illinois Federation of Labor, which was an official arm of the national federation. Walker was ousted, stripped of all his offices, and forbidden even to attend the AFL convention. It was a serious and costly mistake to oppose John L. Lewis.

At the same time, the old local in Panama, Illinois, which had elected young Lewis as its president and sent him to Springfield as a lobbyist was, like most of the other Illinois locals, staunchly with Walker and other officers of District 12 in supporting the Reorganized movement. The Panama local, where Lewis still held his UMW membership, wrote him to return his union card. "You are unfit to be a member of the United Mine Workers," was its blunt statement to its most renowned son. The Springfield group put Lewis on trial for dual-unionism because he had conducted the Indianapolis convention when the true United Mine Workers was the organization that had assembled in Springfield and adopted a constitution. On the other hand, the Indianapolis gathering expelled all the top leadership of the Reorganized who still held UMW cards for the same crime of dual-unionism. Deviationism, whether it be from the word of Stalin, the mores of the corporate body, the rules of the United States Senate, or the commands of a labor union, is a risky endeavor wherever practiced, as people inside organizations continue to behave with predictable consistency in seeking to suppress those who do not conform.

When the shouting and the tumult of the twin conventions subsided, the hand-to-hand and head-to-head warfare began. The combat was in every arena where unions' warriors meet. They struggled in the courts, in the streets and alleyways with bullets and fists, in organizing campaigns, and in propaganda attacks. There was the pen of Ameringer against the rhetoric of Lewis; but it was Lewis who held the official ties to the American labor movement through Green and the Federation. There were the organizing efforts of Howat and Adolph Germer, another unusually able man who was a key figure in the struggle against Lewis, but it was Lewis who had the staff and the money and the trained troops who never questioned the word of their commander. Howat may have believed that he controlled Kansas, but when Lewis suspended every officer of District 14, the coal companies checked off the union dues and forwarded them to John L. Lewis. Coal miners in Kansas were forced to sign loyalty oaths to John L. Lewis, a different kind of yellow-dog contract in labor's history.

But it was in Illinois where the critical battlefield was found. Illinois had been the biggest and most prominent bituminous state; the key rebel leadership had its roots there; the *Illinois Miner,* the information-soul of the Reorganized, was the most potent anti-Lewis weapon; with the destruction of the UMW in Kentucky and West Virginia and its decimation in Pennsylvania, the union miners in Illinois, now more than 60 percent of the total union rolls, would, after all, determine the final ending of the union's own civil war. The brotherhood envisioned by Daniel Weaver was put to its severest rending even in the same mines where the redoubtable Englishman turned his dreams into tablets of history.

Lewis knew he must fight in Illinois or go under, even with his official status and money and authority. Despite the wide respect for Walker and the solidarity of his oldest enemies in the union, Lewis still commanded areas of support in the state. Philip Murray and Frank J. Hayes, the man who preceded Lewis as UMW president, and who had a revival of energies, made speaking tours over the state to stir support for Lewis. In the small mining town of Royalton shortly after the conventions adjourned, there was a bloody confrontation that was to exemplify the struggle in Illinois.

Adolph Germer, the Reorganized's vice-president, and probably its ablest organizer, came into Royalton in southern Illinois to address a local union that was strongly in the anti-Lewis camp. Ray Edmundson, one of the loyal Lewis staff men, assembled a force of three hundred miners from nearby West Frankfort and Zeigler, whose histories of violence in mid-America rival that of any Serbian village. They took their rifles, shotguns and pistols when they marched upon the Royalton local's meeting. This was an advance task force in the best traditions of any guerrilla army, and bloodshed was of little concern. There were bullets and shots and clubs and fists and beaten heads, and a meeting that was never held. Five men were wounded and one supporter of the Reorganized, Barney Davie, was dead. Germer too was badly beaten in another foray into another town. Through every Illinois mining town where there were divided loyalties, union man hunted union man, with bodily harm, from death to unconsciousness, as the immediate objective—all for the passions and power of the true church.

But it was a ruling in the law, not violence, that became the decisive shot in the campaign. The court dispute had begun in 1929, when Lewis had suspended all the officers of District 12 and appointed a provisional government under the unchecked authority given him by the UMW constitution. The elected officers of District 12 filed suit in an Illinois Circuit Court to enjoin Lewis from ousting them and to regain the revoked charter of the district. The case, pending on the court calendar while the rival conventions boiled and the organizing wars followed, had been widened to embrace the issue of which organization was the lawful union. When the opinion was released, it held that Lewis had originally lacked the authority to throw out District 12 and its officers. They, who were elected by the membership, and not the appointees of Lewis, were the true authorities of District 12 of the United Mine Workers of America. (Lawyers may well wonder why other of the numerous victims of the unilateral authority of Lewis under the UMW constitution did not seek the same successful approach in the courts. But the Illinois ruling is the only known legal attack until the current federal government's litigation against the provisional governments inside the UMW.)

But the decision also held that the constitution of the union had not lapsed in 1929 when Lewis failed to call a convention. The true United Mine Workers of America was the union of John L. Lewis, not the Reorganized of Howat, Germer, Walker and Ameringer. The rebels were legally dead, but their major architects were restored to legitimacy and a return to the mother union under the thundering enmities of John L. Lewis. The tension and uneasiness that prevailed led into 1932 and the creation of yet another miners' union that has survived to this day. Lewis had beaten off the Reorganized, the National Miners Union and the West Virginia union, but warfare in Illinois was not to end for many bitter seasons over yet another organization of coal diggers.

The mines in Illinois were struck in 1932. When the contract between the Illinois Coal Operators Association and District 12 expired on April 1, the companies demanded a 30 percent wage cut from the $6.10-a-day base rate. After three months of a shutdown, John H. Walker, back at the head of the union negotiating team, capitulated to the $5-a-day offer. The miners voted 4 to 1 against it and continued the strike. Walker, rejected by his people, unable to end the strike, called on Lewis for help.

Lewis met with Governor Emmerich of Illinois, talked with the producers and agreed upon the same $5 scale that Walker had initiated. The proposal was sent back for a new vote with a message from the president: "The agreement, distasteful as it may be, represents every concession that at this time can be wrung from the impoverished coal companies in a stricken and almost expiring industry." There was no indication that hostile miners were in any better mood than when they repudiated the same offer that Walker had presented.

The locals, voting by secret ballot, sent their returns to District headquarters in Springfield for the tally. At the end of the first day's count, with more than one hundred local unions reporting, the voting showed a landslide for rejection of the Lewis proposal. The tellers took the ballots to a bank vault that night and prepared for the next day's effort that would conclude the referendum.

The tellers went to the bank the following morning, took the ballot boxes, and began a leisurely walk down the street toward union headquarters. A car pulled alongside. One of the men in it was Fox Hughes, a Lewis supporter who was now vice-president of District 12. There was a brief conversation; the tellers tossed the ballots into the car. They then proceeded on to the office and rushed in with the announcement they had been "robbed."

Lewis issued a proclamation. There was a state of emergency within District 12 because bandits had stolen the ballots, thus preventing the completion of the count. The president would have to act in the best interests of the membership. He met quickly with the operators that day and negotiated a "new" agreement. No one has reported how its terms differed from the one submitted to the voters, but the same $5 wage scale was in effect. Lewis issued another edict: since this was a new contract under his emergency powers, it did not need to be submitted to the miners for ratification. He signed it and announced that the strike was over.

"Coal diggers in southern Illinois have been betrayed once more by the reactionary leadership of the UMW," said the *Nation*. The magazine reported the "theft" of the ballots and commented on the lack of indignation in the outside world about the role of Fox Hughes and the UMW in the affair. Labor-watchers of the day, worn by the traumas of the Depression, made their cynical observations too, but nothing was done.

Except by the miners. War—not metaphorical, not a writer's

phrasemaking, but old-fashioned armed hostilities—was the answer. Mass meetings were held to denounce Lewis and the settlement. It was reported that ten thousand miners met in one gathering in Benld, Illinois, on August 14. The next day, at Taylorville, eight thousand angry men surrounded the four big mines of the Peabody Coal Company, carrying shotguns, pistols, pitchforks, ax handles, and every conceivable form of weapon. The miner who even thought of working was risking his life. A week later, there was death at nearby Zeigler, where gunfire killed one and wounded six others. The strikers rallied with a force of more than ten thousand men, almost the equivalent of an army division. Heavily armed deputies halted a night march, injuring another hundred fifty. The National Guard was called into southern Illinois. John L. Lewis announced that twenty more leaders had been expelled from the United Mine Workers for life. The companies, the police, and the union had united against striking coal miners.

The cry for a new union spread through Illinois. By September 1, barely three weeks after Lewis had signed the new agreement, there was a founding convention in Gillespie, Illinois, with 272 rank-and-file delegates. All the old leaders of the Save the Union Committee and the Springfield convention were absent, either silently observing or unhappily supporting Lewis. The Progressive Miners of America, a new international union of mine workers, was formed. Small coal producers in central Illinois, humbled for years by the giants that made up the Illinois Coal Operators Association, recognized the new union. They offered a checkoff of union dues in return for the same $5 wage scale that the big producers had settled with Lewis. Since one of the founding planks at the Gillespie gathering was the $6.10 wage rate, this was almost a death blow to the PMA, but the checkoff insured its survival and the deal was made. There was never in the future any wage differential between mining unions in Illinois.

The Progressive Miners of America, perhaps not worthy of more than a passing footnote, has survived as a minor irritant to the UMW. Small, ineffective and isolated, it has had its own scandals, its crimes, its prosecutions, its sellouts, but after its original hold in Illinois, it has done no more. Its continued existence is a tableau to one more rebellion against John L. Lewis, marked only by its survival, not its accomplishments.

With the gradual decline of the PMA after its own $5 wage settlement, with the capitulation of the old stalwarts of District 12 and the Reorganized Mine Workers, with the graceful withdrawal of John Brophy, the crushing of Farrington and Howat, the loss of funds for Ameringer to publish the now-extinct *Illinois Miner,* and the repetitive demonstration of the authority of John L. Lewis, the president of the United Mine Workers had won all his internal wars by the end of 1932. Not even his public support of Herbert Hoover for President against the challenge and hope of Franklin D. Roosevelt disturbed his defeated rivals any longer. His enemies were destroyed; he was supreme.

6·

If John L. Lewis had departed the labor movement in 1933, or had met an untimely death, those scholars of labor's past would indeed have placed a harsh judgment upon him. His years in office to that point had been filled with the almost virtual destruction of the United Mine Workers of America. It had lost its contracts, its wage scales, its membership. Its once great treasury, the pride of America's unions, was thin and insecure. It had no strength to resist the operators, who could even count on the support of Lewis himself when they needed it.

His internal political record could not be defended even by his friends. No man was ever permitted to defy him. Those who fought him could face almost sure expulsion from the union. Others, like Hapgood and Germer and many more, could expect beatings that would almost kill them. His troops, like the cadre commanded by Edmundson to smash the Royalton meeting, could be expected to use whatever violent means were necessary to compete with the moment's exigencies.

The charge of vote stealing could be maintained, based upon the shameful evidence of the 1926 campaign supplied by Brophy. Lewis hardly bothered denying it. His convenient use of the "robbery" of secret ballots of striking miners in the 1932 strike in Illinois was another example of his ruthlessness. He often supported coal companies against his own men, wiping out an anthracite strike in Pennsylvania in 1931 as another example. His abandonment of other strikers and his failure to rally to other miner battles in Kentucky and West Virginia were notorious.

He was regularly called one of the most reactionary men in American labor, with no program, no vision, no concept of the future. His political support of Coolidge and Hoover enraged many others in the union movement who had a different idea of the course America should follow. His constant redbaiting, even extending to the support given Brophy in 1926, was but one of the demagogic tools he would use whenever it suited his purpose.

About all that could be said for John L. Lewis as the Age of Roosevelt began was that he had survived.

Then the questions arise as to what course the miners might have followed had John Brophy won the 1926 election. Brophy, to his death, always believed that he had won, but in the lost archives of the past, there is no proof that could ever resolve the claims. Could Brophy have saved the contracts? Could he have kept the once great strengths in West Virginia and Pennsylvania from eroding? Could he have organized the Southern producers in any meaningful way? Could he have tamed the wild men in the union and still maintained internal democracy? Could his programs, all of them thoughtfully considered, have succeeded among coal miners? Or would the disasters of the Depression, the fallen price of coal, the hostility of the operators, have weakened the UMW even more had he been president?

Brophy, measured by every commentator of his times, every student of the movement, every aging patriarch who knew him from the past, surely ranks as probably the most decent human being ever to involve himself in the problems of working America. He provided a tinge of scholarship among workers when it was sorely needed. He stood for unshakable integrity when it counted, as in his support of Jim Maurer in Pennsylvania when Lewis was coming to power. His own decision to oppose Lewis was made with the full knowledge of the consequences of defeat, of the fact that he might not be able to provide food for his wife and young children if he lost. His own unwillingness to support every rebel outburst merely because it was anti-Lewis was a consistent devotion to his own ideal of progress for his union. Even his willingness to come back to Lewis and work under him as a loyal servant, as happened later, is a testimonial to the devotion to workingmen that dominated his life.

Yet, one's admiration for the man that was John Brophy only leads to deeper inquiries. He lacked the flamboyance and showmanship to bring men to their feet cheering, as John L. Lewis could. One of his devoted old friends, who worked closely with both Brophy and Lewis, remarked that Brophy could never make a speech the way Lewis could. There was always something lacking. But yet, when one read the text of Brophy's remarks, it was filled with impressive substance. One could hardly imagine John Brophy stirring the hopes of American workers in the CIO days as did Lewis, or even denouncing his enemies with the furor of thunder that Lewis gave forth from the Indianapolis platform in 1930 during the days of the rival conventions.

Did Brophy have the toughness, the resourcefulness, the guile to ultimately triumph in the jungle of intra union politics? Was he not cut more from the cloth of a Weaver or a Siney or a John Mitchell, none of whom could survive within the union? Did not his own willingness to respect the other point of view as compared with Lewis's absolute certainty at all times; his care to insure fairness and due process to the membership as contrasted with the dictatorial edicts of Lewis; his hopes to educate, as compared with Lewis's authoritarian commands—did not these all contribute to his defeat? Brophy could not have rigged the counts of tellers or upheld a "robbery" of strikers' ballots—it was not within him to do so—but it was Lewis who made the great mark in labor history.

Lewis was power and authority, from his girth to his fists to his eyebrows to his booming voice that produced such rhetoric. There was no boom to Brophy, only honesty and incisiveness and, yes, idealism. The word *charisma* had not been applied by the writers of the times as one of their most descriptive clichés, but whatever it was, Lewis had it in abundance over any man who ever walked in the same room with him. The man of gentleness could not stand alongside the man of iron; their themes were too disparate.

One harks back to the theories of Carlyle on leadership. Where stand the Brophys, with their thoughtfulness and honesty, alongside the bruising violence of the bulls of the Lewis stripe? But Lewis, as time proved, had something more than the strong man's lust for dominance, as marked the parallel career of Big Bill Hutcheson of the Carpenters, who left nothing else. Yet even the Hutchesons usually crush the Brophys inside their own organizations.

But what of Carlyle's intuitive insight into reality? The argument could be made that the true idealist lacks it in the world of violence and despotism. But does he lack it because he sees the better side of man, the hope of fraternity that moved Daniel Weaver? Is he the hopeless eternal dreamer who leaves no monuments save memories of his integrity—memories that will evaporate with time—as did John Brophy? Does intuitive insight into reality, which John L. Lewis surely commanded as much as any man, claim its successes because it more accurately measures the cruelties, foibles and passions of fellow citizens? Then, what mighty force inside, or what meat to feed a Caesar, moves the intuitive realist like Lewis to ruthless dominance of those around him, to stamp his own brawny personage upon everything he touches? Are the John Brophys of history, who submerge person to goals and purposes, designed to be followers, not leaders, as Brophy himself followed Lewis in the story we have yet to tell?

There are basically two remaining themes of Lewis and the miners, one of triumph and the other of ultimate tragedy. Brophy might not have produced either. Then, one may ask, who has gained and who has lost, and what is the meaning of it all? And, as we shall inquire again and again, what are the means that men may employ to achieve one and prevent the other? But to approach this inquiry, it is necessary to look again in perspective at the triumphs and achievements of Lewis which were yet to come as he continued to build his cocoon of political despotism that he bequeathed to those who followed.

4. Solidarity Forever

TRIUMPH AND TOTAL DOMINATION

The stricken union arose. It revived. The feat was accomplished in a few hectic months, as in blitz times when wars are won. The incredible campaign it waged became the foundation for years of strife and achievement; it became the launching point for the unionization of American enterprise that structured an industrial society. This in turn made management-labor relationships a matter of grave national policy. It occupied the Congress and the courts and the attention of the public for decades to come. It led to new power bases in American politics. It was a renascence that made organizations of ordinary men more powerful than the individual ethic that had previously dominated the course of a nation.

It was all done in the name of grimy-faced men who mined coal. Its central figure was, of course, John Llewellyn Lewis, whose inexplicable story will need to be fully told by some perceptive biographer of the future. For now, it is his influence on the affairs of other men and how they accepted it or reacted to it, that concerns us.

1·

It was in 1933 that the efforts of a new President stirred such hope among despondent people. Soon after the inauguration, there was quick public talk of a plan of new industrial codes to revive the dying economy. Congressional draftsmen began to put together the words that became the National Industrial Recovery Act. While the Blue Eagle was in its birth process, John L. Lewis read the fine print from drafts supplied to him. The code for each industry embraced concepts of cooperation between managers and workers for the common survival, a necessity in any war effort. But if workingmen were to play any realistic part in the process of recovery, there must be someone to speak in their behalf, to represent their interests. John L. Lewis knew that the only coherent voice had to come from some kind of organized representation, and that meant union. Where there were no unions, organizations would have to be formed. Lewis had the managerial insight to recognize this fact, a reality that has strangely escaped the awareness of so many who devote their energies to the business side of life. Lewis had written in 1925: "Trade-unionism is a phenomenon of capitalism quite similar to the corporation. One is essentially a pooling of labor for purposes of common action in production and sales. The other is a pooling of capital for exactly the same purpose. The economic aims of both are identical—gain."

Consequently, Lewis was surely one of the few men, if not the first, to grasp the organizing possibilities inherent in the legislative proposals that became the NRA. Only Sidney Hillman and David Dubinsky, who represented needle-trades unions, the "intellectuals" of the labor movement, appeared to have an appreciation of the realities similar to that of Lewis.

In early May, 1933, a few days before the NRA was formally introduced into Congress, Lewis called all his organizers and staff men into a general meeting. He explained his understanding of the proposed law. He predicted that it would be passed. He was by now an experienced tactician; he laid before them an entire program. The language of Section 7-a of the new NRA bill was something new in American life. It contained magic words that were to become the fundamental charter of the later Wagner Act and are the foundation of American labor law to this day. Every industrial code was required to have a provision "that employees shall have the right to organize and bargain collectively through representatives of their own choosing, and shall be free from the interference, restraint, or coercion of employers of labor . . ." This was a new freedom, recognized in law for the first time in history. The discharge, the blacklist, the yellow-dog contract, the banishment for even thoughts of unionism, had plagued the fathers of John L. Lewis and John Brophy and all intrepid workmen for decades thereafter. This kind of employer action had been such an accepted practice in American life to that point that few persons even realized that broad words of salvation could change the old realities. They made their greatest impact upon John L. Lewis.

Lewis told his men that the union treasury, or what was left of it, was committed to a new organizing effort to the last dollar. When President Roosevelt signed the new bill into law on June 16, 1933, the UMW organizing campaign was already under way. Staff men poured into mining towns. "The president wants you to join the union," the organizers told coal miners. They didn't say what president; the miners could have thought they meant Roosevelt; the organizers, if challenged, could blithely say, "Why, President Lewis, of course." This line was so effective that one coal company was prompted to issue a notice to its employees that President Roosevelt is not an organizer for the United Mine Workers."

But the urging of a president, whether of a nation or a union, was not enough in itself to cause men to sign union cards. Miners had suffered through a long night. In the territory of once powerful District 2 in central Pennsylvania, where John Brophy had once built a vigilant organization, the checkweighmen were gone, and a miner's "ton" had ballooned up to 2,600 and even 3,000 pounds, for which the pay had dropped as low as 28 cents. Diggers began to complain bitterly, almost with the same kind of resistant spirit that moved men in the Belleville fields in the first days of the Civil War when Daniel Weaver emerged. Despair and hopelessness had dominated coal miners for a decade; gloom had outlived its usefulness. When the national leader in Washington began to act for a country, men believed it was time to act for themselves.

There were still some men of ability who had remained loyal to Lewis during the severe internal wars. Philip Murray, Thomas Kennedy, Van Bittner, William Mitch, and a revived Frank Hayes went into the fields like generals of divisions to enroll the awakening miners. Enthusiasm was so high that miners were sworn into membership by mass inductions. The enmities against John L. Lewis among the staff representatives were swept aside. Organizers who had not signed a new member in years were deluged with requests to join the new army. They told each other in amazement, "By God, the old union is coming back."

By mid-June, delegates in District 5, representing 40,000 miners, came to a meeting to draft plans for bargaining with the operators. In July, some 2,579 delegates came to Charleston, speaking for 160,000 newly organized miners, demanding shorter hours and better wages. Miners in the South were coming into the fold so quickly that organizers were racing from camp to camp to administer the oath of obligation. In areas where the county sheriff and the town police had been the first to greet organizers in older days with stern warnings to get out, there was almost a complete absence of opposition. Frank Hayes wrote in one of his reports: "I addressed a monster mass meeting here in Raton, New Mexico, yesterday. A few years ago our representatives were chased out of this town by the police-protected thugs of the coal operators, but now the mayor of the town gives us the city park for our meeting."

There were reports that storekeepers in the coal towns welcomed the organizers, gave them gasoline for their depression-worn cars, and plied them with encouragement and suggestions. Anyone who could help the thin, ragged, penniless people of the mining camps was welcome. Van Bittner reported by June 22 that the entire northern field in West Virginia was completely organized. Sam Caddy, another staff man, said that Kentucky miners had joined. Philip Murray said that by the end of June there were 128,000 new members in the Pennsylvania bituminous fields. John Brophy's comment a few years later was that desire for the union was so great that the men "organized themselves."

In all of the history of labor unions in America, there has never been any other organizing campaign carried out so quickly with enrollment of so many members as the 1933 UMW drive. The reasons were basically three: the times, the tradition, and Lewis. Not one alone could have done it; but the amalgamation of these factors made it one of the most exciting events of the lives of men like Murray and Bittner, and even moved the emotions of the massive Lewis.

Waves of spirit sweep across an entire people rarely, and only in great moments. The feeling of unity of a nation immediately after the Pearl Harbor attack is one of the best examples. The uplift after the inauguration of a young Kennedy is a somewhat lesser one. It happened in 1933; even those of us who were youngsters old enough to have an awareness of public issues were swept up in it. Tapping a phrase from the late Mr. Justice Brandeis, it was even more than "a brooding omnipresence in the skies." The words of Roosevelt brought stirring, guiding hope. Men were eager to try new ways, to act with boldness, to join together to make an effort to pick up a country. In the mine fields, as later occurred in the factories, fear of the boss had run its course; there was nothing more that could be done to a man. As one young economist who came to Washington said: "The climate was exciting. You were part of a society that was on the move. You were involved in something that could make a difference. Laws could be changed. So could the conditions of people."

Gardiner C. Means, a veteran of the early Roosevelt era, in reminiscing over the times, made these comments: "Talking a couple of days ago with a couple of old New Dealers, we agreed it was a very exhilarating period. There was no question in our minds, we were saving the country." This was the kind of feeling that pervaded a nation and moved coal miners to join the union.

In every mining camp in the country, men knew of the United Mine Workers of America. It had achieved such respect and notoriety under John Mitchell that a grand reservoir of admiration remained, even among the fearful men who dropped out of it in the twenties. Its troubles under Lewis had not removed it from the public prints; its reputation for strength and effectiveness was still far stronger than reality. Sons of immigrants from England, Scotland and Wales remembered the union backgrounds of their fathers. The old stories in the mining towns carried their legends; the old union had never died.

It is doubtful that any totally new union could have emerged in the times to win the adherence of an industrial force. The shell of an existing institution was still there. The traditions of Daniel Weaver, John Siney, and John Mitchell had survived. There was something to join; it once had a powerful voice; it offered an opportunity for men no longer afraid of the future.

The Lewis who made little effort in the twenties to organize anyone had become a driving recruiter in 1933. It was Lewis who called his staff to the contest, even before the proposed law entered the *Congressional Record*. It was Lewis who could see the future, as far as his union was concerned. Other labor leaders were faced with the same decimated membership rolls. Aside from Hillman and Dubinsky, there was little or nothing done in that first renaissance year to renew their organizations. The record reveals that William Green did make mild exhortations to organize after the passage of the NRA, but there was no leadership decisiveness behind his typically mild entreaties.

A few seasons later, when they were working for the same goals, Lewis, in a mellow moment, turned to John Brophy and said: "Well, John, who timed this thing right, you or I?" Brophy's reply was, "I guess you did, John." And then Brophy added, when he later told the story, that Lewis was "a genius on timing."

Again, we are reminded of Carlyle's perception of "intuitive insight into reality." John Brophy writhed in internal discomfort in the 1920's, because no effort was made to organize coal miners. Lewis was unmoved by his entreaties. Was it his insight into reality that persuaded him that it could not be done? Brophy knew the difficulties too, but he wanted to try. But when the true time came, Lewis said the union's last dollar would be put on the line. When the new day came, Lewis was there first, ordering and commanding and directing and instilling a sense of accomplishment in his lieutenants. The miners may have been easy to organize, but the conclusion is inescapable that, without the leadership of John L. Lewis, it would never have been done as fully and quickly and efficiently as it was.

But union membership was meaningless without tangible benefits to fulfill the hope that accompanied the organizing. Coal operators were proposing various NRA codes for the industry, most of them in fragmented and special-interest fashion. Lewis favored a national code for coal, and he held firm. Demands of the nonunion operators for a pledge in advance for an open shop became a further obstacle. Pressure from President Roosevelt and General Hugh Johnson, Administrator of the NRA, forced a committee of company representatives into major negotiations with Lewis and his lieutenants over national code provisions. The demands of the nonunion operators were bypassed; there was surely to be a single national code. Agreement was reached on September 16, 1933, and approved by Roosevelt two days later.

A code was not a union contract, but it removed most of the obstacles to a new agreement. Lewis and his negotiating crew moved quickly into contract meetings with the major Appalachian field producers. After fourteen days, the document was signed. It covered

340,000 miners in the most important bituminous area in the nation. It re-established the basic ton at 2,000 pounds, granted the UMW the checkoff, restored the eight-hour day and forty-hour week. Men could elect the checkweighman, one of the most important figures in a coal mine, for it was his honesty with the scales that determined the kind of pay the men would make. Lewis and J. D. Morrow of the Pittsburgh Coal Company issued a joint statement. The new contract was "the greatest in magnitude and scope" ever negotiated in the United States.

The strength of Lewis and the revived union was to be tested quickly in another critical area almost at the same time the Appalachian agreement was being worked out. The captive mines, owned and managed by steel companies solely to produce fuel for their mill furnaces, had been unusually resistant to unionization over the years. Because their coal was not sold to the public, the national codes had little relevance to their operation, they said. Miners in the captive fields had turned to the union in great numbers in the hectic summer of 1933, as the western Pennsylvania areas around Pittsburgh reverberated with talk of demands, righting old wrongs, bringing back dignity to workingmen, and support for the UMW. Diggers for the H. C. Frick Coke Company along the Monongahela in Fayette County made a demand which might seem mild to most of us, asking only for a checkweighman to give them a fair break at the scales. When the company refused to listen to such rebellious ideas, a spontaneous strike was the result. The sheriff of Fayette County, issuing baronial decrees with the same certitude as in past unchallenged years, simply waved his hand and forbade all pickcting of any kind anywhere. Governor Gifford Pinchot, unsympathetic with the attitudes of the owners, declared martial law and sent three hundred state troopers into the area. The strike spread quickly. Miners in every county in the southwestern corner of the state in all the captive mines heeded the call. Some 60,000 men were refusing to work, and the coal supply for the steel mills was almost gone.

Gunfire and pitched battles and beatings and bloodshed raged up and down the river. The companies were so adamant in their refusal to even meet with the union officials that the two sides were forced to convene in separate hotel rooms with intermediaries carrying messages back and forth. This occurred when General Johnson brought the warring factions to Washington. On August 5, from his Hyde Park residence, President Roosevelt announced a settlement. The men would go back to work. A code would be promulgated for the captive mines. Until it was ready, a special board would hear grievances of the men.

Miners were enraged. Such a settlement gave them nothing after the desperation of the strike and the risks to their lives. There were shouts of sellout against John L. Lewis. Only when Roosevelt sent his special emissary, Edward F. McGrady, an Assistant Secretary of Labor and a former AFL vice-president, to plead with the miners to go back to work did the strike subside, but only temporarily.

As meetings over code provisions dragged on, men once again began to walk out. The steel owners, fearful that recognition of the UMW in the mines would be a prelude to unionization of the mills themselves, fought against any acceptance of the union. Governor Pinchot repeatedly urged that the union be recognized, as the only way to have peace in the Monongahela Valley. By September 12, more than ten thousand miners were out and more were joining the picket lines each day. There was more bloodshed, and a few days later, the strike was once again almost complete.

Lewis watched the tension grow, and then he moved. When the Appalachian code was announced in mid-September, he immediately called for its application to captive mines. There was a fetching equity in his logic; there were now more than ninety thousand walking miners along the Pennsylvania hillsides to add power that made the logic more persuasive. As negotiations dragged on in Washington, coal inventories in the coke plants and steel works went lower and lower. Governor Pinchot announced in early October that the state's production was down to a fourth of capacity. More ominous, he said, looting of food stores had begun as hungry men became desperate.

The steel companies were compelled to accept the wage and hour conditions of the Appalachian settlement. But recognition of the union and the checkoff were anathemas. The mediator of the dispute was the President. Roosevelt called leaders of U.S. Steel into the White House on October 7 for his own private version of a trip to the woodshed. Three days later, the owners said they would recognize a voluntary checkoff, not to the union, but to "representatives" selected by the miners. By the end of October, the dispute was compromised. The union would ask the men to return, the checkoff would be granted, the terms of the Appalachian agreement would be applied, and elections would be conducted by the National Labor Board, which was then no more than an early committee appointed by the President under the executive authority given him by the NIRA.

The men did return and the elections were quickly held. There was no United Mine Workers on the ballot at all. Men could vote for a slate of John L. Lewis, Philip Murray and Thomas Kennedy, who happened to be the three top officers of the UMW. The slate of names won a great majority of the elections. The Labor Board then ruled that the steel companies still did not have to recognize the UMW, but that they must sign agreements with Lewis, Murray and Kennedy as individuals. This fiction, a face-saving farce, left many dangling issues, but by early 1934 agreements had been signed with owners of the captive mines. The dark hills of the bottom corner of Pennsylvania were never the same again. The union was almost back to its days of highest membership.

2·

John Brophy returned.

Events made it inevitable for him, and likewise for John L. Lewis to accept him. Brophy, restless in his family-feeding job with the Columbia Conserve Company, caught some of the same inspiration that was taking hold of the awakening labor movement in 1933. He quit his job with the Hapgoods and came back to Nanty Glo. It was his own little town; there was his old local union; it could surely use his help. Shortly after he arrived, he wrote a series of articles for the Johnstown *Democrat,* where his name was well known. He explained what the NRA could do for the miners. He too had a vision of the future. Word spread quickly through the echelons of the UMW in Pennsylvania, and up to the top, that John Brophy was back.

The first overture was not long in coming. Philip Murray, against whom there was little enmity from any faction, was often the useful liaison between Lewis and old enemies. Murray called and said Lewis would like to talk to Brophy. The UMW president was at the AFL convention in Washington at the time, and Brophy made a special trip there to see him. The fierceness of the past had subsided; Brophy was surprised at the cordiality. Lewis was alive with conversation. He told Brophy what he had been doing, of the hopes for new organizing, of how the UMW was coming back. It was almost as if Lewis wanted Brophy to interview him. Then Lewis turned to the reason for the meeting. Phil Murray always had great confidence in you. Why don't you see Phil Murray in Pittsburgh. There were neither promises nor suggestions. But Brophy went quickly to Pittsburgh to see Murray.

When he arrived, Murray was ready with an assignment. Go to Illinois and find out what's going on with the Progressive Miners, and report back. Brophy smiled softly and said that his report would not be merely something to please Lewis. He went there, talked to miners over the state, and predictably wrote that the best way to unite Illinois was to return self-government to District 12. Lewis just as predictably ignored the report as if it had never been submitted.

The assignments through Murray continued to come. But there was still penance to pay. Brophy wanted his membership back, even though he was on the payroll of the international union. He was forced to write a petition to the executive board "requesting" that his previous expulsion be vacated. A formal reply came from John L. Lewis. Permission had been granted for Brophy to become a member on "probation," ineligible to run for any office until his full rights had been restored by the executive board. There could never be any political threat from John Brophy again as long as he held this kind of second-class citizenship. But there was work to be done, and Brophy was to become one of the most useful men around Lewis in the next seven exciting years.

3·

Caught up in the enthusiasm of the UMW resurgence, Lewis pleaded for greater organizing effort inside the American Federation of Labor. By 1934, there was constant talk of organizing the big basic industries, like steel and auto, and others that were relatively untouched by unionism in America. The craft unions said it should be done group by group, millwrights inside the plant, carpenters inside the plant, and the other skilled trades, one by one. The Bricklayers, Carpenters, and Machinists were dominant powers in the Federation. As with children protective of their turf, their jurisdictional lines had to be sacredly observed. But there were no crafts in coal mines, as every man who worked in and around the pits belonged to one and the same union. Lewis had little sympathy for ancient craft lines; it was industrial unionism, which meant every man in the plant under one roof of brotherhood, that appealed to him. That was the way to organize, he said, and Sidney Hillman supported him. The issue was widely debated at the 1934 convention in San Francisco. Resolutions for new efforts came out of the gathering, but the rhetoric was still in craft-union terms.

Most Americans could presumably care little for the terminology that fills the labor histories of the times: craft unionism versus industrial unionism. The question was widely discussed and widely debated in 1934 and 1935. At bottom were the jealousies and prerogatives of men, conservatives in their own traditions, unwilling to risk that which was familiar and that which made sense within the confinements of their experience. Lewis, who took the industrial-union side, was likewise accustomed to his position, and had no discomfort in clinging to it. The Hutchesons, the Tobins, and the Wolls, most of them aged in years and in outlook, adhered to their ways, which were those of the past. The needs of men were on the side of John L. Lewis.

There were but the feeblest efforts of the Federation chieftains to organize after San Francisco. At meetings of the Executive Council, Lewis bluntly told them of his disappointment at the pace. His biting criticisms served only to stir the rulers into defensive rejoinders. He was like the Brophy of a decade earlier, urging more and more work in the field, to organize the unorganized. Convinced that nothing would be accomplished, he began to plan for the 1935 AFL convention at Atlantic City. He talked confidently with three men, Murray, Brophy, and the union's lawyer, Henry Warrum. With Brophy's assistance, he had prepared a series of strategies for attacking the hierarchy when the convention assembled.

He rose on the floor to make one of his most memorable speeches, his "seduction with words" talk, much of it directed at the negativisms of Matthew Woll. He first answered the question of why he was so critical of the efforts that he had been forced to endorse a year earlier.

"Well, a year ago at San Francisco, I was a year younger and naturally, I had more faith in the Executive Council. I was beguiled into believing that an enlarged Executive Council would honestly interpret and administer this policy—the policy we talked about for six days in committee, the policy of issuing charters for industrial unions in the mass-production industries. But surely Delegate Woll would not hold it against me that I was so trusting at the time. I know better now. At San Francisco they seduced me with their words. Now, of course, having learned that I was seduced, I am enraged and I am ready to rend my seducers limb from limb, including Delegate Woll. In that sense, of course, I speak figuratively."

His voice boomed eloquently. The labor movement, he said, "is organized upon a principle that the strong shall help the weak." In pleading for further organization, he said the delegates must "heed this cry from Macedonia that comes from the hearts of men." If the delegates rejected the minority report on organizing, which Lewis supported, he must accept the judgment as that of closed minds. If that happened, the enemies of labor would be overjoyed. Lewis said it this way: "High wassails will prevail at the banquet tables of the mighty."

His words moved only the chroniclers of a later time. But it was a physical blow at his seducers that stirred the delegates and added to the Lewis legend. The Mine Workers' delegates were grouped not far from the Carpenters, where Big Bill Hutcheson lent his commanding presence to guide the floor strategies of the old guard. When delegates who spoke for industrial organization were on the floor, Hutcheson arose to interrupt with points of order time after time, almost like the technique of Senator Joseph McCarthy years later. Lewis became increasingly annoyed. "This thing of raising points of order all the time on minor delegates is rather small potatoes," he said.

Hutcheson, near the same aisle where Lewis was returning to his seat, had a scornful rejoinder. "I was raised on small potatoes. That is why I am so small." He stretched to his fullest ponderosity as he said it.

"Pretty small stuff," Lewis said again.

The two were almost side by side as Hutcheson spoke again. "We could have made you small. Could have kept you off the Executive Council, if we wanted to." Then, close witnesses heard Hutcheson call Lewis a "bastard."

Lewis pivoted quickly and swung his hardest right cross. He smashed Hutcheson squarely in the face and drove him back across a Carpenters' table, scattering papers, glasses and furniture as he fell. There were shouts and curses, and masses of carpenters and miners moving toward each other in the aisles. There were enough peace-makers on hand to call an end to it, as Hutcheson arose to wipe the blood from his face. Lewis stood calmly in the aisle, adjusting his collar and tie, and with aplomb, he relighted the cigar that had never left his mouth. William Green, in the chair, nervously upheld Hutcheson's point of order, if anyone remembered what it was. But John L. Lewis had scored a blow for all the unorganized workers in America.

The convention ended in turbulence and discord, perhaps as Lewis knew it would. He passed the word that he wanted to have breakfast with a few men on the last Sunday morning before leaving Atlantic City. He brought John Brophy, Philip Murray and Tom Kennedy from the UMW. Sidney Hillman, his strongest supporter on the issue of new organization, came with David Dubinsky of the Garment Workers, Charles Howard of the Typographical Union, and two others. The times demanded action, he told them, and he intended to have it. He would have new plans and new ideas for organizing the leaderless workers of America. He asked them to meet with him again in Washington at the UMW's newly located headquarters in the Tower Building.

Here was the leadership determination of Lewis asserting itself. Other men knew, too, what must be done, but it was Lewis who called them together, who told them what was required, who pounded his heavy fist on a table and said it would be done. They met again, and it was the beginning of the CIO. It was only a com-mittee then, and that was what they called it. It was to be the Com-mittee for Industrial Organization within the American Federation of Labor. Lewis told them he would be chairman of this new, ad hoc committee. There was no doubt about it. He told them also that John Brophy would be the director of the new committee, drawing his pay from the Mine Workers. He selected Charles Howard as the secretary, and said that the three largest unions represented, the UMW, the Amalgamated Clothing Workers of Hillman and the International Ladies Garment Workers of Dubinsky, would each put up $5,000 to start. They would hire organizers under the direction of Brophy and move quickly to sign workers everywhere.

Lewis cared little for the reactions of the rulers of the Executive Council. The mutterings of the sinful words, "dual-unionism," were echoed, and there were calls for the Committee to disband. William Green, at the urging of the Executive Council, asked that it be done. He arranged with Lewis to speak at his own union's convention when the UMW met in Washington in January, 1936. Lewis met this new approach with his own resignation as a member of the Executive Council.

Lewis was supremely confident of his position when he addressed his own delegates. His old enemies had been dissipated. The man who commanded the most respect among all of them from the past, Brophy, was working closely with him. There was an air of movement, of meaning, of progress, of growth, not only in the still-gaining UMW, but in all of industrial America. Old miner visions were coming alive everywhere, and when Lewis told them of the new committee and of the spending of UMW funds on it, he was loudly cheered. He told them that unless his own delegates ordered him to cease and desist, "all the members of the Executive Council of the American Federation of Labor will be wearing asbestos suits in hell before that committee is dissolved."

William Green was accorded the rostrum to address his old brothers. He urged them to have patience with the AFL and support its policies, stay away from the divisiveness that had been created, and help Brother Lewis return to the paths of righteousness.

Lewis showed his mastery of the drama of command. He raised his arm and called upon the delegates who had changed their minds because of Green's speech to rise. Then he coldly turned to his old compatriot and intoned: "The chair sees two delegates."

Lewis was now ready for the *coup de grâce*. He prepared for the reaffirmation of his position with his most pedantic phrases: "Again, the question recurs upon the fiat of the Executive Council of the American Federation of Labor, read to this convention as an ultimatum by President Green. It demands that the President of the United Mine Workers of America, with his associates on the Committee for Industrial Organization, like hoary slaves at night, scared to their dungeons, dissolve, disband, cease and desist with reference to the Committee for Industrial Organization. Let those delegates . . . who believe that the President of the United Mine Workers should comply with that request rise to their feet."

The majestic quiet that is usually such a part of the scene followed. "The chair sees one delegate arise." No hoary slaves were scared back to their dungeons. Then, Lewis put it to them once again. He asked all the delegates who supported him in his efforts to stand. The conductor was leading his orchestra to an emotional climax. The assemblage arose as a body and cheered and cheered, almost as if their leader had waved a baton. Lewis calmly waited until they subsided in their seats, let silence come over the hall again, and then turned to a red-faced and humiliated William Green.

"President Green, you have received the answer of the United Mine Workers of America to your ultimatum."

The rulers of the Executive Council repaired to their legalisms, almost as if they were unaware of the history that was settling its unfavorable scroll upon them. Franklin D. Roosevelt was in the midst of an exhilarating campaign for his second term in the White House. Workers were signing union cards all across the land. The Executive Council of the American Federation of Labor convened solemnly to start the process of expulsion of its errant supporters of "that" Committee. It acted in the summer to suspend the Mine Workers and the other unions that worked with Lewis. Final expulsion would have to await the convention in the fall in Tampa, when the accused organizations could not even vote against their own excommunication. Lewis certainly must have recognized the doubtful legal grounds of the Executive Council, but there was more to do than to resist actions which were becoming more meaningless week by week. But Lewis was determined to make it as uncomfortable for William Green as was possible.

A "Dear Bill" letter went out, asking Green to support as a "loyal son" the policies of his own union, the United Mine Workers. Green's reply was that he was bound to honor the laws of the AFL. He cited past history where the Federation had given its aid and as-

sistance to the UMW, and asked for recognition in kind. Lewis replied again:

> All this is beside the question. I am not concerned with history.
> Rather I am concerned with the problems of today and tomorrow.
> You do not deny that the American Federation of Labor has frit-
> tered away two years of valuable time without effectuating the or-
> ganization of a single worker in the steel industry. You do not deny
> that your Executive Council is even now scheming to eject your
> union from the house of labor. You did not deny that the crime for
> which such ejection will be punishment is the crime of lending aid
> to the unorganized workers and seeking an expansion of the numeri-
> cal strength of the American Federation of Labor. Your lament is
> that I will join you in a policy of anxious inertia. Candidly, I am
> temperamentally incapable of sitting with you in sackcloth and
> ashes, endlessly intoning, *"O tempora! O mores!"*
> It is, of course, needless to discuss further the points of honor in-
> volved. You will make your own decisions. For myself, I prefer to
> err on the side of America's underprivileged and exploited millions,
> if erring it be.

The division was irreparable. Lewis had boldly taken into his Committee new unions that had direct jurisdictional conflicts with the International Brotherhood of Electrical Workers and the Metal Trades
Council, some of the oldest and most powerful of the crafts. Green
now faced the same fate in his own union as did all the others who
opposed the positions of John L. Lewis. A "member" of the UMW
named John L. Lewis filed charges under internal union law against
one William Green for conspiracy to suspend the UMW from membership in the American Federation of Labor contrary to the laws of
said Federation. Accused member Green was also charged with failure to observe the policies of the UMW, fraternization with avowed
enemies of the United Mine Workers, and distortion and misrepre-
sentation of the objectives of the UMW. The date for his trial was
selected as November 16, 1936, the same day that Green as president was to gavel into order the annual convention of the American
Federation of Labor.

The trial of William Green was solemnly conducted with the defendant *in absentia*. The verdict was guilty as charged. The tribunal

ordered that Brother Green cease and desist from his unlawful activities; failing to do so, he would be expelled for life. The expulsion came, and the president of the American Federation of Labor was faced with the fate of not being a member of any union. The solution was to award him a card from the Musicians' Union. This provoked another of Lewis's scourges of Green, with comparison to the fiddling of Nero while Rome burned.

The greatest days of John L. Lewis were at hand. His Committee was the talk of industrial America. Its heart came from the United Mine Workers. John Brophy, as its working head, brought back old UMW compatriots, even though past enemies of Lewis. He signed on Adolph Germer and Powers Hapgood, his own lieutenants from Save the Union days. When Brophy told Lewis he wanted them, Lewis hesitated only slightly, asking if it was necessary. Brophy said he needed men who knew how to organize and who believed in him personally. Lewis answered quietly, "All right."

Brophy's pay, and that of many others, came from the UMW treasury. Brophy set up regional offices around the country, again supported by Mine Workers funds. Allan Haywood, another former miner from Illinois, was placed in charge of the New York office. Germer worked in the rubber campaigns in Akron. Hapgood was everywhere, trouble-shooting with Germer and Brophy and finally with the auto workers in Michigan. Van Bittner was busy in steel, along with Philip Murray, who headed up that campaign. William Mitch, another of the UMW's most successful organizers, went into steel to work under Murray and Bittner.

The big breakthroughs were in auto and steel. These were triumphs of John L. Lewis. He went personally to Detroit during the sit-down strike and negotiated directly with officials of General Motors and Governor Frank Murphy of Michigan. The most dramatic stories of his forays have been told by Saul Alinsky in his biography of Lewis. When General Motors capitulated in 1937, John L. Lewis and the CIO were the most common words in American conversation after F.D.R. Big steel, too, was successfully organized and the fame of Lewis grew even more.

It was UMW money that backed the efforts of Lewis and his men. Lewis received no salary as the chairman of the Committee, nor even after it became a Congress in 1938 as a full labor federation to rival the AFL. But his UMW paycheck was his income during those years. The UMW made "loans" to the CIO in 1936 and 1937 sufficient to provide 83.4% of the total cost. At the 1938 UMW convention, Lewis reported loans of $50,000 to the CIO, the sum of $475,000 to the Steel Workers Organizing Committee, and another $99,000 to a textile committee. There was a payment of support money of $180,000 to Labor's Non-Partisan League, the political arm that preceded the Political Action Committee, as well as an outright contribution of another $30,000. By this time, more than two million dollars of Mine Workers money had gone into the founding and support of the Committee. Even with these expenditures, the revival of the union starting in 1933 had been enough to bring its treasury up to a cash balance of more than 2.5 million.

John L. Lewis and the United Mine Workers had made labor unions a new force in the nation's life. He was at the height of his successes and his notoriety and his dramatic impact on all of a country, but ahead there were political crises which would turn Lewis away from all of labor back to the Mine Workers, where his handling of events continued to make him the absolute master of the union that stood first in any roll call of associations of men.

4·

The organizing of industrial America was one of the two great events that made John L. Lewis such a dominant figure both in his own union and in the nation's labor movement. The other was his use of the strike weapon, in wartime and in peacetime, to win gains for the United Mine Workers.

During the period just prior to World War II and culminating in the year after, national strikes in the soft-coal fields followed so quickly that the rememberer of the times can hardly distinguish one from the other. Yet each strike welded the power of Lewis, solidified the membership of the union behind him as it never was in the 1920's, and gave him even greater authority within his own house.

All this happened at a time when the national leadership of Lewis was in diminution. He destroyed himself so thoroughly within the CIO by his great blunder against Roosevelt that the remainder of his national career was to be spent back in his own union. Some said it was his vanity; others laid it directly to his unachievable desire to become Vice-President, or even President, of the United States; there are those who lay it to the overplaying of the theatrical sense of destiny which he thought guided him. Yet even in these defeats in a grand design, he was able to exert the strongest portions of his will and his inflexible leadership in such a way as to literally end all opposition to him and his policies within the United Mine Workers.

His first major clash with Roosevelt came in 1937, so soon after Lewis had given the first support of his life to a Democratic candidate in the election of the year before. It came during the days of the Little Steel strike, shortly after the killing of ten workers by Chicago police outside a Republic Steel plant on Memorial Day, 1937. F.D.R., when asked at a press conference about the warring faction, uttered a Shakespearean quotation of his own: "A plague o' both your houses!"

Lewis fumed until Labor Day, 1937, before answering. In recounting the dead and injured in the steel campaign, he turned one of his most eloquent shafts against Roosevelt. "Labor, like Israel, has many sorrows. Its women weep their fallen and they lament for the future of the children of the race. It ill behooves one who has supped at labor's table and who has been sheltered in labor's house to curse with equal fervor and fine impartiality both labor and its adversaries when they become locked in deadly embrace."

There was a growing coolness between the White House and the most important labor figure of the day. Lewis was there occasionally for meetings, and at the 1938 UMW convention he intoned that "Roosevelt was the only President in our lifetime who has tried to give a square deal to the common people of this country." But there was much private grumbling; mutterings of "fair-weather friend," "unreliable," and a later statement to Saul Alinsky that Lewis had "discovered the depths of deceit, the rank dishonesty, and the double-crossing character of Franklin Delano Roosevelt." Some of his pique went into his famous invective against Vice-President Garner, in another of Lewis's memorable deflations of another person: Garner was a "labor-baiting, whiskey-drinking, poker-playing, evil old man." The Vice-President never recovered in the public eye.

Yet the 1939 UMW strike, settled long before Pearl Harbor, was won with at least the tacit assistance of the government. Lewis demanded the union shop, and when the operators balked, the entire bituminous industry, now almost fully unionized, was shut down. Lewis said he was willing to send the miners back if the settlement were retroactive. Roosevelt had written to the parties urging settlement, but had said nothing of the UMW offer to resume work. Lewis addressed a scornful note to the President. "Failure of the Roosevelt Administration to approve or sustain the Mine Workers' offers to keep the industry in operation caused many coal operators to believe that they had carte blanche from the Government to disembowel the Mine Workers' Union if they could. In consequence, your Department must accept responsibility for its own administrative blunder."

But there was to be no "disemboweling" that year, or any season thereafter. Lewis, in the strategy of word-hurling that he used so well, told doleful stories of "dietary deficiencies" and implied that the political consequences were "obvious." The President was more demanding in his appeals for a settlement. The pressure was unremitting against the operators. They yielded. And whether Lewis gave the White House credit or not, one operator bluntly said, "We might hold out against John L. Lewis . . . but we can't hold out against both Lewis and President Roosevelt."

Lewis had won a total victory in the 1939 strike. Even though the mines had been under contract to the UMW, the malcontents, the free riders, those who philosophically did not want unions, and others who did not want to join for one reason or another could always remain outside the fold in what was still an "open shop" in labor terminology. But the union-security clause, which required every man to sign and pay his dues to keep working, was an entrenchment of the union to the fullest and was a convincing demonstration of the leadership strength of Lewis in keeping men out of the pits when it counted. This was merely the prelude to the bigger strikes that were to come.

The final break with Roosevelt and the resignation of Lewis from the CIO came the next year. Lewis opened his campaign against the President at the 1940 UMW convention in January, long before the third-term talk had caught the country's attention. "I am one who believes that President Roosevelt will not be a candidate for re-election. Conceding the Democratic National Convention could be coerced or dragooned into renominating him, I am convinced that, with the conditions now confronting the nation and the dissatisfaction now permeating the minds of the people, his candidacy would result in ignominious defeat."

The story has been often told that Lewis proposed to F.D.R., even after his remarks at the January UMW convention, that the miners' leader run as the Vice-Presidential candidate on the same ticket. There were those who maintained that Lewis wanted to become President of the United States; that after his achievement in building the CIO and becoming almost the second-best-known person in the nation, he considered only the top office as befitting his talents. But Roosevelt, the fox, the master politician, holding the kind of command authority that Lewis had used so well inside his union, was outmaneuvering Lewis in a game that the UMW head could not possibly win. When there were important appointments for labor, where the CIO must be represented, Sidney Hillman was selected. When Lewis attacked the administration during the spring and summer months of 1940, Hillman was always available with a thorough, complete answer. Philip Murray and John Brophy announced early for Roosevelt, and Tom Kennedy too. At least Lewis did not force his brooding anger upon his closest associates. Leaders of other CIO unions also announced for the President. Lewis was isolated in his own house.

Lewis endorsed Wendell Willkie in October and then went on a nationwide radio hookup to make his own election appeal. He denounced Roosevelt with the same vehemence he had poured on his enemies of old. The President, he said, was consumed by an "overweening, abnormal and selfish craving for power." This familiar charge had been made against Lewis a hundredfold. The President demanded that Americans throw away their "priceless liberty." This too had been an oft-uttered phrase at UMW conventions over the years. Lewis, in building to his climax, boasted of labor's strength, and tolled off the names of the unions that he had aided over the years. Then he offered his own form of a bombshell:

> It is obvious that President Roosevelt will not be reelected for the third term unless he has the overwhelming support of the men and women of labor. If he is, therefore, reelected, it will mean that the members of the Congress of Industrial Organization have rejected

my advice and recommendation. I will accept the result as being the equivalent of a vote of no confidence, and will retire as President of the Congress of Industrial Organization at its convention in November.

When the speech was ended, Sidney Hillman told those around him, "John L. Lewis is through. This is really the end for him!" The election results, of course, were overwhelming. In the industrial areas of the North and East, where labor's vote was heaviest, Roosevelt won enormous victories. Would Lewis keep his word and step down from the leadership of the organization that he had founded, nursed and built to such prominence?

When the third convention of the Congress of Industrial Organizations assembled in Atlantic City shortly after the election, Lewis was still in full command. Only the Amalgamated Clothing Workers under Hillman was taking a strong stand that Lewis must go. There was a growing movement to insist that he stay. A single statement from him that he would reconsider would have settled it. Many have speculated as to why the statement never came; vanity, they submit, was too great. When he opened the convention, he intoned, "In just a day or two, I will be out of this office." But there were delegates with huge buttons, "We Want Lewis." "Draft Lewis" banners filled the halls. As the convention moved into its second day, there was considerable doubt about what would happen.

Lewis was still the headmaster, suppressing opponents and excoriating his enemies. His quashing from the chair of an errant voice demonstrated his control over every moment. When the *CIO News* was criticized for its pro-Willkie slant, Lewis took full responsibility and said he would do it again. The convention proceedings recorded a "boo" by an individual or two.

Lewis reacted immediately. He called out, "Will the gentleman who booed please stand up so I can identify him?"

There was no movement on the floor.

"He must be a brave man," Lewis said. "I would like to see him. If he really wants to boo I will appoint a committee to escort him to the platform here and we will have him put on an audition. We will see how scientific he is in his booing." No man could withstand the authority and scorn of Lewis at that point.

When the Amalgamated Clothing Workers brought up a resolution on the second day to resume negotiations with the AFL for unification, the bitterness and anger of John L. Lewis came pouring out. David Dubinsky and the International Ladies Garment Workers, who had been with him since the Atlantic City breakfast of five years earlier, had already left the CIO and returned to the AFL, along with Max Zaritsky of the Hatters' Union. Lewis had words for all of them, starting with Dubinsky.

> He has crept back into the American Federation of Labor. He abandoned his fellows and he abandoned what he claimed was his principle. And he has gone into that organization on his adversary's terms. He is crying out now and his voice laments like that of Rachel in the wilderness, against the racketeers and the panderers and the crooks in that organization . . . And Zaritsky, he was the man representing the Millinery and Cap Workers. He said, "Me too." And now above all the clamor comes the piercing wail and the laments of the Amalgamated Clothing Workers.

Lewis was inviting his former ally who had turned into his principal foe, Sidney Hillman, to leave; and if that occurred, there would have been no obstacle to the draft of Lewis.

But as to reaffiliation with the Federation, Lewis told the delegates how difficult it would be, especially with the men who ruled the Federation. Their rulers who had not listened to him in past years were given scathing summations of disrespect.

> We have explored every proposition. What have we all been doing? I have been an explorer in the American Federation of Labor. Explore the mind of Bill Green? Why Bill and I had offices next door to each other in the same corridor for ten years. I was a member of the same Executive Council that he was for one year. I have done a lot of exploring in Bill's mind and I give you my word there is nothing there.

Then it was the turn of the other patrons of the Executive Council.

> Explore Matthew Woll's mind? I did. It is the mind of an insurance agent, who used his position as an officer of the American Federation of Labor and a member of the Executive Council to promote

his insurance business. [Woll was the president of the labor-sponsored and -supported Union Labor Life Insurance Company, which was his principal business function in the labor movement.] . . . Explore Tom Rickert's mind, of the United Garment Workers, who was on the Negotiating Committee? I did, and here is what was in his mind. He said he did not propose to let the Amalgamated Clothing Workers into the American Federation of Labor if he could help it . . . Explore the mind of Bill Hutcheson? I did. There wasn't anything there that would do you any good. So what? Waste more time on unprofitable explorations?

There was a tension and an uneasiness over the convention. The angry mood of Lewis, the looming repressions against those who stood against him, the growing movement to urge him to reconsider, brought Sidney Hillman to one of his most skillful moments. He asked for the floor and made the response that both interred John L. Lewis and made way for his successor as president of the CIO. He began with smooth praise, telling of the great privilege of having associated with Lewis. Then he delivered the unretractable coup to the quieted delegates.

I regret that John L. Lewis will not be the leader of this organization. I know there is nothing else he can do and will do and will agree to do but what he believes to be the best for the organized labor movement. I have great respect for a man who in a crisis stands by his guns . . . It is my considered judgment that when John L. Lewis steps down there must be a demand for Phil Murray.

There was a recognition that Hillman was right, that it must be done, that the founder and the inspiration had charted his own course and must be kept to it. Another Mine Worker, Philip Murray, who had always been faithful to his master, was even urged by Lewis to accept the CIO leadership. Lewis placed Murray's name in nomination two days later. All that remained was the valedictory; few had seen Lewis shed tears in public before.

All the rest of his years were with the Mine Workers.

The next strike crisis came in 1941, shortly before Pearl Harbor. The UMW had won increased benefits for miners in the bituminous fields in negotiations that summer. With these contracts secure, Lewis moved against the captive mines, whose steel-company owners negotiated separately from the major coal producers. Wages and other benefits won in the coal industry could hardly be denied by the steel lords. But the old unsettled issue of the union shop, to require every miner in the captive pits to join the UMW to keep his job, was brought to the top of the list by Lewis. Before the breakdown in negotiations, Benjamin F. Fairless, the president of United States Steel, used the old arguments against the union shop in his talks with Lewis—"John, it's just as wrong to make a man join a union if he doesn't want to as it is to dictate what church he should belong to." Lewis always replied with the traditional labor retort: "It's wrong to have men getting the benefit of better hours and conditions won for them by the union without giving a penny to help support the union."

In mid-September, with the nation preoccupied with the war in Europe and consciousness of defense needs, men in the captive mines went on strike over the unsettled issue of the union shop. The government had already created a National Defense Mediation Board to try to settle major labor disputes, and it took jurisdiction. Lewis agreed to a thirty-day truce and the miners went back to work. Again, the recurrence of in-and-out-of-the-pits at the orders of Lewis was established in a familiar pattern for years to come. Many union leaders, once a strike is ended by sending the membership back to work, have found it extremely difficult to have them leave a second time. But it was never that way with Lewis in command.

When the end of the truce neared, Lewis gave no indication of keeping the miners at work. President Roosevelt appealed to Lewis and his members, "as loyal citizens, to come now to the aid of your country. I ask that work continue at the captive coal mines pending the settlement of this dispute." Roosevelt's message had stressed that there must be uninterrupted production of coal for making steel, "that basic material of our national defense." This plea came in late October, six weeks before the Japanese attack. Lewis replied curtly. This was a fight only between the union and "a ruthless corporation." "If you would use the power of the State to restrain me, as an agent of labor, then, sir, I submit that you should use the same power to restrain my adversary in this issue, who is an agent of capital. My adversary is a rich man named Morgan, who lives in New York."

Lewis said he would meet with Roosevelt and with J. P. Morgan, who he said was the real power behind United States Steel, "for a forthright discussion of the equities of this problem."

But the miners went out. They left the pits the day Lewis wrote his reply to Roosevelt. The President asked again that the men return to work. The American Federation of Labor, through a statement issued by one of its spokesmen, cried betrayal, and it added: "Lewis today is the most cordially hated man in America. His scornful refusal to consider the best interests of the nation, his deliberate attempts to embarrass the national defense program, his bitter feud with President Roosevelt, his insulting arrogance are more than the American people can stomach." Lewis was attacked in both houses of Congress and by the President. Writers in newspapers and magazines and commentators on the air added their rebukes.

Two days after the strike resumed, Lewis went to the White House with Myron Taylor of U.S. Steel to talk with Roosevelt. When he came out, he told the men to go back to work again, but only until November 15. The full Defense Mediation Board was to study the dispute further. But Lewis refused to pledge that he would abide by the Board's decision if it should be unfavorable. And it was, as AFL representatives surprisingly joined with management to vote against granting the union shop. This caused all the CIO representatives to walk out, totally destroying the effectiveness of the Board, since it needed labor's full participation to function.

Lewis scheduled another walkout for November 17. Roosevelt called him to the White House again, along with other officials of the union and of the steel companies. The President gave one of his sternest lectures. It was his "indisputable obligation" for national defense to see that coal production for steel not be stopped. He said there would be legislation if needed. "I am telling you this with absolutely no element of threat. To this conference I am stating a simple fact." But the President went on to tell Lewis directly that the government would never compel the nonunion miners to join by government decree. "That would be too much like the Hitler methods toward labor."

Lewis was unmoved. Silence and a scowl was all that the President received. Not only would the captive miners leave their pits on November 17, but the word was out that it might be necessary to shut down every coal mine in the country to "preserve the integrity" of the union's agreement with the commercial bituminous producers. The previous criticism of Lewis was mild compared to the new rounds of denunciation. The front page of *The New York Times* on November 17 implied that the army would be used to break the strike.

On the day of the call, November 17, the in-again-out-again routine was repeated. Coal miners did not work, and the captive mines were silent. The men had walked out three times in less than two months. There was restlessness in the commercial collieries over what new order might come from Lewis. Roosevelt again appealed for a return to work.

From the viewpoint of a tactician determined to win his battle, Lewis's handling of the captive-mine strike to this point had been unquestionably brilliant. His enmity toward Roosevelt fueled his defiance. But even that could not have fully accounted for his unwillingness to yield; it required the resoluteness, the implacability, the strength of John L. Lewis; lesser men would have succumbed at earlier stages of the crisis. Perhaps Lewis knew that if he refused to give even a step, he would ultimately win. By this time, attacks, even from the President, had little effect upon a man who was accustomed to receiving vital blows from blunt men in the union movement. The threats of new laws from Congress were not enough to convince Lewis, for the nation was not yet at war. He would hold until someone else broke. Even when the pressure against him was heaviest from the White House, when Roosevelt suggested binding arbitration, Lewis undertook to lecture and chide the President. A judicial decision, Lewis said in response, would be "difficult under existing circumstances. Your recent statements on this question, as the Chief Executive of the nation, have been so prejudicial to the claim of the Mine Workers as to make uncertain that an umpire could be found whose decision would not reflect your interpretation of government policy, Congressional attitude, and public opinion."

It was Roosevelt's move, and he came back with another proposal that led the way to the total triumph of John L. Lewis. It came as another proposal for arbitration, but this time the President named the arbitrators. One was to be John L. Lewis for the union and another Benjamin Fairless for steel management. The third man, whose vote would decide the dispute, was to be John R. Steelman, director of the United States Conciliation Service. John R. Steelman was perhaps the best friend Lewis had in the government; he was an outspoken advocate of the union shop. The pressure on the steel companies to accept in advance a man with the views of Steelman indicated that Roosevelt had convinced them that it was their turn to do their duty for their country. Lewis was aware enough of the realities to know that he had won; he promptly accepted Steelman; the men went back to work; the arbitration tribunal solemnly convened.

The decision was announced on a Sunday that happened to be December 7, 1941. It was, as expected, 2 to 1 for the union shop, Steelman and Lewis on one side and Fairless on the other. Its result brought little reaction. There was greater business at hand now that Pearl Harbor was in ruins.

The 1941 victory, with its strategy of the repetitious chain of strikes, prepared Lewis for his next confrontation with his government two years later, when industry contracts expired. Wartime controls dominated the economy. When negotiations began, Lewis announced that he wanted a $2-a-day wage increase, "nothing more, nothing less." He coupled this audacity with an attack on the War Labor Board, the agency that was charged with approving wage rates, because it gave no just treatment to labor's needs. "Assuredly labor, despite its present weak and vacillating leadership, cannot long tolerate such economically paradoxical and socially unjust treatment," said Lewis. The one leader who was not "weak and vacillating" in returning from two years of silence dismissed the danger of inflation. He made an impassioned case for his members, even though the familiar cries of the critics caused it hardly to be heard.

Food prices had gone up astronomically, said Lewis. The small stores in the mining towns were not controlled by the ceilings of the Office of Price Administration. His members were aware that the nation was at war, and they wanted to play their parts as men and citizens.

> To do that the miner must eat, and he must eat strong meat. He needs strong food. He must have it. The nature and the hazards and the laboriousness and the strain of his industry require it, or his bodily strength disappears, his resistance is lowered, and he becomes a victim of the ills that follow malnutrition and bodily weakness

. . . When the mine workers' children cry for bread, they cannot be satisfied with a Little Steel formula. When illness strikes the mine workers' families, they cannot be cured with an anti-inflation dissertation. The facts of life in the mining homes of America cannot be pushed aside by the flamboyant theories of an idealistic economic philosophy. Neither can these facts be suppressed nor concealed to appease employing coal corporations who smugly hope that the government will chastise the mine worker for daring to make known the miserable facts of his existence.

Collective bargaining in any meaningful sense stopped, as the operators made no wage offer, preferring to let the War Labor Board settle it. The expiring contract was extended for a month to May 1 at the request of President Roosevelt. When a three-man panel of the WLB opened hearings on April 28, the UMW declined to appear. The union had appealed to the public for the first time, taking full-page advertisements in newspapers to tell its side of the story. Its emphasis was on added compensation for portal-to-portal pay as a means of breaking loose from the rigid wage formulas of the War Labor Board. The story of miners' trips in and out of the pits with no pay for such use of their time in travel was portrayed as a wage injustice entitling them to more money.

Without waiting for the expected adverse ruling of the War Labor Board, the coal miners of America left their work on May 1. The government immediately announced seizure of the mines, placing Secretary of the Interior Harold L. Ickes in charge as the top manager. Upon another appeal by Roosevelt, the miners went back two days later to start the familiar pattern of work for a while, strike for a while. When the War Labor Board issued its ruling on May 25, denying the pay increase and granting only vacation benefits and other minor concessions, picks and pails were dropped again. The miners went to their picket lines with the solidarity of an army.

This was a strike against the government. All the other walkouts had been against the operators, even though the administration had been a close and intimate party to the proceedings. After the seizure of May 1, miners had gone back upon request. The Smith-Connelly Act forbidding wartime strikes was rushed through Congress, and even though its harsh and ultimately unworkable provisions caused a Roosevelt veto, it was easily passed by huge majorities incensed at the action of Lewis and the miners. Roosevelt as commander in chief issued another "order and direction" to the miners to return on June 7, 1943. Lewis "recommended" that they go back until there was a final settlement of their claims, and back again to the pits they went.

The spigot was still being turned on and off. When the final War Labor Board directive was issued on June 18, giving little of consequence to the miners, the third walkout began. Roosevelt called it intolerable and said the acts of Lewis and his committee had "highly stirred the anger and disapproval of the overwhelming mass of the American people." A CBS correspondent in Cairo read a soldier editorial from the army newspaper *Stars and Stripes,* after describing a cartoon portraying Lewis throwing dirt upon the grave of a soldier in Africa. These words were spread over the national radio network:

> Nor is John L. Lewis a traitor to his government alone. He has betrayed by his excesses the cause of union labor with which he has so long been identified. He has betrayed the spirit of the democracy which gives him the right to move against the welfare and will of America's millions. He has betrayed the belief of the American soldier that this would be a war in which the individual's gain and the individual's interest would be sublimated to the common purpose. Speaking for the American soldier, John Lewis, damn your coal-black soul.

Lewis, secure in his belief that his tactics would bring benefits to the miners, again agreed to send the men back, but imposed another deadline, this time to October 31. He had stated that if $1.50 a day could be gained on the portal-pay issue, this might solve the problem. In the meantime, his man in Illinois, Ray Edmundson, had negotiated an agreement with the Illinois producers that allowed $1.25 a day for portal-to-portal travel time and added an eighth hour to the previous seven-hour day, with time and one half for the eighth hour. If this could be approved by the War Labor Board, it would amount to an added $3 a day to the miners' pay when Lewis had originally asked only for $2! When the War Labor Board rejected the agreement in October, coal miners in all the fields once again started the familiar strike.

On November 1, the government again seized the mines. Some form of acceptable agreement was imperative, and Lewis met with

Ickes to find a formula. As usual, there was a solution to an insoluble problem when one party, so incensed at the refusal to grant justice to its position, showed the determination never to yield otherwise. There was an allowance of forty-five minutes for travel time, with pay. Lunch periods were reduced from thirty minutes to fifteen minutes, and with the addition of more work time to the day, coal miners were able to bring home an additional $1.50 a day without shattering the national wage formula. Lewis had won again.

The last of the great strikes of Lewis came after the war had ended. It brought more of the nation's wrath against the Mine Workers, resulted in the largest fine ever levied against a labor union, and produced a Supreme Court decision that twisted and bent the law to fit a particular situation, as is too often the case. Contract time came at the end of March, 1946, and the UMW, like most of the organizations that had been held back during the war, had many new proposals. The establishment of a health and welfare fund was first submitted that year and won. The first strike came early, as an anxious government watched. Weeks dragged into late May. When coal stocks were nearing their end, and with no movement from any party, the government used its lingering wartime powers to seize the mines again. Lewis met with Secretary of the Interior Julius Krug, who had been named by President Truman to run the mines as Secretary Ickes had been chosen by Roosevelt. The contract, popularly known as the Krug-Lewis agreement, was signed in the oval office at the White House. It was another triumph for the UMW. The welfare fund was created, financed by a royalty of five cents on each ton of coal mined. Wages went up, and there were new benefits throughout the contract.

The summer that year was peaceful, as the government prepared to turn the mines back to their owners. Disputes arose in September over vacation payments; there was another serious wrangle over what weights would be used for calculating royalties to the welfare fund. Lewis said the government was reneging on its agreement, and there were repeated clashes with Krug. A new strike call went out for November 20, 1946. The government moved in the United States District Court in Washington for an injunction against the walkout, receiving a sweeping order from Judge T. Alan Goldsborough. The brinkmanship of the past had been with the executive and the public;

there was no reason for a miner strike to yield to a judicial decree. While miners struck, contempt-of-court citations went out against Lewis and the union.

A hearing was quickly ordered on a combined charge of civil and criminal contempt. On December 3, 1946, while the strike was still in progress, Judge Goldsborough handed down his findings of guilt. The United Mine Workers of America was fined $3.5 million, a sum to stagger even its healthy treasury. Lewis was personally assessed $10,000. This was a far more biting blow than the denunciations of Presidents and editorial writers. Four days later, Lewis told the men to go back. A speedy, direct appeal to the United States Supreme Court was perfected as a part of the agreement to go back to work. A majority of the justices sustained the government, upheld the personal fine against Lewis, reduced the union's fine to a mere $700,000 if it complied with the court decree, and mangled the law of labor injunctions into a confusion that still exists. Lewis yielded. He had finally met an authority that possessed a superior power, whether it was rightfully exercised or not. Even in defeat, he had won a sympathy from old rivals in the labor movement who recognized the implications of federal might; and he was still endeared to his members for his willingness to undergo a punishment for their interests. Lewis was so mighty now that he could be restrained only by the government and the United States Supreme Court. Mineowners, mere mortals they, when the collieries came back to them, were hardly of the caliber to deal in the future with the demigod. Labor-management relationships in the coal mines were to move into a new era, where the strike was no longer necessary, after a lesser stoppage in 1948 was settled. But the recognized solidarity of the men was a force at every bargaining table, where the acknowledged leader of the coal industry in America was not a business tycoon but the president of the United Mine Workers.

5·

Complete, unquestioned authority over the organization of men that was the United Mine Workers was not yet achieved when the rebuilding began in 1933, even though Lewis had won all his fights for control. Old issues, unresolved although they were brought up again and again, were there to plague the president. When the new era began, there were bitterness and hostility toward Lewis throughout the mine fields from those who knew and could not forget the past. The same goals of self-government still stirred men. Those who opposed the president must be dealt with; even old comrades would have to be expelled, like valiant Bolsheviks whose continued presence brought discomfort to men in command.

The provisional governments which Lewis had imposed over the districts irritated many of the same delegates who rose and cheered at each movement of Lewis in his handling of William Green at the 1936 convention. Even though they applauded efforts at organizing outside the mine fields by the creation of the CIO, there was still rebelliousness over the provisional districts. At the convention that year, only two districts of any importance outside the narrowly confined anthracite areas were allowed to elect their own officers. Since Lewis appointed the heads of the "provisionals," and these presidents filled a majority of the seats on the executive board, that body was totally subservient to the top officer. The only antidote to one-man rule of the Mine Workers was the annual convention, where delegates independently elected from mining-camp local unions could still speak their own thoughts. But the appointive power ran through the echelons much deeper than merely at district levels; the staff men could often influence local unions in their choice of delegates; favored and trusted men could be given important assignments that renewed their loyalties to the political leadership.

The rebirth of the union by 1936 brought in turn some of the restlessness of the past about the centralized control over the organization. One of the delegates at the 1936 gathering took the floor to start a chain reaction of cries for local autonomy. The first speaker said, "They tell you to leave all questions pertaining to the autonomy of any district in the hands of the International Executive Board. How many men in this convention know how many members of the Board are elected officially? They are appointed men, all except three . . . They have a majority, and on any question coming before that Board you know what the consequence has been."

A man out of District 17 in West Virginia threw a direct challenge at his brothers. "I want to see if you men have a backbone or if you are jelly. Most of us get nervous in the presence of men who have power over us." Another delegate from John Brophy's old territory of District 2, which could no longer elect any Brophys to represent it, said, "Throughout my district the question of autonomy seems to be the most important subject . . . We believe if we select our own representatives we should select better men than we are having now and we will accomplish more than we are accomplishing now."

Delegate Houser from District 21 took up the call for free elections. "We feel if we are given the privilege to elect our officials the same men of the District will exercise discretion and will select officials that are good, honest union men, not politicians or political has-beens, but labor leaders from the heart. They will not elect a man who has been in office for twenty-five or thirty years and has become legal-minded and politically inclined . . . Our machinery has got to be a political machinery and we have lost the pulse beat of the workers, and it should be brought back close to the rank and file."

The man who held the chair permitted the debate to run for a time, as he usually did. Then steady, loyal Philip Murray took the floor and started the counterattack. He used the unusual argument that because the union had been so largely reorganized since 1933, it was in reality only three years old, and he implied that such youth was not ready to make its own decisions. If this internal dissension continued, the security of the union itself could be menaced. But it remained for the master to take his customary turn on the rostrum as an advocate and deliver the blow that always buried the proponents of union elections. "Business efficiency" was the theme stressed by Lewis again and again.

"It is not a fundamental principle that the convention is discussing," he said, "it is a question of business expediency and administrative policy as affecting certain geographical areas of the organization. It is a question of whether you desire your organization to be the most effective instrumentality within the realm of possibility for a labor organization or whether you prefer to sacrifice the efficiency of your organization in some respect for a little more academic freedom in the election of some local representatives in a number of districts."

He then selected pieces of case histories from defunct districts to demonstrate their lack of "efficiency" and their inability to govern their affairs. Then he asked them what they wanted, efficiency or some implied horrible alternative. He made it sound as if the advocates of elections were foolish dreamers. "After all, what is involved in this? Well, a chance for some of our energetic, spirited young men, active and vigorous, ambitious, which they properly should be and of which we are proud, to run for office in the organization. That is all that is involved in it . . . But what do you want? Do you want an efficient organization or do you want merely a political instrumentality? That is all that is involved in this matter—business administration, effective internal policies, and no denial of the fundamental principles of democracy. But learn to walk before you run and learn to wait while you train some of these young men who come upon this platform today to be the successors of Van Bittner and President Mark and the men from these other districts."

It was time for the roll-call vote, with its preordained outcome. The tally sheet showed 3,169 for the position of John L. Lewis and only 1,132 for those who wanted to elect their district officers.

But the issue still refused to die. In 1938, when Lewis by this time was the most widely known and respected labor leader in the land, at the top of his prestige and authority, with success at every turn, there were still challenges to his appointive authority. Aware that the issue would arise again, the *United Mine Workers Journal* printed a lead article before the convention warning of a conspiracy on the autonomy issue. It was an employer plot centering in District 17 in West Virginia, instigated by hired agents from the hated Baldwin-Felts Detective Agency. The article said, "Autonomy in West Virginia at the present time would turn the whole organization of the United Mine Workers of America into the hands of certain labor-hating coal companies and their Baldwin-Felts thugs. Such a change would mean a return to the long hours, poverty wages and frightful working conditions that scourged the industry before the United Mine Workers of America rescued the miners and their families from those awful conditions."

Delegates who were not intimidated rose on the floor to attack with more bitterness than had been evident two years earlier. One man said, "You are going to leave it up to your executive board. It has been that way before. Have they granted autonomy to any district? No."

Again, Murray and Lewis made their arguments and the outcome was evident enough to call only for a rising vote. When the great majority of the delegates left their chairs, there were only a few remaining to call out that they wanted to be recorded in favor of autonomy. The futility of making the same unsuccessful pleas year after year was there for all to see.

But it arose again in 1940, as Illinois miners wanted District 12 returned to them. Ray Edmundson, appointed president by Lewis, said the advocates of such heresy were secretly in the pay of the hated rival, the Progressive Mine Workers. Self-government should never be restored in Illinois until the Progressives were erased from the state, he said.

There were still streaks of independence and rebellion in some of the districts, and when it surfaced, the outcome was even more provisional government and less autonomy. The anthracite regions had been primarily aloof from the internal wars for many years, and as a consequence, had been allowed to run their own affairs. In 1941, when the union by referendum voted an assessment of fifty cents per member per month to build up its strike fund, there was particular resentment in the anthracite fields, where the men had not been involved in the major work stoppages. Out of forty-two local unions in District 7, thirty-eight sent representatives to a conference to call a strike against their own union in protest against the assessment. When John L. Lewis came to Hazleton, Pennsylvania, to ask them to go back to work, he was booed far beyond his capacity to control. He settled the strike by agreeing to an international union commission to consider the anthracite objections to the assessment. The rebels, at the height of their disobedience, had also wanted the unpopular district president, Hugh V. Brown, ousted. Lewis turned this to his advantage. Brown was removed, but another provisional government went into effect, with Lewis appointing the president as usual.

Lewis likewise went about eliminating his old lieutenants from the top ranks of the union. Brophy, whose status had never been secure, even though he was an intimate part of the start of the CIO, had to go for the second time. His disfavor with Lewis came when he began to receive too much support from other leaders within the CIO. In 1938, when Charles Howard, who had acted as secretary to the Committee, died, Brophy took over the duties as acting secretary as well as director of the organization. The founding convention of the Congress of Industrial Organization was at hand, where the Committee would be succeeded by an appropriate federation of unions. It was generally assumed that Brophy would have no opposition for the secretary's job that was to be second in command. Lewis however considered it an ideal position for his daughter, Kathryn, and first brought up his plan at a preconvention luncheon with Philip Murray and Sidney Hillman. Both of them said it would be a mistake; Brophy was entitled to the job. Lewis responded that the selection of Brophy would place too many miners at the top, even though the suggestion of daughter Kathryn would have brought the same result. Murray, who was a CIO vice-president along with Hillman, offered to resign if that would eliminate the problem concerning Brophy, but Lewis would not have it. The subject was dropped, but Lewis soon let out the word that he wanted youthful James B. Carey to hold the secretary's job. His wish was the acclamation of the convention. The following year, without a word, he abolished Brophy's job as national director. This demotion, along with ill health that substantially reduced his activities in the important days of 1940, ended Brophy as a figure of first-rank importance in the CIO, although he gave it many more years of useful service. With his rejection by Lewis in 1938 and 1939, Brophy knew there was no place for him within the UMW, and he never made an effort to exert any further influence within his old union.

The most poignant of the Lewis purges within the UMW came against Philip Murray, who had worked more closely with him than any other human being. Lewis had named Murray his successor as president of the CIO and had stood affirmatively against the self-doubts that Murray possessed about his ability to do the job. The year after Murray became president found Lewis occupied with the 1941 strike and Murray at work both on the steel campaigns and adjusting to his new position. Early in 1942, Lewis announced his support for an "accouplement" with the American Federation of Labor, in keeping with the country's sense of unity so shortly after Pearl Harbor. When a report broke on the first page of *The New York Times* that Lewis had met secretly with Daniel J. Tobin of the Teamsters, now even more powerful in the Federation than Hutcheson and Woll, and worked out a plan for William Green to retire as the price of merger, with younger secretary George Meany to become president of the united federations, Philip Murray was deeply hurt. He had not been consulted. Then President Roosevelt ignored the talk of merger by asking both the AFL and CIO to appoint three-man committees to meet with him on the war effort. Murray countered by omitting the CIO's most prestigious name, John L. Lewis, from the committee.

The old comrades were now far apart. Murray was asserting his independence, his manhood. Lewis, because of his enmity toward President Roosevelt, with whom Hillman and Murray were now favorites, was almost ignored within the CIO. Murray was soon to be humiliated within his own union, even as he was being chosen as first president of the United Steelworkers to go with his honor as premier officer of the CIO. When he entered the Mine Workers Building in Washington to attend to his vice-presidential office, he found an oppressive silent hostility. Saul Alinsky wrote: "He was shunned by his colleagues as a moral leper, traitor and Judas Iscariot. Those who still liked him were panicked with the fear that fraternization with Murray would be interpreted as being anti-Lewis."

Lewis called a meeting of the International Policy Board in Washington for late May. There was no agenda nor any intimation of why the group was being called together. Lewis is reported to have said, "Let Murray's conscience tell him what the agenda will be." Attacks on Lewis within the CIO had become frequent, and Murray too had made unfavorable comments. There had been a number of irritating incidents between UMW forces, particularly parts of District 50, and CIO officials.

The Policy Board met in a basement room at the UMW headquarters where mementos of Lewis adorned the walls. There were cartoons, photographs, testimonials, and even a portrait. Any unhappy miscreant summoned there could not escape the glower of the master no matter where he diverted his eyes. Murray was attacked for holding two jobs now that he had been selected to head the Steelworkers. When Murray protested that Lewis had held many positions at one time, the rejoinder was that never for any outside pay. Lewis overlooked the fact that Thomas Kennedy had been elected lieutenant-governor of Pennsylvania under the George Earle administration, and had drawn his state pay check at the same time he kept his post as secretary-treasurer of the Mine Workers.

Murray tried to assert his status as president of the CIO; Lewis interrupted him and told him, as he would address a small boy, "You may talk when I am through." Lewis replied to the attacks on his patriotism: "I am just as good an American as my former friend, Vice-President Murray." Murray was referred to in acerbic terms, he was denounced by his old compatriots, he was subjected to scorn and derision, reducing him to tears and impotence. After three days of ridicule, Lewis ignored the charges prepared against Murray and said he was ready to act under his constitutional authority to remove officers of the United Mine Workers. He simply handed down a verbal edict: the office of vice-president was vacant; he appointed a faithful unknown, John O'Leary, to fill it. Philip Murray was to curse John L. Lewis for the rest of his life.

The next to go was another of the faithful soldiers of the past, one of the most talented organizers ever turned out by the Mine Workers. Van A. Bittner had worked with Murray in the steel campaigns; he kept his loyalty to the Scotsman after Murray's banishment by Lewis. Bittner was still president of District 17 under one of Lewis's provisional appointments. He was summoned to the office of Lewis and was asked, "Would you like to resign now, or do you want the International Policy Committee to ask you to resign?"

When the Mine Workers assembled for their 1942 convention, the inevitable resolution to leave the CIO was reduced to a routine matter of business. The vote was 2,867 to 5 to follow the direction where Lewis pointed. Before another year was out, Lewis turned toward the American Federation of Labor to rejoin the men he had maligned so often. He was a lonely figure even among the Hutchesons and the Wolls; the CIO he had founded was full of men who joined the rest of the nation in denouncing him. He was to live out his legacies inside his own organization, the United Mine Workers, where there was no one left to stand against him.

6·

When the era of the great strikes came to an end, following as they did the achievement of bringing the organizing of industrial America to life, John L. Lewis was in control of a United Mine Workers of America that was far different from what it had been in the past. The right of men to vote for their own leaders, from local unions up to the important district officers, and then on to their own selections for the top executive positions, was ended. Lewis simply had no intention of permitting the membership to elect district officers, and he imposed that will on his followers. Every man who had dared oppose him over the years was in exile or banishment. The inquiring spirit of the English, Scottish and Irish immigrants who came to America to dig coal had died out. The desire for learning and the Weaver spirit of brotherhood had been relegated to a forgotten footnote of history. No other labor organization was so thoroughly in control of one man; at the same time, no other was nearly so powerful.

Many have asked questions as to the whys of the power and authority of John L. Lewis, particularly when coal miners marched in and out of the mines at the mere suggestion of their union president. During the days of achievement, the easiest explanation was money. By 1949, the wages of coal miners were the highest of any workers in the fifteen basic industries in America. From 1940 to 1948, despite some rise in prices, the economic progress of coal miners was phenomenal. In 1940, their hourly rate of pay was 85.7 cents in the North and 80 cents in the South. By 1948, it was $1.63 per hour in all the bituminous mines. In 1940, there was no travel-time pay, but eight years later, there was an hour of compensation for each miner, in itself a substantial benefit. There was no vacation pay in 1940; in 1948 each miner received a $100 payment for his vacation. He even had pay for lunchtime at another 81.5 cents, adding another half hour to his check. There was more money in shift differentials. Take-home pay had more than doubled because of the stretching of the work week from the seven-hour day originally won as a great advance to a prolonged week of 48 hours.

By 1948, the welfare fund, unknown before the beginning of World War II, was functioning with payments of fifty million dollars a year coming into it. For decades, coal miners had bought their own tools and equipment. In 1948 the companies paid for them. Where money mattered, coal miners, even discounting the price rise of the times, had more than doubled their economic position. There could never be any more impressive testimonial to the benefits of unionism where there was a unanimity of purpose.

The economic-gain rationale is surely an important factor, but it is only half the story, and perhaps the lesser half. Unanimity of purpose did not exist in the 1920's when approximately the same number of men produced the same amount of coal that came out of the ground after World War II. There was disarray, misery, lack of direction, lack of spirit, and total subservience, not to the will of John L. Lewis, for he was not able to impose it, but to company management. Had the same solidarity prevailed that made the campaigns of the 1940's so successful, could the miners have won big wage gains, stopped the assaults on the security of their union, and compelled the coal industry to accept their strengths as a fact of life? Most likely, as long as one concedes the same solidarity. But even to assume that it was possible under the circumstances is an adventure into fantasy of the past. If John L. Lewis had been as democratic as John Brophy, could it have been done? No matter what kind of leader Lewis was—or Brophy either for that matter—the most likely answer is that, given the milieu of the times, the ethics and the acceptance and the mood of America in the 1920's, there existed no giant, no apostle, no Caesar, no Solomon, who could have led the miners to the rewards of a decade later.

The first ingredient, as it is in any revolutionary thrust, is a desire of the people. This does not mean vague yearnings, or fireside wishes, but a resoluteness born of bitterness that ripens into a passion for betterment. It too often appears that this resoluteness cannot come about until desperation triumphs over acceptance of one's lot. Just as the New Deal would never have been possible without the collapse of the country in the Great Depression, so the rejuvenation of the United Mine Workers of America would not have been possible. The movements and tides of history on a national scene are repeated again and again in lesser concentric circles as a product of revival. The proponents of a disaster theory of progress can assemble powerful examples to sustain their argument.

John L. Lewis happened to be there when it happened. If the miners had not demonstrated their desire to come back into the union —"organized themselves," as Brophy put it—the talents of Lewis would not have been turned to their welfare. But it was Lewis who launched the organizational campaign, who sensed the readiness of the men, who "timed it right," as he boasted to Brophy. When he gave to them, they reciprocated, and when they showed their willingness to strike, the massive cycle of escalation for improvement was begun, each act imposing a new foundation for new rewards in the future.

They went west together, the miners and Lewis. This began to produce the spiritual *accouplement* (to borrow a word from Lewis) that is a necessary ingredient in any leader-follower situation where there is a phalanx of common action. Lewis responded to it just as much as did the men. He captured the essence of it in another of his memorable phrasings, when he said, "I have never faltered or failed to present the cause or plead the case of the mineworkers of this country . . . not in the faltering tones of a mendicant asking alms, but in the thundering voice of the captain of a mighty host, demanding the rights to which free men are entitled."

This reciprocity of reactive spirit, once it started and began to catch hold, fueled by achievement, spiraled to the unity that made the great strikes possible despite the furor of a nation, and made Lewis indeed the captain of a mighty host. A miner's wife in Pennsylvania wrote McAlister Coleman: "You know how we used to feel about John L. Well, now I figure he's right and we will go out for him one hundred percent." Reporters and commentators ventured into the field to find out what miners thought of Lewis and were greeted with unremitting praise. *Fortune* and the *Saturday Evening Post* published postwar encomiums from working miners everywhere pertaining to the achievements of John L. Lewis and their admiration for him. Unsolicited tributes in verse and story from coal miners rolled into headquarters and were often printed in the *United Mine Workers Journal*. Thomas Kennedy, in a burst of emotion at the 1948 UMW convention, in attacking the government for trying to isolate Lewis from the miners, said, ". . . if they think they can separate the membership of the United Mine Workers of America from its President, John L. Lewis, then they certainly have a ridiculous situation in mind. It would be about as reasonable to expect to separate His Holiness, the Pope, from the Catholic Church, in the world . . ." Whether mawkish or not, good Irishman Kennedy was indubitably right about it.

At the same time that he won the devotion of the rank and file, Lewis never relinquished control of the political realities of union life. Although he had effectively destroyed his opponents even before the rebuilding of the union, he used his successes on the national

scene as a means of virtual enshrinement within the UMW. This be-
fitted his personality and his vanity—and even his talents. His ability
to control a convention, his unsurpassed eloquence in situation after
situation, his pitiless denunciations of all who opposed him, his fierce
bulk to oppress lesser men, his unyielding position on any issue once
he adopted it, all began to build the image of the king.

Thus it was that the United Mine Workers of America, as an essentially voluntary organization of men, became a labor-union form
of constitutional monarchy by the end of World War II. Other labor
men have succeeded in establishing virtual dictatorships in their precincts, but none with the total success of John L. Lewis. Powerful
men of business have mastered complete control over many corporations; political men have achieved total hegemony over cities primarily, and exerted lesser, but pronounced, powerful influences over
states; there has been domination of many societies of people by
"strong-man types." The fact that it is such a recurring pattern adds
fascination to its frequency.

The union phenomenon is illustrative of the obediences of all men
who form groups for whatever purpose. Lewis, under union law, had
to stand for election time after time. But no one ever opposed him
after 1926 to the day he retired. Political men may have irrevocable
ties to their cities and states, and cannot escape the citizenship of
their countries. But coal miners are not totally wedded to the mines,
as was proved when so many left the pits in the Depression. They
have only the traditions of their fathers and their own fears of a hostile world on the outside to hold them in the union that has become
a part of their lives. Their route to escape, if they desire, is indeed
an accessible one. Their submission to Lewis, in the end, was a willing one.

And, would not any body of men, under the events that marked
their lives, have done the same?

5. License to Kill

MY LAI ON THE HOME FRONT

Demonstrators filled the city streets. They marched in anger, bitterness, frustration. There were shouts and demands. The mayor had summoned the National Guard to preserve "law and order." The Guard stood its ground, blocking the intersections of downtown. There were no weapons in the crowd, only cries for redress. The menace was great, the course was easy, arms were lowered, the firing began. It was an execution; twenty-six dead men were counted when the frightened demonstrators fled the scene.

Across the same state, to the east, in another city, there was a demonstration in the streets at about the same time. The mayor mobilized the police and handed out arms to other good citizens who were prepared to stand firm against the marchers. Newspapers were writing about "revolution." The mayor, like a commanding general, moved his army to a quick confrontation. The orders were to shoot to kill, and one volley point-blank was enough. Three leaders of the marchers were dead; there were wounded all around; this demonstration too was ended.

This was the nineteenth-century way of handling street demonstrations. The marchers were coal miners, whose only complaint against the system was that they wanted more pay for their work. The year was 1877. This was Pennsylvania, not the West of the gunslinger and the frontier marshal. The first slaughter took place in Pittsburgh, the second in Scranton.

Ten years later, there was an even more brutal episode when anthracite miners wanted more money. They decided to march from Hazleton to the town of Latimer to dramatize their demands. The sheriff and his deputies met them on the road and, in the high imperial fashion of sheriffdom of the times, gave the order to disperse. There was the predictable disobedience, the predictable surging forward of the men. The sheriff, exercising his authority, gave the order to fire. As men in the front ranks began to fall, other marchers began to run in all directions. This was easy game for the deputies; this was human prey for the armed huntsman. The firing continued. The victims piled up, shot in the back. There was a count of eighteen dead and forty wounded as a lesson to those who would dare disobey the order of the sheriff. There was enough decent recoil to require a trial, which had not occurred in the Pittsburgh and Scranton killings of the past. Predictably, the jury, far more angered at the demonstrators who "got what they deserved," brought in not-guilty verdicts with the same finality as the volleys that killed coal miners. Obscure chroniclers of the past have called it a massacre, as it surely was, far less known than the killing of only five patriots on the Boston green, and surely even more reprehensible.

One may reflect on the parallels of a century later, when National Guardsmen killed college students in Ohio and went equally unpunished. One may also reflect upon the irony of those many working citizens who applauded the youthful protesters when their grandfathers had been killed by official bullets for marching against their own versions of injustice. One may also reflect upon the appropriateness of the French phrase, *"Plus ça change, plus c'est la même chose,"* as befitting a century of progress. Or, perhaps the Kent State killings in 1970 serve as a reminder that the slaughter of demonstrators in the past was not merely a measure of an uncivilized era of a now compassionate people.

John L. Lewis was indeed a reflective historian as he commented on the 1937 Republic Steel massacre when he intoned in his Labor Day speech, "Labor, like Israel, has many sorrows. Its women weep their fallen and they lament for the future of the children of the race." The United Mine Workers of America can count more casualties of innocents than any other organization of men in all of America's past. No other union comes close, nor perhaps any body of men, aside from the red tribes of the plains.

In every period prior to World War II, the history is the same. Coal miners were killed because they acted as a group to further their cause; violence and bloodshed were almost endemic to their struggles. The stories are remarkably similar in strike after strike, the responses repeat themselves, the reactions of men follow as if a script writer had laid out the consequences which would inevitably emerge. Little wars erupted, as in the anthracite strike of 1902, which bears mentioning only because of its commonness. The coal companies hired their guns, and gave them commissions as special police. Strikers were killed, and angry miners retaliated, as they so often did. In Shenandoah, Pennsylvania, one merchant suspected of selling ammunition to the company deputies was seized by an angry mob of miners and beaten to death. When the company men killed another miner, state militia came into the area. The shooting and killing continued; dynamite ripped out trestles, bridges, homes and stockades. In September of 1902, the *New York Tribune* published its inventory of blood. It reported that fourteen men had been killed, sixteen others shot from ambush, and another forty-two seriously injured. Trains were attacked and wrecked by bitter men. Schoolboys went on strike against teachers whose fathers or brothers were working in the mines while the strike was on. There was a residue of death over eastern Pennsylvania that lingered in the memories of men for all the days of their lives.

As a leader of coal miners, John Lewis was spawned on the cheapness of life, from the ease with which men killed each other with guns to the perpetual imminence of death underground. He saw it everywhere, in all his experiences and in all his awareness. He saw it in its ugliness, in its frequency, in its pervasiveness. He saw it in all manner of men. He saw it in Ludlow, in Mingo-McDowell, in Harlan. He saw coal miners do it too, in Herrin, where blood flowed in more brutality. How it affected his own unconcern at tactics of his men in the late years of his life is difficult to assess. Perhaps as a man of combativeness, of strength, he may have reveled in it, may have accepted it as a part of soldierly manhood, eye for eye and tooth for tooth. Or it may have shaped his own views of the inherent nature of the human animal, in the deepest cynicism of "every man has his price," a view that many thought he held. Or, it may have brought him "many sorrows," although the evidence for this reaction is not readily available.

Three episodes plus one other selected from the many do illustrate how men act when unrestrained, when their passions are permitted, when there is no guidance, whether divine or legal, to control their aggressions. Their distances in years do not detract from their realities, any more than armies and combat in South Vietnam detract from the realities of the slaughter of women and children. The killing of coal miners in Pennsylvania in the 1870's and the killing of college students in Ohio in 1970 leave their lessons, as does the conduct of men in Colorado, West Virginia and Kentucky in the 1910's, the 1920's, and the 1930's, and also in Illinois in 1922. And in our decades, as well.

1·

Colorado coal mines were struck in 1913. It was like the Pennsylvania struggles of years before and the West Virginia combat of later seasons. The companies owned the towns, the houses, the land, the mayors, the police, and literally the souls of all who entered. The miners wanted a union. It was their quest for self-respect, their yearning for a voice, the same touchstone of spirit that caused men to form and build the United Mine Workers of America into the most imposing association of working people in all the decades before the right to organize became the law of the land. They signed cards in the United Mine Workers and asked their lords to meet with them in recognition.

The Colorado Fuel and Iron Company, owned by the Rockefellers, led the other companies in the campaign to suppress the union effort and remand the men to docility. When the strike call came, the owners were ready with their arsenals. In the mining counties, the sheriffs were summoned. There were mass inductions of deputies and the issuance of arms. Trains from the East began to bring new men, lured by the promise of work, unfamiliar with the darkness and danger of coal mines. The Colorado Fuel and Iron Company, in its demonstration of might, brought in a specially built armored railroad car to transport its guards and strikebreakers. It was aptly dubbed, "The Death Special." To all this, when an emissary of the Secretary of Labor made an appeal to John D. Rockefeller, Jr., came the reply that the situation was being handled by men in the West.

Strikers were told to get out. Every house, company-owned, was ordered vacated when the work stopped. The tent cities that accompanied every such contest were laid in friendly fields nearby. Miners too brought their firearms and ammunition, and like wary armies in the night, they patrolled their uneasy barricades. There were occasional shots, like Palestinian border incidents, and killings began to accumulate on both sides. The governor, who had made an unsuccessful effort to mediate, sent in state troops to control the territory. Determined mineowners, with no intention of ever recognizing the United Mine Workers, kept their power pressures upon whatever peaceful instincts the higher authorities possessed.

The National Guard troops, instead of protecting the peace, became another auxiliary army of the owners. When the revered Mother Jones, who, like a wandering Johnny Appleseed of miner organizers, came to Colorado to help her "boys," she was seized on sight by militiamen and deported to Denver. Irrepressible, she came again to the scene. This time, she was bodily carried into a nearby hospital, put to bed under guard, and held for nine weeks without being permitted even a word with the outside world. Such was due process of law and legal rights for people in Colorado who happened to support coal miners.

An investigating committee headed by a Colorado law professor made a report that received the ultimate silence of some of the work of commissions of our own time. It told of the abuses of the militia and pleaded that certain officers be compelled to resign, including a particularly bloodthirsty lieutenant, Karl E. Linderfelt. A Congressional committee came from Washington in early 1914 to investigate. There was enough good behavior while the committee was there to cause the governor to remove most of his troops, leaving primarily one company under the command of Linderfelt on duty at the Colorado mining town of Ludlow.

Ostensibly searching for a missing boy, Linderfelt marched into the Ludlow tent city to demand his return. Louis Tikas, a leader among the many Greek miners on strike, maintained that the lad was not in the colony. Linderfelt was enraged and took Tikas, James Fyler, the secretary of the local union, and another miner as hostages. There were outbursts, and Linderfelt ordered an attack. He smashed a rifle over the head of Tikas and then led his men in pouring bullets into the bodies of Tikas, Fyler, and the other captive while soldiers were rampaging through the tents, burning and shooting. In addition to the three murdered miners, two women and eleven children were dead when it all ended. The obscenities of Vietnam had their earlier American precedents.

The Ludlow massacre produced a new round of warfare in Colorado. Miners over the state brought their guns. There were attacks along a wide front, as coal mines were captured like French villages. Men were killed on both sides, buildings and offices were burned, and this time it required United States Army troops to put an end to the civil rebellion. Proposals for settlement came from the White House, but coal owners turned down every plea. There was to be no recognition of the union. By the end of 1914, the strike was ended, lost, and the union was dead in Colorado.

The forces of law, responsive to the victors, began a round of indictments. Not Linderfelt nor any agent of the owners, but only coal miners and their leaders were accused. John R. Lawson, who headed the UMW leadership in the state, was put on trial for murder, was found guilty despite lack of evidence that he had ever fired a gun at anyone, and was sentenced to life imprisonment. Some 162 other miners were indicted for various crimes against the peace and dignity of the people of Colorado. Lawson won an appeal on a procedural point in the state supreme court, causing his conviction to be set aside. There was no inclination to try him again. There was no need to bother.

2·

In the low corner of West Virginia in the counties of Mingo and McDowell and Logan were great coal deposits along the Tug River. The big companies, despite scores of UMW cards in the pockets of miners, had managed to avoid dealing directly with the union even during World War I. The UMW was strong in West Virginia in the upper Panhandle near the Pennsylvania deposits and in other regions in the state. One of its ablest men, Frank Keeney, was the president of District 19 in Charleston, and it was his campaign in 1920 to win in the "outlaw" counties. As pressure for recognition of the union grew, the coal companies responded with the familiar pattern of mass evictions, discharges for mentioning the word "union," paying for deputy sheriffs, and mobilizing the forces of law to maintain the kind of order they so desired.

There were pockets of sympathy in the mountain towns for the brothers who worked underground. Young Sid Hatfield, whose fathers had survived the bullets of McCoys, was the one-man police force of the tiny village of Matewan, the subsite of many mining families in this faraway portion of noncivilization. Families and uncles and cousins of miners who dreamed of the union were being thrown from their shanties to the roadsides. Hatfield, along with a group of miners, confronted two of the Felts brothers, Albert and Lee, whose operatives had been active in the Colorado campaigns, and who had brought the notorious Baldwin-Felts Agency to West Virginia to fight the United Mine Workers. Hatfield expressed his frontier indignation at the evictions; the Felts gang was in no mood to accept words from a local hill marshal. They had their version of high noon; there was gun fighting of the most primitive kind. Hatfield at least knew his enemy. He managed to kill both the Felts brothers, who died along with four others of their mercenaries. There were three dead on the union side.

The authorities of McDowell County, beholden to the lords of enterprise, brought murder indictments against the marshal of Matewan and the other miner survivors of the eviction battle. The passions of jurors were with native men; Hatfield was acquitted. But the processes of the law were still compliant. A summons went out to Hatfield to appear at the courthouse in Welch, the county seat, for a further inquiry. He went with his pal, young Ed Chambers, and their wives. They left their guns at home; they "didn't want no trouble."

When they started up the courthouse steps, they saw C. E. Lively, an old Baldwin-Felts detective who had served time in Colorado for a murder that could not be ignored. The girl bride of Ed Chambers told her widow's tale later. "Sid turned a little to wave at Mr. Collins. Just then he was shot in the back.

"I saw him falling. I looked at my husband, and he was falling loose from my arm. Lively and a man with heavy-rimmed glasses were shooting. I was begging, 'Oh, please, Mr. Lively, don't shoot Ed any more.'

"He was already dead then. With me begging like that, he just walked down to where Ed was lying with his right cheek on the stone landing and put his gun behind his left ear and fired twice."

Lively too went on trial, but this time there was to be no "miscarriage" of justice. Self-defense it was, said his lawyers, and so the jury voted.

The tent colonies that had aroused the passion of Sid Hatfield were plentiful along the Tug River. They were an integral part of the UMW's campaign of wickedness, said the operators. The union had planned them for men who had been "induced" to strike. Workers and their families were supported in "idleness." The tent colony, it was said, was primarily a weapon of offense for the United Mine Workers and not a relief institution. This view was blandly accepted by the "good people" of West Virginia. The Red Cross denied relief to evicted strikers; no "Act of God" had brought them to their troubles; there was plenty of food, clothing, and shelter if they only would go back to work. The Y.M.C.A. in Charleston said the strike was a controversial issue; the "Y" could do nothing; besides, one operator had made a large contribution toward a new wing on the building. Charleston ministers bemoaned that there was considerable "immorality" in the tents. McAlister Coleman, who went to the scene, told a quite different story.

> Sheriffs and their company-subsidized deputies, with an eye for melodrama, would generally choose the hour just before dawn for their eviction jobs, and if the weather was foul so much the better. Fortified by liberal potions of white mule and ostentatiously showing sawed-off shotguns, high-powered rifles and revolvers, they would descend upon a sleeping town. Along the cinder streets in front of the company houses, each the drab counterpart of its neighbor, they would march, huddled together, until they came to the home of the miner on whom the order had been served. If the door didn't open at once to their pounding, they would break it in and come piling through to pull the digger out of bed and stand him up against the wall at the points of their guns. Then they would herd the women and children out into the street and go to work on the mean furnishings of the place . . .
>
> I once drove up on a union truck loaded with tents and food to the outskirts of a town where an hour before sunup six families had been set out. Through slashing rains, our truck sloshed along a valley trail to the coal camp, where we found the women in drenched house dresses trying to calm their frightened children. They had taken refuge under the shed back of a small church. The men were standing ankle-deep in the creek water that had over-

flowed its banks and was swirling past the doorsills of the company houses. In the sulphur-yellow water there was a confusion of broken bedsteads, cribs, chairs, tables, toys.

When the tents, many of them used by the Canadian army in World War I, were up and when there was gathering around the communal cooking pot, group cohesiveness began to take hold. The mountain women were able to joke about the pleasures of camping out; the air was a little bit freer. The accommodations provided by the companies had brought no dignity to their lives. The typical town was alongside a stony creek bed and a railroad track that ran in to pick up the coal cars. The tiny houses, drab and unpainted, showed sagging porches and missing steps. Open coke ovens often showered them with soot and grime. The sulphur fumes "were kind choky," said one stoic wife; she didn't think they did her baby much good. The shabby privies outside were the principal collection place for the swarms of flies that visited every table top. The streets were masses of mud when it rained, as it does so often in West Virginia hills; and in the dry times, there was the dust that could be added to the oven soot. Typhoid was a constant killer in Mingo and Logan counties—far more even than in other backward parts of the state. There were no printed words to read, no songs to hear, nothing except ugliness and sloth to the mind and soul; and yet men of authority, with willing listeners, used words to portray the United Mine Workers of America as an evil institution in West Virginia.

Once committed, the tent soldiers repaired to their weapons, too. Some of them had been at St. Mihiel and Argonne; they organized squads and patrols, commissaries and mess halls; Regular Army officers who came in later with federal troops marveled at the military skills of these erstwhile army privates. Almost by common acceptance, there was a battle uniform of blue overalls with red handkerchiefs around the neck. Women with nursing experience taught others, and they formed a nurse corps; they proudly wore caps with crude hand letters, "U.M.W. of A." atop each one. There were guerrilla forays into Logan County, where Don Chafin, the most hated and cruel of all the sheriffs of the coal counties, maneuvered his deputies to smash the union. In 1921, even with United States Army troops in the area, the miners mobilized an army of six thousand men, gathered at a ball-park encampment in Madison, West Virginia. They were preparing an open attack on Chafin and his deputies. Frank Keeney came to plead with them to disperse and return to the tents.

A lifetime of indignity had erupted. Too many men had died along the mountainsides; Keeney was ignored; the order to attack was given. War correspondents, such as Floyd Gibbons, were there to report this home-grown war to the Eastern newspapers. As the miner army marched out, the 19th Infantry of the United States Army, with planes and heavy weapons of intimidation, moved between the combatants; federal authority was recognized; miners turned back to their tents.

Their intensity subsided. Despair replaced the exhilaration of preparation for battle, and as so often occurs, descent from the peaks of expectations produced a malaise of hopelessness. Frank Keeney was seized and indicted for murder; he had fired no more shots than had John Lawson in Colorado. William Blizzard, a subdistrict director under Keeney, who lived to sign many miners in West Virginia in 1933, was put on trial for treason. The evidence was too transparent; both men were acquitted.

A Senate committee, reflecting the sensitiveness of the times, had had words for both sides, but had reserved its strongest verbal severities for the union. Its conduct was "absolutely indefensible. Men have been killed, property has been destroyed, telephone wires cut, trains commandeered and misused, and a march of some thousands of men organized and policies carried out which bordered close on insurrection." Perhaps it was, but it was ended, and so was the hope of men in Mingo and McDowell and Logan counties for a dozen years, until new events brought a new national mood to the mountainside coal towns.

3.

Harlan was like McDowell, as McDowell was like Colorado. It wasn't far to the west; it had coal and feudalism and all the power of the operators to resist the union. But it was a different decade, and there was a new law in Washington; however, mine companies had no more intention of recognizing the law than they had of accepting the union. Efforts to organize in Harlan County before the New Deal had been met with the crudest kind of American feudal power; there was no pretense of law or rights or justice. Phrasemakers of the day had called it "Bloody Harlan," a shaft so appropriate that no one hesitated to use it. Men could be killed with the same apparent lack of conscience that followed the shooting of a squirrel off a high tree branch.

There was the usual script: mass inductions of deputies, with their pay coming from the coal companies; union organizers told bluntly to get out of town or be killed; pronouncements of all the local rules pertaining to the evils of the union; the justification for shooting two-legged animals, if any were needed. Only one thing was missing, the tent colonies. The ease of throwing together a mountain shack had made the company towns not so common in Kentucky. Mine Worker organizers came in 1935, after Mingo and McDowell and Logan had succumbed to their New Deal drives in West Virginia. Hired gunmen patrolled the roadways to fire at homes, ambush the crossroads, and snipe at every identifiable representative of the union. Every hotel room that housed a UMW organizer was a preparation pen for a raiding party. Just as there was a Linderfelt in Colorado and a Lively in West Virginia, there was a legal killer who gained his fame in Kentucky. Old Ben Unthank was chief of the black hats; his deputy sheriff's badge was the ostensible authority for his weapons and his armed legions that ruled southeastern Kentucky.

The most ruthless killing was that of a twelve-year-old boy, whose father, a union organizer, had been warned to leave because the gang was on its way to get him. When the deputies arrived to find the father gone, they shot dead his young son, Bennett Musick, as another lesson in how Harlan was run.

There were ample witnesses to a series of killings. When Senator Robert M. La Follette, Jr., conducted his investigation under authority of Senate subpoenas on deprivations of civil liberties in 1937, eyewitnesses named unpunished triggermen time after time. An organizer would be led outside and killed in view of all who happened to be near. Nothing was done to the eyewitnesses; they could better spread the fear; there was no authority to interfere with the "rights" of deputy sheriffs. The findings of the La Follette Committee aroused the nation; federal indictments against mine owners and gunmen for conspiracy to violate the rights of workers under the Wagner Act threw the force of a higher law into Harlan. Its long story was a triumph of the legal power; the Harlan coal mines too were eventually organized.

4·

There was a degradation of decency on the union side, too. It happened in 1922, a fearful year, a turbulent year, one of turmoil and blood all around in labor's warfare for survival in the hostile environment that was "normalcy" in America. Soldiers, federal and state, were everywhere in the mine fields. A strike in western Pennsylvania brought 1,100 state Guardsmen to stand watch. In Colorado, where residue from Ludlow simmered in bitterness, the governor had to call out the Guard again. Unrest in Kentucky brought more Guardsmen, as soldiers with rifles and bayonets patrolled the highways, broke up union meetings, stopped miners from even talking to each other in the streets. The National Guard was called out in Indiana, New Mexico and Utah. Detachments of United States Army troops, in addition to the maneuvers in West Virginia, were called into the mine fields at the request of governors in Pennsylvania, Tennessee, Wyoming, Utah, New Mexico, Oklahoma, Kansas and Washington.

Illinois was the least fruitful ground in the land for strikebreaking. The Southern Illinois Coal Company decided to work its strip mines in Williamson County despite the UMW strike that had shut down all mining operations in that part of the state. This was union territory, as solidly united as were Colorado and West Virginia and Kentucky on the company side. The sheriff was a former coal miner elected by the political force of his old compatriots. The storekeepers and town clerks and business interests were dominated by people from families with ties to the mines—not absentee owners but home-bred workers.

To play the dangerous game of working the strike scene, the company imported a man from Kansas who liked to boast he had tamed every wild strike started by the irrepressible Alex Howat. The new superintendent was C. K. McDowell, who carried a shattered leg from a Kansas bullet, and whose pronounced limp along with the gun and holster on his hip brought him the enemy name of "Old Peg." Old Peg wasn't to live long in Williamson County.

McDowell was warned by every knowledgeable man in the countryside. National Guard leaders told him bluntly to stop bringing in strikebreakers from the slums of Chicago and get out of the coal-stripping business while he was still intact. McDowell roared his defiance, proudly showing his arsenal of rifles, sawed-off shotguns and hand grenades. More armed guards to protect his strikebreaking imports was his answer. One of his gunmen, in an idle moment, penned his fancy to a local lass, telling her how he whiled away his time: "I have been sitting up here on the bank waiting for a goddam coal digger to stick his red neck out. They give us all the white mule we can use, a high-powered rifle and ten dollars a day."

An eruption came, as it usually does. On June 21, 1922, in mid-afternoon of high summer, a young striker talking with friends in a farmyard a half mile from the mining site was scored with a high-powered rifle, dead through the heart. The story came back that it was McDowell himself who limped to the top of the bank with his weapon, telling his guards that he wanted to get a striker so they could all be sworn into the militia to save money. Guns from every household were grabbed by angry men, and by twilight, a task force of a thousand men and boys was advancing in military fashion on the mine. Ex-soldiers wore French helmets, and there was a single ancient airplane to support the citizen army.

Shooting went on all night. McDowell's defenders, overwhelmingly outnumbered, had machine guns behind their barricades, and steady bursts held the attackers off until dawn. A cook's apron, white enough to make a flag, was hoisted at sunrise by McDowell men, and a wave of cheering attackers swept toward the embankment. Machine guns opened up, and men went down. But later in the morning, McDowell himself called out that he had enough, and this time the miner army took over the defense works. The prisoners were lined up for a march to Herrin, four miles away, to be loaded on the next train to Chicago, to be told never to return.

As the march began, anger at McDowell went out of hand. Two cursing miners pulled him from the ranks of the enemy and dragged him down a small side road. The captors and captives stood quietly at a crossroad as a volley of shots sounded. Two grim silent men returned alone. McDowell's dead body, filled with bullets, was found in the lane later that day.

A new crowd of armed men from Herrin, who had not been in the all-night shooting, met the marching column outside the town. There was no longer any leadership, any control, any thought. The frightened McDowell men were lined against a barbed-wire fence and told they could run for their lives. The remainder was gore and bestiality, human beings acting with an unleashed passion against others. The mob began to fire into the strikebreakers, and then charged directly into the fleeing survivors, shouting for more blood. Dead and wounded were all around, some were caught in the woods, throats were sliced from ear to ear, and McDowell guards and McDowell strikebreakers were hanged from tree branches and left dangling. Six others caught in the woods were dragged into Herrin, made to crawl on their hands and knees in the streets through to a small cemetery on the edge of town. An open trench was dug, they were tied together, and rounds of bullets were poured into their bodies long after all life had departed. Seventeen other stripped and mutilated bodies were put on display in Herrin. Its telling and retelling, and rereading after the years, can only remind one of what he saw at Dachau in early May, 1945, on the day after his division occupied that unspeakable horror.

Two hundred men were indicted for murder, most of them union miners. Indignation, far more than that which had followed the Ludlow massacre, filled the front pages and editorial columns of the nation's newspapers, already alarmed at the labor unrest of 1922. The Chicago Chamber of Commerce raised a fund to pay for special prosecutors to go to the aid of Williamson authorities to seek convictions of the "depraved" miners. The trials began in October and wound down to a dreary conclusion the following spring. The aroused citizens of Williamson County who sat on the jury would not find against their own for atrocities against strikebreakers—not any more than would a West Virginia mountain jury convict Sid Hatfield for killing Felts brothers; not any more than would Pennsylvania or Kentucky veniremen punish deputy sheriffs; not any more than Southern juries of the past would render true bills against white men for killing black men. Not one man was found guilty.

5·

What are these forces of ugliness that induce men to kill their fellows with far less compassion than the deer hunter, who at least must surely recognize that he slays beauty? Are the Pennsylvania deputies who gleefully gun down defenseless men in flight and Herrin townspeople who do the same, pulling similar internal triggers? Why do Linderfelt and Lively and Unthank and Illinois miners who summarily executed Old Peg McDowell and so many of his men feel so unrestrained in what they do? Is the life of man "solitary, poor, nasty, brutish, and short," as Hobbes and other theorists have held? Or do the poets of the soul inscribe a more persuasive brief on behalf of essential good?

There are students of men's violence who argue this ethereal subject from opposing positions. Some say the aggressive drive in man is innate, that violence may be instinctive, that the brute resides in us all. The social theorists support a different proposition. Frustrations of life and society breed violent behavior, promote its eruptions, and leave men no recourse but to resort to it. That cruelty and violence and inhumanity abound in men can be doubted by no one; that anger and bitterness and frustration bring homicide is equally indisputable. From all the mineworker events, from all that has been revealed by these episodes of blood, there are certain conclusions which must be reached to make meaningful any future view of the social structure. The beauty-or-beast inquiry may be left to probing scholars of man's nature; we shall search for contemporary answers to his government.

There were indeed great frustrations which caused coal miners to fight back in Ludlow and West Virginia, and perhaps a common bond of believing in defense of a way of life in southern Illinois. However, there is some evidence that the major Herrin atrocities were committed by town hangers-on who only joined the battling miners after the night shooting had ended, whose own internal lusts were turned loose. If this be so, add them to the Linderfelts and Livelys who utilized their licenses to kill. But what social frustrations would allow these kinds of gunmen to kill men with such lack of hesitancy, such exhilarating willingness? What zeal would draw the deputies to accept the badge of authority that offered the weapon to kill the people? What brought McDowell from Kansas to Illinois to break another union strike?

The evidence is simply that men will kill others when they are permitted to do so.

This same conclusion follows from every episode we have discussed and from every other one we have encountered. Linderfelt could kill at Ludlow, and Lively could fire bullets into Sid Hatfield and Ed Chambers, because it was an acceptable thing to do in the society in which they lived. (Likewise, does not the same theory apply to young Calley at My Lai?) No restraints inhibited them; there was cultural encouragement to kill. Pennsylvania deputies and West Virginia deputies and Kentucky deputies who shot strikers were acting out the ethics approved by their leaders. The John D. Rockefeller, Jr., who told probers that events in Colorado were being handled by men in Colorado was content to allow them the license to carry out the accomplishment of their goals. The governors of Colorado and West Virginia and Kentucky, and yes, even the good sheriff of Williamson, powerless though each of them may have been, acquiesced in the license. The cultural juries who voted essentially to punish the victims, whether by acquitting their killers or bringing in verdicts against Lawson in Colorado (as well as every other cultural juror, South or North) stamped their agreements with bloodshed.

Thus, we move from these unhappy excursions to another period, only a short time ago in our lives, which leads more directly to the ills of an institution of men, that once great and grand union of coal miners which shows us so much about behavior of organizations of men. There was force and brutishness on a massive scale in a time when the law provided a recourse. This, as we shall see, was surely a prelude for the rejections of life that came afterward.

6. Mineworker Muscle

PRELUDE TO MURDER

When World War II was finished and John L. Lewis began his era of consolidation of the union's triumphs over the bituminous industry, there remained one major source of irritation to the entire structure. Throughout Kentucky and Tennessee were scores of nonunion mines, many of them small, many run by local operators, many of them in the aggregate turning out enormous tonnage for the market. There was also a major new customer—the Tennessee Valley Authority. The TVA too was in an era of postwar expansion, with a heavy demand for coal, all based upon competitive bidding as befitting a government operation.

The nonunion operators, paying substantially under the union-industry wage scale, and with no requirement to pay royalties into the Welfare and Retirement Fund, were securing numerous contracts with the TVA as their bids repeatedly undercut the major producers tied to UMW contracts. The big companies were concerned, the union was frustrated, and the stability that both sides sought was under stress. As the TVA called for more and more coal, new mines were opened each month in the southern Appalachian deposits and more nonunion operators entered the field to threaten the UMW-industry wage pattern.

It was the union's task to deal with this problem. There were only two possible solutions: organize the mines or close them down.

Either could be difficult, costly, hazardous. There was a law now that protected the right to organize, and an election machinery through the National Labor Relations Board that provided the way to peaceful resolution of organizing campaigns. The problem there was that miners voted by secret ballot, and if the union lost the election, the mine was free to continue its nonunion operation. With the higher pay of UMW contracts and with the expanding hopes for welfare and retirement through the new fund, coal miners would so obviously benefit by voting for the union that those of us who reside in neutral amphitheaters might have difficulty understanding how the union could ever lose. But those of us who have been there know the more chilling realities of the "free" electoral market place.

The union was destined to lose, over and over again. (Union organizers face the same struggle in every industry, as workers repeatedly vote their fears and their conditioned employer loyalties and reject the promise of benefits that come with every union contract.) Small-village miners in Kentucky and Tennessee had none of the union traditions of the descendants of Welsh and Scottish miners in Pennsylvania and Illinois and of the strange union solidarity that grew up in West Virginia a long time ago. When mineowners fought back with thinly concealed promises of their own, attacks upon the union, and "predictions" of closing down the mines if the union came in, the ballot boxes were inundated with "No" votes. The UMW was defeated in election after election, even though it scored its occasional triumphs in the over-all debacle.

The election pace was pitifully slow. Even when a small mine was won and the industry contract came in, there was the real threat of a loss of business to the owner who could no longer bid successfully against the remaining unorganized companies for the lucrative TVA contracts. It was an almost all-or-nothing proposition: all the mines had to be captured to stabilize the entire wage structure, or the campaign would be surely lost through gradual deterioration, undercutting of standards, and the eventual threat to the UMW's entire position in TVA country,

Tactics more dramatic than an appeal to the uncertainty of the ballot box had to be used. There was one method all the hill men and small operators understood. Bullets and dynamite and sheer muscle had always been persuasive factors in their regions; they were a hundred times more eloquent than a union leaflet; they made men sit up and pay attention. Practitioners of such manly arts abounded in those parts of Appalachia; all that was required to unleash them was leadership and direction and money.

The UMW command headquarters in that part of the country was in its District 19 in Middlesboro, Kentucky, a small city on the western side of the Cumberland Gap. From Middlesboro, staff representatives and organizers could move out into all of southeastern Kentucky and the Tennessee areas down toward Knoxville and westward into the central part of the state as far as the coal deposits went. District 19 had fallen under the control of John L. Lewis long before, when he made it a provisional district and thereafter appointed all its officers and directors. These men from Middlesboro were some of the key actors in the campaigns of a decade of turbulence. The money to run the activities of District 19 came from Washington; these same "activities" led into hundreds of thousands of dollars of adverse jury awards in later seasons. Only a few miles from this headquarters center across the line in Tennessee was the small town of LaFollette, laid in an area of many violent Mine Worker deeds, and the home locale of the genesis of the killing of Jock Yablonski, according to several confessed participants. All this, and everything about it, is enveloped into one of the most unwholesome episodes, tragic, sad and unsavory, in the story of any body of men.

1·

The first effort to crack the Meadow Creek Coal Company in central Tennessee came even before the end of the war, in 1944. The method was the ballot box, and it failed. In an election run by the National Labor Relations Board, the Mine Workers were badly defeated. In late 1946, there was another campaign, as J. W. Ridings, who sat on the International Executive Board as a representative of District 19, came from Middlesboro to lead the drive. Some mines were won in the area, but the men who worked for Meadow Creek wouldn't sign UMW cards. A year of intensive organizing work produced nothing; the time had come to do it another way.

On the morning of January 12, 1948, representatives and organizers and local union officials, along with unattached coal miners and other recruits, assembled in Sparta, Tennessee, about twenty-two miles from the Meadow Creek mine. There were two hundred of them. They pulled out in a convoy along the highway, heading for Meadow Creek. Men with guns dropped out of the cavalcade to block the roads leading to the mine. The afternoon shift was changing at 2:30 just as the lead car pulled up in front of the mine opening. Ernest (Spooner) Stultz, another International representative out of Middlesboro, jumped from the lead car to face one of the mine foremen and tell him the mine was being closed down. A truck pulled in front of the mine commissary, its empty bed to be used as a platform for the speakers. Ridings and Hugh Brown, another staff man, stood on the truck bed and told the frightened captive workers that the mine "would not run another day unless the company signed a contract with the union."

Roads were sealed with the efficiency of a police operation. Most of Meadow Creek's coal went out by truck. The drivers who were loading when the "persuaders" arrived were told to get out. Those who approached the roadblocks were turned back, with a menacing rifle waved in their faces to emphasize the seriousness of the business at hand. The next day Spooner Stultz drove into Crossville to the east to visit a local coal dealer whose trucks worked the Meadow Creek route regularly. Stultz bluntly told the owner that his place would be blown to bits if he sold the coal that had been hauled to his yard from the mine. The trucking of coal from Meadow Creek was totally stopped.

W. T. Ray, the owner of the company, and his foremen, along with a few men who slipped through the roadblocks, continued to work the mine with low output. The Tennessee Central Railroad had run a spur track to the mine two years before, and now the railroad was called on to bring in cars to haul out the coal. On June 23, a dynamite blast destroyed the track and stopped rail shipment from the mine. Two union members were quickly arrested and lodged in the county jail in Cookeville, the county seat of Putnam County. Another District 19 staff man named Bell, as two federal courts later noted, made regular visits to the cells with food and cigarettes.

There was a carefully directed campaign to win over the men who were afraid to go back to work. Every storekeeper in the area was visited and told to give groceries to the men who had left the Meadow Creek mine. The UMW paid the bills. During the campaign, more than $70,000 of union money went to merchants for food and necessities to support the men who didn't go back.

With the trucks stopped and with the rail track destroyed, there was one more visit to the mine to call upon the few men still working.

Workers were lined up at gunpoint for curses and threats and directions not to go back underground. Willard Clemons, another union official, led this cadre; his talk aroused men to fight back; three days later he was shot from ambush by a brother of one of the men he had intercepted. Clemons recovered from his wounds and two years later wrote John L. Lewis asking for money to compensate him for the hazards he had endured. The UMW constitution contained a prohibition against paying sick benefits or damages of any kind to any member. But a union check was drawn for $5,000, was signed by John L. Lewis, was sent to J. W. Ridings, and was hand-delivered by him to Clemons. This too became evidence in a later trial to help prove liability against the union.

After the visit of Clemons and his men, owner Ray had enough. He called Ridings and said he was ready to sign. On July 13, 1948, they met and the agreement was executed. Meadow Creek Coal Company was now a union mine. Ridings had one further request. The boys in jail over in Cookeville for the dynamiting of the railroad—well, charges against them had to be dropped. This occurred too, and the mine began to operate.

Meadow Creek later fell upon competitive times. Owner Ray couldn't continue to win his bids for TVA contracts against the lower rates of the nonunion diggers. Meadow Creek went down, and afterwards a damage suit was brought against the United Mine Workers for the 1948 campaign. It was not until November 4, 1957, that the first verdict was rendered—a judgment for the company for $400,000, upheld on appeal, and eventually paid out of the UMW treasury. Meadow Creek may have been won once upon a time, but the permanent record reveals that it was irrevocably and ignominiously lost.

2.

Not too far to the southeast from the bloody southern Illinois coal fields are big deposits in western Kentucky. District 23, covering all that part of the state, had its headquarters in Madisonville, a coal town just east of the Kentucky Lake country. Western Kentucky too had a mass of nonunion mines after World War II, and the economic pinch on union miners was as severe there as it was in the Appalachian sections. There were abortive organizing efforts in 1946, but after the "success" of the Meadow Creek maneuver, the same tactics were imported to Madisonville in 1949.

The campaign brought an army to Hopkins County. The companies were big and far more powerful than smaller Meadow Creek in Tennessee. West Kentucky Coal Company was the leader of the holdouts, operating several profitable mines. West Kentucky was working six days a week; the eighty-six union mines in all of District 23 were down to three days. Again, union coal was undercut; the jobs and economic welfare of members of the United Mine Workers were truly in jeopardy. The same call went out: organize the nonunion mines or close them down.

Miners came down from Illinois and Indiana, and all across Kentucky, to take part in the drive. Ed J. Morgan, who had been successively appointed as District 23 president by Lewis for more than fifteen years, turned the campaign over to Earl Suver and Arthur Chaney, two of his staff organizers. Suver and Chaney assembled a force of two thousand men on the morning of June 29, 1949, all along Kentucky State Highway 85 east of Madisonville. There were cars, trucks and buses, and then a marching foot patrol, six or seven abreast. The convoy, followed by its foot soldiers, marched into the East Diamond mine of the West Kentucky Coal Company soon after the first shift started.

Suver and Chaney led a task force into the mine office. Ray Cobb, the superintendent, was told to get the men out of the mine. He asked if it could wait until the shift was ended. Chaney said, "It's that same damned old story. We have heard that a lot of times. We are going to talk to your men now. What are you going to do about it?"

By this time the sheriff of Hopkins County had arrived, along with a Captain Jones of the Kentucky State Police. Cobb appealed to them for help. When the sheriff asked whether the men could go back to work after the talk, Chaney said, "What in the hell do you think we are all out here for?" Then Jones told Cobb that there were too many men outside; he could not "control them" or "handle them." The workers had better come to the top.

As the men came out, they were herded into a large circle. Suver told them of the benefits of UMW membership and of dire things that might happen if they did not join. Chaney told them the mine would be organized if they had to "guard" it twenty-four hours a day. The men were to go home now and "wash the scabs out of their clothes." Chaney told them to come that night to the home of Jim Dunlap, another District 23 staff man, to sign their cards and take the obligation. He then asked for a show of hands of all those who would be there that night. Only a few hands were raised.

"Get 'em up! Get 'em up, you sons of bitches!" The roar came from the massed throng around the captive workers. Every hand went up; with "alacrity," as a National Labor Relations Board trial examiner later found.

When the work at East Diamond was done, the caravan went on to the company's North Diamond mine. The same scenario was repeated, with the sheriff and Captain Jones witnessing in full view. Chaney told the North Diamond men, "They say it is against the law for us to do this, but it isn't and we'll do it." His legal analysis was mistaken; ten days later the Circuit Court of Hopkins County, Kentucky, issued an injunction against all the UMW tactics in that county. The National Labor Relations Board made extensive findings on the same conduct and ruled that it violated federal law as well as the strictures of the Commonwealth of Kentucky.

The campaign went on all day June 29 and again on June 30. Six major mines in the vicinity of Madisonville were visited. The same task force moved in on the mines in the same fashion, with the sheriff and Captain Jones on the scene each time, making no effort to interpose. At the Homestead strip mine, the party grew rougher. One slow-moving worker named Curlee started for his car without hearing the indoctrination speech. Two men grabbed him, another smashed him in the mouth, breaking his upper plate, causing profuse bleeding. Every hand was raised at the call without hesitation. At the close of the talks, men were told where to report that evening. All were instructed to go home at once, wash the scabs from their clothes, and not to return until the mine was under contract. There were curses and threats and dire predictions of what might happen if a second visit were necessary. The finding of an NLRB trial examiner, summarized in one long, incredible sentence, doing its own brand of violence to legal writing, tells the story of the campaign:

> The invasion and seizure of the mines by this large group of UMW men, numbering 2,000 or more, of such size and fixed determination that the sheriff and State patrol officers professed their

inability to halt or stop them in their announced purpose to invade and shut down the mines, the imposition of their demands upon the mine officials, as the officers of the law advised that there was "no other choice" if "violence and property damage" were to be avoided, the consequent shutting down of the mines, the "rounding up" and taking into custody by squads and groups of UMW men of the mine employees working in the mine yards and buildings, the enfolding of the mine employees coming out of the mine or from the pits as they reached the mine yards by impenetrable masses of UMW men, the "herding" by UMW men of all the employees into one group and their complete encirclement and imprisonment by solid masses of UMW men, and the speeches then addressed by the UMW leaders, agents and spokesmen to the captive employees, while thus encircled by this overwhelming and inimical superior force, to the effect that this group of UMW men had shut the mine down, that they would not permit or allow the mine thereafter to operate or the employees to resume work until the Company signed a UMW contract and the employees joined the Union, and ordering the employees to forthwith leave the mine premises and not return to work until they had joined the Union, that if the employees attempted to resume work without having first joined the Union the UMW would come back and stop them, would see that they did not work any more, that the UMW meant business this time, that if they had to come back "it would be bad," that the UMW had the nonunion miners outnumbered, and other similar both implied and expressed threats to exert force and violence against the employees if they attempted to resume work without first joining the Union, effectively conveyed threats and warnings that the nonunion employees would be subjected to punitive action and economic reprisals, and physical force and violence, if they did not obey the ultimatum given them to forthwith cease work, leave the mine, and not thereafter resume work without first joining the Union, and constituted a course of conduct creating an atmosphere of terror and fear and exceeding the bounds of peaceable action, which was reasonably calculated to, and did, in violation of Section 8 (b) (1) (A), restrain and coerce the nonunion mine employees in the exercise of the rights guaranteed them by Section 7 of the Act, among which is the right to refrain from joining a union.

The "atmosphere of terror and fear" failed. The state-court injunction was obeyed and the invasions stopped. But there was a better way to organize the West Kentucky Company. The entrepreneurial maneuvers of John L. Lewis with Cyrus Eaton, the Cleveland tycoon, led to Eaton's financial control of West Kentucky by 1951. Under new management, West Kentucky signed. Dollars were far more effective than muscle, and the western Kentucky campaign was ultimately more peaceful and more successful than the battles that were to be resumed in the East, when the real bloodshed began.

3.

The continuing campaign to break the nonunion mines moved eastward again to Kentucky and Virginia. The far-western tip of Virginia was covered by District 28 headquarters in Norton, likewise under the control of leaders appointed by Lewis under the "provisional" government structure. The Virginia campaign also had its recalcitrants. Its aftermath too wound up in the courthouse, this time in legal papers that contained detailed allegations of dynamite and blood.

A staff representative named Charles Minton turned into a plaintiff against his own union. He filed suit in the Circuit Court of Wise County, Virginia, in February, 1952, claiming damages of $350,000 for loss of his job. He said he had been fired because he had refused to commit murder. He had been a busy man with dynamite, so he said, blasting stubborn collieries into oblivion, but he was not yet ready to kill a man for hire.

Minton's pleading, filed by one of the most responsible law firms in southwest Virginia, spread the story of the "organizing" campaign. He was called to the District 28 office in Norton to meet with Allen Condra, the acting president, along with Michael Widman from Washington headquarters. Widman told them that Lewis was very unhappy with the lack of organizing progress. "Damn the lawsuits; we will take care of them," were instructions from the top, said Minton. He stated he was then called into another room by George Griffiths, secretary of District 28, and told specifically to blow up the mine substation of the Gladeville Coal Company near Glamorgan. Minton then spelled out how he and another man "in the middle of the nighttime" did go and set off three cases of dynamite that blew up the Gladeville station. Then, a series of other dynamitings were detailed, all of which had occurred.

The Gladeville Company stubbornly continued to resist. Minton was then called to a meeting in Knoxville with an "agent extraordinary" and "personal agent of John L. Lewis." He was told he had been selected to kill C. P. Fugate and Harry L. Turner, the two owners of the Gladeville Coal Company. He would be paid a handsome reward. He would be furnished the finest legal counsel. If he went to prison, his family would be well supplied with funds.

In his pleading, he named the "agent extraordinary" as Tony Boyle, who was then administrative assistant to John L. Lewis.

During the federal investigation of the Yablonski murders in early 1970, the story of Charles Minton's lawsuit became known. Agents who went to the county courthouse in Wise, Virginia, found that court files had disappeared. The lawyer who drew the pleading for Minton was dead. Minton himself was found and brought to Cleveland to testify before a federal grand jury. Apparently he knew little or nothing of the later Yablonski crimes. His own case against the UMW had long ago been settled—quietly and out of court. Its most prominent visibility was in the old files of *The Coalfield Progress*—of Norton, "In Old Virginia, a Friendly Newspaper, Serving a Friendly Community"—which printed the story in front-page headlines when the case was filed. Minton had refused to kill Fugate, and for that he was fired, read his declaration. The record further sayeth not.

Minton's charge that Tony Boyle told him to murder a mineowner has never been proved, and the truth of his charge will probably always remain unresolved.

4·

The Meadow Creek, West Kentucky and Norton campaigns were mere warm-ups for the big drives that followed in Middlesboro country in 1959.

By the spring of that year, the status of the UMW in eastern Kentucky and Tennessee was somewhat critical. Whether the tiger was made of paper, or whether the growing roster of nonunion companies would be brought into line was the big issue in the coal fields. By March, there were 176 holdouts against the 1958 industry package. Such massive recalcitrance could break the union in the territory. The old terror tactics, only half successful in the past, were again brought into action.

More than ever, TVA dominated the market. By 1951 there were no more rivers to dam. Hydroelectric power had reached its capacity. At nearby Oak Ridge, the Atomic Energy Commission was using one half of the entire TVA output of electrical energy by 1956. Other markets were crying for power, too. TVA managers made the decision to turn to steam, and this meant more coal to burn. In the ten years that followed the completion of the water-power projects, twelve new steam plants had been put into operation. By that time, TVA had become the largest coal purchaser in the world. It bought one tenth of all the coal sold in the electric-utility market in the United States. Its coal consumption grew twenty times over in that one incredible decade of expansion, from a million tons in 1950 to the higher figure in 1960. By 1956 the TVA was using 78 percent of all the coal mined in Tennessee.

This brought hordes of new entrepreneurs to the mountain country around Middlesboro. As the TVA issued call after call for bids on new coal contracts, the diggers and the strippers and the "dog-hole" operators, some of them as small-time as a shovel and a truck and others with manpower and equipment, began to dig and bid. John L. Lewis unburdened his rhetoric as early as 1954 to excoriate the TVA for its low-bid policies, which meant nonunion coal.

For the key to profits was to keep away from the union. Getting coal to the market place with the lowest cost was the way to win succesful bids. The welfare-fund tax of forty cents on every ton of coal was alone enough to make the difference for many operators. In addition, there were enough hungry mountain men to work below the union wage scale to make pay-cutting the sharpest money game in the area.

As the eager entrepreneurs took vast leases of Tennessee and Kentucky lands noted for coal deposits, there was another economic chess game to play to beat the union, the government and the law. There is an old federal statute from New Deal days, known as the Walsh-Healey Act, which requires companies selling to the government to meet the prevailing wage scale in the area. This usually means union wages, as labor-management contracts ordinarily set the prevailing standard. To escape the union and avoid paying union wages and yet meet the government's requirements of union wage scales in order to win the TVA contracts was not too difficult for the clever hill-country lawyers who were as astute in corporate manipulations as their more worldly brethren in the Wall Street canyons.

The technique was to create a string of paper corporations, all in the family. There were a mining corporation and a trucking corporation and a tipple corporation to receive the coal at shipping points. The tipple company might buy a few tons from the dog-hole boys at a low rate in order to maintain the fiction that it was an ordinary business concern, despite the fact that the stock was owned by the same man, with his wife, children, brothers and cousins, who owned the trucking company and the mining company. It was only the tipple company that sold the coal to the TVA, even though it bought the coal from the trucking company that bought the coal from the mining company. The few men who worked around the tipple could be paid a rate that equaled the union scale in the absence of a contract in order to meet TVA's requirements of compliance with the Walsh-Healey Act.

This was only a small part of the total wage cost, since the major part of the man hours came in the mine. And even the tipple companies could escape paying the forty-cent royalty as long as they could hide from a UMW contract.

The mineowners maneuvered to evade the law by their legalisms and the Mine Workers maneuvered to evade the law by cracking heads. The new gold-rush people played on the needs of hungry miners who were desperate enough to work for low wages. The union played on the oldest fear of all, death. The same conduct that characterized the Meadow Creek and West Kentucky campaign had been brought into action around Middlesboro in 1954 and 1955 to seed the memories of the mountain people. One of the early defiant operators was Clifford Osborne, who fought the UMW in 1954 after he secured one of the big TVA contracts. His lawyers obtained an injunction against the union in a Kentucky state court that year after the first outburst. Buttressed by the paper order, he leased more land, hired new men, and secured his own tipple in Jellico, Tennessee.

The Kentucky court order stopped at the state line. Ed Daniel and Taylor Maddox, two staff men from Middlesboro, rounded up new gangs to visit the Osborne mines in Tennessee. Drivers were stopped, pulled from their trucks, pushed, cursed and threatened. Coal was dumped on the ground. Osborne's lawyer moved into a Tennessee courthouse at Jacksboro and obtained another restraining order to try to stop the new assault.

With each new ploy, the union adjusted its campaign. The tipple in Jellico became the strategic point. Crowds of miners filled the streets of the little Tennessee town, stopping every truck. Spencer Douglas, an active local miner, became a deputy sheriff; every driver who came into town was hit with a warrant for operating without proper equipment.

As the struggle with Osborne became the major contest, restless men, while waiting, visited the small nonunion mines. Mineowners named Boots and Cox were severely beaten. An old man named Van Huss was hit by a band of marauders. His workers were made to strip him naked, whip his bare buttocks, and "baptize" him in a nearby pool. His mine was halfway between Jellico and LaFollette.

Inside the town of Jellico, the blockade of the tipple drove Osborne to the wall. He closed his mines. Some of the others shut down with him, while a few others signed the industry contract. Osborne was later to sue for damages in federal court and win a verdict of $215,000, all paid out of the UMW treasury in Washington.

The 1959 campaign began with a strike call against all the marginal operators who had failed to sign the 1958 national contract. Most of the holdouts argued they couldn't meet the new scale and keep their TVA contracts. As soon as the strike began, on March 16, the shooting started. Rifles began firing from the hillsides on the first day, sniping at trucks as they moved along mountain roads.

Mine Worker convoys began to patrol the roads. Twenty cars rolled up before the small mine of Woodrow Smith on Stinking Creek in Knox County, Kentucky. Smith was told to sign or else. He began to shout his defiance. A group chased him up a small hillside near the mine. State police arrived too late. They found Smith's body with six bullets in it. The troopers broadcast the call of cold-blooded murder. By the next day, they had arrested six UMW men, including a staff representative from Middlesboro, all charged with murder. One of the gunmen, John Henry Warren, signed a statement, went on trial in London, Kentucky, in July, was convicted over his plea of "self-defense" and was sentenced to life imprisonment behind Kentucky walls.

The first truck driver was killed a few days after Smith was murdered. The message to all mineowners and drivers was unmistakable. The Kentucky National Guard came into the area, but was no match for snipers and dynamite. Frightened operators pooled their resources and set up a radio transmitter near Hazard, to send out strike bulletins and give advance warning of raids. The transmitter lasted only a few days until another dynamite blast ripped it apart.

Since the state courts had not stopped the campaign against Osborne in 1954 and 1955, it was the turn of the federal judiciary this time. The National Labor Relations Board was called in; its lawyers filed suit for an injunction in the federal courthouse in London, Kentucky; on April 30 a broad restraining order was issued against all of District 19 and District 30 in an effort to stop the warfare in eastern Kentucky.

The United States Court of Appeals for the Sixth Circuit in Cincinnati later described the union's Kentucky operation. "The campaign was conceived and prosecuted on a grand scale. Spectacular and varied methods were employed. Mass picketing was instituted at the tipple sites, on the highways, on railroad sidings and at the mines. Pickets, sometimes numbering more than a thousand men, roamed throughout the area in motor convoys. The persuasion of sheer numbers was supplemented by more violent and forceful methods. Trucks were stopped at the tipples, and on the way to and from them; their loads were dumped onto, and off, the highway. Mine and tipple workers were beaten. Strong threats of violence were made to the independent truck drivers to persuade them to discontinue transporting coal from the mines to the tipples."

The court went on to describe how tactics changed after the issuance of the federal court's injunction. The roving car convoys stopped. Dynamite at night continued, taking out railroad tracks, bridges, tipples and unguarded trucks. The word was spread among the working miners, "when the leaves come out on the trees" more convincing methods would be used. The green of springtime came early in Kentucky to afford protective cover from the steady gunfire that hit the tipples where armed guards patrolled. One railroad spur leading to a tipple of the Flame Coal Company was dynamited eight times. Flame too won a heavy damage verdict against the union.

On the Tennessee side, the diggings around Jellico were hit with the same methods. The White Oak Coal Company had lived with a

UMW contract for several seasons, but it too was a holdout in 1959. UMW staff organizer Ed Daniel, who had led the Osborne campaign in 1954–55—assisted by another representative, William J. Prater, who was charged in 1972 in the Yablonski murder—took over the White Oak program. It started with the usual convoy, made up of more than two hundred men. They pulled into White Oak Mine No. 1, pulled the 75-man crew off its stripping operation, and told them no more work without a contract. A blockade was thrown up to stop every truck. Squads from the hillsides put bullets through tires, truck beds and cabs. Truck drivers poured in their resignations.

The tipples in Jellico were again prime targets. The blockade had stopped Osborne and his allies, and strategy once successful was ripe for renewal. Another holdout, Gilchrist, was operating two tipples in Jellico to handle his own coal and that of the White Oak mines. At midnight, on May 6, 1959, carefully timed explosions obliterated both tipples; the blast shattered windows along the main street of Jellico a block away. Ed Daniel slept in his home in Jellico that night; he, like everyone else in town, was shaken by the blast; his earliest response was a morning walk down the street to view the damage. Prater, in bed in the Eblen Hotel, showed similar nonchalance. He went back to sleep, got up at his usual time, had breakfast, walked down the street, and called the sheriff to find out who had been arrested.

Even with the tipples in Jellico destroyed, White Oak kept trying to operate with other locations to process its coal. A trucker named Randolph, who had been moving White Oak coal, was visited by Prater and told he would be shut down. "Mr. Prater, what legal right do you have to shut us down?"

"I don't need a legal right," Prater said. "I take my orders from Washington."

One of the most feared striking forces in the Jellico area was the "Overall Gang." A burly roughneck named Hubert Bailey led the crew. Prater went with Bailey outside the town, to a restaurant owner who specialized in handguns; four revolvers were bought there. Bailey and his boys marched through the Jellico streets day after day, like hired gunmen in Tombstone years, dominating the conversation of the sidewalks. Bailey would take them into Malcolm Jackson's restaurant for their meals. He signed the tab. The bills for every meal were paid by the United Mine Workers of America. Bailey charged gasoline at local stations; this too was paid out of UMW dues money.

Bailey liked to talk, as well as throw around his authority. Arnold, the chief operator of White Oak, was his prime target. "As long as the Union is paying us twenty-five dollars a week and furnishing us plenty of dynamite, Arnold is not about to go back to work," Bailey boasted. These comments came back to the witness stand a few years later, when another enormous damage-suit verdict was enrolled against the union in *White Oak Coal Co. v. United Mine Workers.*

In early July, Ed Daniel summoned 150 men to a night meeting. "We have been accused of doing the damage around here," he said. "We might as well go full-blast ahead."

On July 13, 1959, Arnold's strip-mining equipment, two power shovels and a bulldozer, were torn to pieces by a blast after midnight. One man who had been hired to guard White Oak's property had previously talked with Ed Daniel to find out if he should stay on the job. "I would rather you didn't work at that," said Daniel. "The boys like you, and they don't want to hurt you and don't want to get hurt."

"I got to work at something."

"Well, you can make more money working with a wrecking crew. One night's work will pay you more than you can get from Arnold for a month," warned Daniel. The old man said, "I don't want that kind of job." Like so many other tellers of the violence of the times, he too turned up on a federal court witness stand to add his bit to the legend.

The shooting and the killing went on into June and July. Trucks were constant targets. One strip operator who closed down, Jess Fessler, of Sunbright, Tennessee, had moved his bulldozers to a flood-control project he had undertaken for the U.S. Army Engineers. He relaxed his viligance in the belief his troubles were ended. One shot from ambush killed him on June 8 while he stood outlined in front of his equipment; his slayer was never caught. There were more bombs and more dynamite, with some of it coming back at union officials as well. By the end of June, there were enough damage suits on file in the United States District Court for the Eastern District of Tennessee in Knoxville to total claims of more than fifteen million dollars. Many more were to follow, eventually to take a terrible toll on the UMW treasury.

By November, the campaign had wound down, almost as if exhausted by killings and dynamite and mob dominance and the multiplying legal claims against the union. An announcement of the end came from Washington. John L. Lewis and the big coal operators had sought to eliminate nonunion coal in their 1958 contract with a protective wage clause. The union's 1959 efforts in Tennessee and Kentucky were to "organize" something quite different from contract language. Lewis and the operators used as an excuse the Landrum-Griffin Act, passed by Congress in late 1959. The new law tightened secondary-boycott provisions of the Taft-Hartley Act, which they said might affect their contracts. To anyone knowledgeable in the law, the new legislation made no difference; the Middlesboro campaign was not even close to the law's requirements long before Congress passed the Landrum-Griffin Act, as so many of the later court judgments demonstrated.

The law is often a convenient excuse; it could be turned on and off to meet the exigencies of the situation; the deeper reason was that enough killing had occurred. Fortunately for man's survival, fits of distemper have a way of eventually ending their bloody courses.

5·

It could be called a revolt of the union men in the mountains; some of the more sympathetic observers at the time attempted to label it so. But the inescapable conclusion is that it all came from Washington, where the old man was in his last years. Violence and terror itself were as much a part of the program as if they had been written into a script by someone at UMW headquarters.

For Middlesboro does not stand alone. It was more like one part of a ten-year war, begun at Meadow Creek in 1948 when some of the tactics of the Illinois violence of the 1920's were brought up to date. The use of motor convoys, full of armed men, sealing off crossroads, blockading mine outlets—like miniature *Panzer* divisions—required planning and direction. In case after case, it was found that UMW staff representatives organized the convoys, convened the gunmen, did the talking, gave the orders, and built the atmosphere of a backwoods breed of Attila's warriors.

The campaigns of dynamite were directed with unerring precision. Targets were carefully selected and areas were reconnoitered; grave-

yard hours were prime time. There was recruitment and camaraderie
and protection among the spear carriers. "The boys like you, they
don't want you to get hurt." There were visits to jail cells with food
and cigarettes and moral support; lawyers were hired to defend the
unfortunates who were caught; there were hired gangs and hired guns
and free-flowing expense money. When the 1959 campaign began,
the International Union began to pour money into District 19 by its
device of "loans." Some of the monthly shipments of money from
Washington to Middlesboro reached $425,000, more than $14,000
each day. In the calendar year, almost two and one half million dollars was "loaned" by the UMW to District 19. The financial sustenance to the marauders was more than enough.

The continuity of the attacks flowed from Meadow Creek up to
West Kentucky, where men were brought from Illinois and Indiana,
back to the crushing of the Osborne Company, into the massively
planned and executed 1959 campaigns, a consistent course of conduct for eleven years, subsiding only in rest periods between affrays,
as armies of the field rest their brigades while commanders plan to
capture new pinnacles. District headquarters men were its field commanders in every case; its general staff was in Washington.

The military concept of command responsibility must be applied.
Not only does a general become charged when a private on the line
wanders astray, but in any tightly run organization, the man at the
top carries the burdens. John L. Lewis was an unusually prescient
leader. One of his great strengths over the years was his infinite
knowledge of what transpired in every district headquarters. The
men who worked there were his chosen appointees. District 19 was
under his complete dominance for decades; no man could darken its
Middlesboro halls without his approval. Tony Boyle was his administrative assistant in those years and worked closely with him. But
the word of Lewis was law at UMW headquarters. He was as aware
a leader in 1948, when Meadow Creek began, as he was in his later
dealings with the West Kentucky campaign, and on through the years
of the 1950's. There is no plausible rationale for blaming the viru-
lence of 1959 on underlings who worked without the knowledge of
the aging patriarch. If John L. Lewis did not personally plan it, he
personally permitted it, authorized it, paid for it and, when it did
not work, personally brought it to a close. It is a conclusion not

pleasing to his admirers or to any of us who appreciate his achievements, his lasting phrase-making, his defiant courage and his considerable contribution to the history of our times. Its full awareness
cannot be evaded, even with the dolorousness that it brings. It was
another side of an intensely gifted human being more complex than
the conflicting varieties of the souls of most of us.

No other union in all of America's labor history has ever used a
systematic prolonged program of violence and terror to achieve its
goals. The trampling of opponents by Teamster lords in the higher
days of Dave Beck and Jimmy Hoffa was never done on a planned
coordinated scale like that of the UMW campaigns. Rough, insensi-
tive, hardened men, callous and unconcerned, like scattered indige-
ous progeny of a power-oriented society, often wielded Teamster
authority; but they were usually sensitive to the pressures of law and
the views of those whose ultimate dominance counted; there is no
evidence that there was ever a concerted campaign. In addition, some
unions have been invaded by gangsters who have used their brutali-
ties, but this is hoodlumism, pure and simple, not trade-unionism. On
the other hand, the great mass of the labor violence in America has
been directed against oppressors of labor—as the coal miners' violence so often has been—and many workingmen have been killed in
the process. Most often, the authorizers of the slayings were the employers of labor, not the men who tried to organize.

Thus, the conclusion is unassailable: the United Mine Workers of
America stands alone as the only union in America's history to undertake a concerted, directed, planned, financed and calculated campaign, over a sustained period of time, of violence, terror, dynamite
and killing of other men.

Apart from its futility, from its fears, from the human lives it destroyed, there could never have been a rational argument to support
it. As long as there was some semblance of law in Kentucky and
Tennessee, it was certain to meet a proscription. If the states were
unable to curb it, there was the federal government, and it was eventually the federal power that made its continuation no longer workable. The National Labor Relations Board and the federal courts,
unintimidated by mountain mores, took a terrible toll. Literally millions of dollars, all dues money from the pockets of working coal
miners, was wasted—not just misspent or merely badly invested, but

diverted to intrinsically evil purposes, if one accepts the reality that beating and terrorizing and killing are evil purposes.

When one authorizes or condones that use of physical power against other men, starting with a push or shove, or a curse or a threat, or a compulsory herding into captive bunches, the next step is invariably a blow or a punch. The bullet follows so easily. Once the mark of harm has been cast, pain inflicted on another human body becomes so acceptable that the ultimate blow of death is the next step, almost without hesitation—a dark, unhappy sequence that step by step heightens the savagery of man. This happened at Ludlow, in Illinois, in West Virgina, in Harlan, in earlier days in Pennsylvania, and in every other precinct where force was the governor. History's stories are so full of it that only a blotting of the mind can ignore it.

Then why did Lewis do it? Despite his erudition, his whole life had taught him that sheer force was the most certain way to triumph. He had employed it successfully in his struggle against his enemies in the union, whether Howat or Farrington or Brophy. Powers Hapgood and Adolph Germer, with their words and reason, were troubling annoyances. A good bloody beating silenced them for a while and, better still, broadcast a forbidding message to all those who might like to join them. He saw the raw violence of employers too, and its tragedies moved him to heights of eloquence. His mastery of the strike weapon, with the power that made it work, undoubtedly fueled the sense of destiny that he once embraced. There was no longer any sense of conscience about it, he could employ raw force as could a reckless gambler whose passions obscured the consequences.

His life was turbulence; his sensitivity to human existence had been dulled. When there were no political restraints upon him, he ignored the potential legal ones. He behaved like his corporate counterparts; they permitted and, yes, authorized violence against workingmen in the labor wars; he permitted and, yes, authorized violence against all men, be they frightened or fearful or resistant or confused. Perhaps he possessed more insight than they, and certainly more eloquence, but authority unhampered would be wielded in the same manner.

Just as Lewis bequeathed the legacy of political despotism to Tony Boyle and his other successors, he left them violence as an integral way of life within the union. He taught it to them, he guided them in it, his acceptance of it was their acceptance of it. And when there was a serious political threat to the regime he created, the acceptance of it made it most logical to physically destroy the enemy who challenged that regime. It was in this milieu that Jock Yablonski, the opponent, with his wife and his daughter, could be gunned to death in their beds, just as dynamite could eliminate an offending coal tipple, or stubborn mineowners could be shot down, or frightened men could be herded into a circle to be told what to do, or convoys of terror could roam over a countryside.

It is no argument to say that its victims in Middlesboro country were cheats and chiselers, as many of them were. Or that they spread their own brand of fear over deluded workingmen who had no free choice, which was so often the case. Or that they dealt in human misery by driving standards so low that every miner's bread would be imperiled, which was indeed a practical possibility when millions of tons of nonunion coal went to market. All the accumulated wrongs of the others—and they were multitudinous—surely cannot justify the killing of a single man, if one places any value on human life at all. In addition to its gruesome ethics, its strategy was wrong, destined for an ultimate failure that eventually and inevitably settles over similar adventures of violence. It ended with as many nonunion miners as before, with millions of dollars in court judgments, with bitterness and frustration, and with a stain on the name of United Mine Workers of America that saddens every man who believes in the intrinsic value of unions of working men and women.

Regrettably, as late as 1968, years after the departure of Lewis, some of the same tactics were still in use. In the mountain regions of Pennsylvania, approximately sixty miles east of Pittsburgh, in District 2, an independent group known as the Southern Labor Union, which had done some organizing in Tennessee, had secured a small outpost. The Mears Coal Company operated a processing plant in Dixonville, in Indiana County. In mid-January, 1968, an abandoned office building of the company was blown apart by dynamite, reminiscent of old-style campaigns.

Pennsylvania state police, aware of rumblings among men in the area, warned the Mears management to expect a major visit late in the month, even naming the day it would happen. On January 30,

1968, a convoy, led by a District 2 representative named Telk, brought nearly a hundred men to block the roads around the Mears property. A large gang of men went to the scalehouse to call the men from work and to talk with Charles Mears and Earl Bence, partners in the business.

"You sons of bitches brought the Southern Labor Union in, and we are going to send them back to Tennessee!" "We will blow this place off the map!" "You will either become United Mine Workers or we will get even." These were some of the shouts that went up from the crowd. Telk asked Mears what he was going to do about the SLU. Mears responded that his operation was covered by a legal contract with the Southern Labor Union.

"You hear those men out there hollering," said Telk. "This is not going to satisfy them. They want you to get rid of the Southern Labor Union." There were more threats. One of the crowd told Mears he would not operate again. A county sheriff on the scene helped disperse the crowd, after Mears ordered all his employees off the property.

Later that day, nearly five hundred men surrounded the Mears operation. Earl Bence tried to get back to his plant, but was unable to do so. He stood by and watched men move up to the old office building and methodically put it to the torch, where it burned into a pile of ashes.

In December, only a few weeks before, a crowd, assisted by Telk and DeGretto, the UMW director for District 2, had invaded a high-school building where the Southern Labor Union had attempted to hold a meeting. A man named Plavi, who tried to start the meeting, was pulled down from the stage, grabbed and held by two men while a third smashed him about the head with his fists. Plavi was dropped to the floor in front of the other frightened SLU men. The chief attacker turned to them with a question of whether anyone else wanted to take it. Plavi spent sixteen days in the hospital because of this beating. Telk and DeGretto stood by to watch the action. For this and the old-style convoy attack upon the Mears property, the National Labor Relations Board found District 2 in violation of the law.

The United States Court of Appeals in Philadelphia, in methodically affirming the NLRB decision, said: "It is apparent that the massing of pickets on January 30 was a prearranged and coordinated effort. In addition, Telk and two UMW local presidents served as spokesmen for the crowd, and their conversation with a Mears Company officer echoed the crowd's shouted coercive and intimidating threats. . . . The burning of the dynamited Mears Company office building was plainly action taken in consonance with the earlier made threats against the Company for employing SLU members."

This episode, arising so recently in the old district of John Brophy, came in the time of Tony Boyle. Its pattern was depressingly similar to the Kentucky-Tennessee campaigns that were so familiar to Boyle, the international union's executive board, and to every other observer who has paid attention to what has happened to the United Mine Workers of America.

This is bitter irony indeed for a union that was begun with a concept of brotherhood among all men, with a belief that it was knowledge, not a bludgeon, that brought power, and with a hope that men could unite rather than destroy.

7. The King and the Counting House

MANEUVERS WITH MILLIONS

The third legacy left by John L. Lewis was entrepreneurism. Unlike his examples of despotism and violence, his talents for high finance and management were never quite emulated by his successors. Despotism required only a lust for power, a common yearning among men. Violence required only the crudities of the human beast, which reside in most of us. But manipulation of money and corporations required a particular kind of financial *élan* which only a few men possess. Lewis had this aptitude in great quantities; the men who came after him were of more ordinary stuff.

It started with the buying of a bank. At least, the effect on the membership began then, although Lewis had earlier assayed minor forays into managerial enterprise.

The operation of a bank by a labor union could be a noble endeavor, as shown by the conduct of one financial institution owned and managed by the Amalgamated Clothing Workers of America. Other unions too have owned banks, none of which has been shown to be detrimental to the interests of the people who provided the money. Like the universal examples of fire and water, so much depends upon the use to which the element is turned. Given the power thrusts and manipulative skills of John L. Lewis, the venture of the United Mine Workers of America into the banking business had its portents for abuse; it likewise had its accomplishments, as any skilled advocate could demonstrate. However, it fueled the entrepreneurial soul of Lewis; the fortunes of coal miners became secondary. Lewis could always argue, as he did so powerfully, that his one-man rule was a direct benefit to miners; the use of violence was never publicly praised, but those who would explain it could say that its purpose was to organize coal miners, which would benefit all.

But the residue of the bank operation affected the lives of people in a manner Lewis probably never foresaw. It helped remove an institution as an entity from its own constituency, the membership. It left its own form of desolation over the coal fields. Its inevitabilities later led to an awareness among men who mined coal that the union was indeed isolated from them, alienated, no longer caring for their interests as they had fervently believed Lewis did. This, of course, was essential fuel for the revolt that came later. It produced a corruption of the Welfare and Retirement Fund itself; it helped turn union leadership into a nobility that treated coal miners like peasants in their fiefdoms; it blunted the great human issue in coal mining, personal safety. It cost lives of miners, it deprived families of the benefits most of the nation thought they were receiving, it led to the inner rot of what had once verged on the noblest associations of working people.

Without access to official UMW records, the timing and circumstance of the bank purchase are cloudy. As the Welfare and Retirement Fund began to accumulate money, John L. Lewis began to look for a place to keep it. The National Bank of Washington, an aged and somnolent District of Columbia institution, was easily accessible to a take-over from a faction with capital. John L. Lewis began to make inquiries, and in late 1948 or early 1949 the union bought a controlling stock interest in the bank. One of the obscurities of the purchase is that the *United Mine Workers Journal,* the twice-a-month official publication of the union, said nothing about it. Had the bank been bought as an aid to Mine Workers, to further the welfare of their union in order to bring more benefits to them, some favorable mention ought to have found its way into the news that went out to the membership.

John Owens, the union's secretary-treasurer, had a folksy explanation of why the bank was bought when he defended the UMW's financial policies at the 1964 convention. It all started when he had trouble cashing his pay check, so he said. When he came to Washington as an officer of the union, part of its money was kept in the Lincoln National Bank in the city's financial district.

"After I became Secretary-Treasurer," Owens said, "I went down to that bank with my pay check. They wouldn't cash it until I—an executive of the bank—go over and say it was all right to cash my check. My name was on every check that had been paid out of that bank for a few months. But I didn't care about that. The next month I went back, and I had to go in to another officer. I didn't care about that. I told him to take a good look at me so he would recognize me next time. They said, 'All right.' So I went back again in another month. I thought I was going to have to show them my vaccination to prove that I was John Owens."

This was heady stuff for miners in convention, when it was cheering time and praising time. Owens went on. "So we decided that we would transfer our funds into another institution. But our funds were never welcome. We were a labor union headed by John L. Lewis, and the awful coal miners that he represented. So they didn't want to have anything to do even with our money.

"So we found after a while the oldest bank in the city of Washington, organized in 1809—Patrick Henry and other great patriots of this country deposited their money there and it was recorded by handwriting."

Owens then told of the purchase of the bank and lapsed again into the kind of sentimentality plus financial muscle-flexing that must have made every delegate proud.

"That little bank right off of Pennsylvania Avenue has been there since 1809 and was managed by a president that had been going down to that bank every day, and he used to be the bookkeeper and he would copy off the deposits in longhand upstairs over the main entrance to the bank. He worked in that bank and was president when we acquired it. He knew every account there was in the City of Washington that was trustworthy, that was sound, just like that. We gave that old gentleman a new chair and a new desk and told him to sit there so he could be counseled with, and we were going to put a new president in and elect a new board of directors, but his salary would go on just the same. And the old gentleman lived a few years and passed away. But that bank grew until we absorbed the Liberty National Bank, the Hamilton National Bank, and the Anacostia Banks. It had some $28 million in it when we bought it. It has now eighteen large banking units in the great capital of the United

States. It has got $432 million of assets. We invested $23 million in stock and it is worth on the market today $72 million."

When the Liberty National Bank was absorbed by the Washington Bank, John Owens surely had no further difficulty in cashing his pay check. But the cold financial realities of the transactions were on a far more businesslike basis, as one would expect when banks were bought and sold. Soon after the UMW outbid a competitor bank, Lewis began looking about for his own man to run the establishment. He found him in Barnum L. Colton, a Washington bank official who knew banking and how to use money to promote power under the leadership of Lewis. In 1949, Colton was made president of the National Bank of Washington, UMW officials went on the board of directors, and the financial empire began to grow.

After the initial introduction of Lewis to Colton, the Mine Workers president laid out his program at their second meeting. Lewis told Colton he was going to put Welfare and Retirement Funds into the bank, transferring all accounts which had been kept to that point in other Washington banks. By April 30, 1950, there was more than $36 million in deposits in a checking account in the National Bank, drawing no interest and swelling the bank's available money for financial management. The bank's new affluence allowed it to buy other banks, as the Owens report indicated, which made the National Bank of Washington a powerful and prestigious force in the city's commercial circles. As deposits from the Welfare and Retirement Fund poured in, this money grew to more than 20 percent of all the time deposits on hand and more than 30 percent of demand deposits. Here was the monetary leverage to accomplish the kind of things that John L. Lewis wanted.

Employer trustees of the Fund, to their credit, resisted the use of Fund money in the bank. But under the legal structure, there were three trustees, one from the coal operators, one from the union, and one supposedly neutral. It required two of the three votes to make a decision, and Lewis, who acted as union trustee and chairman, always had the vote of the "neutral" trustee, Josephine Roche. Never in the entire time that Lewis lived did Miss Roche ever once vote contrary to his wishes. When the major shift of Fund money was made to the bank in 1950, the coal operators' trustee, Charles L. Owen, confronted Lewis and Miss Roche with a demand that the money be withdrawn and deposited elsewhere. He stated for the record:

"It is undoubtedly the law that a trustee should not deposit trust funds in a bank which he controls or in which he has a substantial participation. Amongst other criticism, he may cause the dividends upon his stock to be enhanced by the Bank's use of a large deposit of his trust's funds for loan purposes. Also, conflicting interests may arise; or, losses may occur." Owen correctly foresaw events of the future; he continued to protest; he made no impact upon Lewis or a complacent coal industry, which could have acted to attack the "neutral" capacity of Josephine Roche, but never did.

The eloquent roars of the Lewis of the warring decades subsided into the inscrutable smiles of an Oriental potentate. He simply ignored Owen. Miss Roche sat silently, and when Owen had finished his protests, Lewis called for the next order of business. Stenographic notes were taken of the trustees' meetings, transcribed, and turned over to Josephine Roche for composition of the "official" minutes. The protests of Charles Owen were calmly and quietly eliminated from the official record.

With the purchase of the bank and the use of Welfare and Retirement Fund money, Lewis literally had millions at his disposal, all out of three sources: the union treasury, the bank, and the Fund itself. He was ready to compete in the money markets with any entrepreneur, prepared to use his millions as he alone saw fit. In his behalf, it must be said that at no time was there any personal profit for John L. Lewis; his gratifications were not in greed, but in power. Judge Gerhard Gesell, of the U. S. District Court in Washington, found in 1971, in the Welfare Fund case: "There is no suggestion that Lewis personally benefited, but he allowed his dedication to the Union's future and penchant for financial manipulation to lead him and through him the Union into conduct that denied the beneficiaries the maximum benefits of the Fund."

About the time of the take-over of the bank and the shift of the Welfare Fund money into it, Lewis was consorting with a new ally and grand financial adviser, Cyrus L. Eaton. Eaton, in his own manner, was almost as remarkable a man as Lewis. Operating out of his offices in the Terminal Tower in Cleveland, Eaton dealt in vast holdings around the world. He combined daring and brains with a financial insight that must have been extremely pleasing to John L. Lewis. Eaton knew the coal industry probably better than most coal magnates, many of whom were objects of scorn to Lewis, who always believed he could run the industry better than any of its operators. Eaton knew how to manage money, make deals, and parlay the fine principle of leverage to its utmost advantages.

Eaton's favor with the Mine Workers and Lewis began to show publicly in 1948 and 1949, when stories about him began to appear in noticeable positions in the *Journal.* An appearance of Eaton before any Congressional subcommittee, no matter how lowly or insignificant, was worth a news story in the *Journal,* a development reserved for no other person in America outside the labor movement. Eaton, a "Cleveland industrialist and financier," told a Senate Appropriations subcommittee in June, 1949, of a squeeze on small business. He testified in November before a House Judiciary group on money monopoly. Such esoteric subjects and appearances unnoticed in the more formidable daily press were "newsworthy" items to readers of the *Mine Workers Journal,* who were undoubtedly deeply concerned.

After having lost the violent campaign to organize the West Kentucky Coal Company in 1949, Lewis was now prepared to use money where muscle had failed. Cyrus Eaton began to buy shares of the corporation. Companies dominated by Eaton began to buy shares. The union itself made direct purchases of stock. Barnum Colton became involved also, directing investments into company stock. By 1952, Eaton and his allies had won control of the board of directors. More Mine Worker money was coming in, and the following year, Eaton became chairman of the board. In 1953, the West Kentucky Coal Company, previously a bitter holdout against unionization, signed the National Bituminous Coal Wage Agreement. There was now money to pour into the Welfare Fund to rest in the bank to provide additional leverage. West Kentucky, with Eaton's direction, turned to buy another major nonunion operator, the Nashville Coal Company. By 1958, the United Mine Workers had loaned or invested $25,456,156 in the two companies. No other union has ever organized employees in such fashion.

The methods of handling money in the West Kentucky maneuver had some unusual features seldom seen in the ordinary business world. Loans were made to Eaton and he in turn would put up company stock as collateral for the loans. He could turn over the West Kentucky stock at any time to satisfy his notes in full. The promissory note read: ". . . and I shall have no liability for any deficiency in the value of the collateral below the amount due under this note." This was a simple no-lose, no-risk proposition, a kind of guarantee ordinary mortals never receive. If the value of the stock went down, only the union could lose. If it went up, the union could not gain—only Eaton.

Barnum L. Colton, the bank president, was likewise a beneficiary of such favored financial treatment. John L. Lewis made loans from the UMW treasury directly to Colton—twelve million dollars on one occasion and thirteen million on another. This was an easy fortune for Colton, costing him not a dime. He bought other bank stock to be merged with the bank he headed and joined Eaton in buying control of the West Kentucky Company.

"When you need money, call on me—or call on us," Lewis told him. The "me" was the more correct terminology.

While the buying into West Kentucky was in progress, the union's vast affluence with its bank ownership was an important source of money to other coal operators. Between 1953 and 1963, eleven major loans totaling approximately $17 million were made to various operators. "Some of these were risky and unjustified," Colton said. The UMW then put up secret collateral to back up the loans of the bank. Colton explained that for "ethical" reasons, the bank did not tell the coal companies that the union was behind the loans. One loan was defaulted in 1959. The UMW had posted $1.5 million in collateral. As a bookkeeping device, the union turned over a check in the full amount, plus interest.

Apparently, there was never a question raised inside the UMW. When one views such casual handling of a million and a half dollars of the money of coal miners without mention or notice, despite the publishing of financial reports, the recognition of the ultimate authority of John L. Lewis in every phase of UMW life is seen again. It was simply incredible.

The West Kentucky venture, too, was a financial disaster.

When Eaton won control with UMW money, the company was a profitable enterprise. By 1958 and 1959, under its union contract whereby it met the union scale and made royalty payments to the Welfare and Retirement Fund, West Kentucky was suffering heavy losses. The union contract was not the millstone, however; other companies were meeting their financial obligations and thriving. The morale of management was gone; there were no further incentives. Its stock went down from the $25 paid for it to around $11 per share. It fell behind in its royalty payments, which in turn caused the union to pour more money through new loans into its own company. By 1963, after Lewis had retired, the union under Boyle had liquidated its entire West Kentucky holdings. It lost eight million dollars of Mine Worker money in the process.

Old John Owens justified that financial foray too, at the 1964 convention. "We didn't want to be in the coal business. We had nothing to do with the operation of the mine. It was just an investment that has paid millions of dollars to the Mine Workers of America. There have been paid out over $90 million in union wages to those men down there, and there have been paid into the Welfare and Retirement Fund $24,496,483.54. And we sold stock at a loss on my books for $8 million loss . . . But we got it back in the $24 million paid into the Welfare and Retirement Fund. We got it back in human freedom that has been established. We got it back in wages paid to the men in that industry down there, and we got it back in the protection of the wages they were destroying in all other mines in America."

Like so many other rationalizations of human effort, there was some truth and some tragedy in it, some pieces of achievement and some parts of folly. But the Welfare Fund was not the union treasury; the loss to the dues payers was staggering. One might argue that Owens had a point in his reference to the stabilization of the industry. But the greater harm was that it was done in secrecy by one man's decision and one man's power, with even the few who were privy to it not daring to raise a single question. When outside sources began to suspect that Mine Worker money was financing Eaton to buy the Nashville Coal Company, the institution behaved as so many other bulwarks of society have behaved in recent years—it lied about it. Lewis wouldn't talk at all, as became his style in his later years. But a UMW official issued a flat denial. Cyrus Eaton himself smiled and said to a reporter, "There's not a word of truth in that story." But the UMW's records irrefutably confirmed the union's role.

During this period, Lewis and Cyrus Eaton began a double-teaming advance into electric-utility stocks, using Welfare Fund money and Mine Workers money interchangeably as needed. Since public utilities were becoming principal users of bituminous coal, following the same pattern established by the TVA, the Mine Workers launched a major campaign to persuade the utilities to deal only in coal produced by union miners.

Cleveland and Kansas City were the first two major target areas. In early 1955, the Welfare Fund bought 30,000 shares of Cleveland Electric Illuminating Company stock. From the union treasury, another favorable loan went to Eaton to enable him to purchase 20,000 additional shares on his own. As high finance operates, Eaton then went on the board of directors of the Cleveland company. The Fund at the same time bought 55,000 shares of Kansas City Power & Light Company stock and lent Eaton $27,000 to buy another block of shares. The Fund would then turn over its proxy to Eaton. By 1958 even the employer trustee was playing the same game. Henry Schmidt became the operator trustee on the Fund in that year, and since his own company was selling coal to utilities, he enthusiastically joined Lewis in voting to use Fund money to buy utility stock.

More money went into Cleveland Illuminating in 1962 and 1963, as the Fund bought an additional 90,000 shares. With Eaton's drive, it was union coal that was now being bought. The Fund bought stock in Union Electric, Ohio Edison, West Penn Electric, Southern Company, and Consolidated Edison, all to exert its influence on the coal-buying policies of those companies.

This arrangement, in its use of Welfare Fund money, was an unlawful breach of trust, as found by Judge Gesell in the 1971 Washington decision.

> This intimate relationship between the Union's financial and organizing activities and the utility investment activities of the trustees demonstrates that the Fund was acting primarily for the collateral benefit of the Union and the signatory operators in making most of its utility stock acquisitions. These activities present a clear case of self-dealing on the part of trustees Lewis and Schmidt, and constituted a breach of trust. Roche knowingly consented to the investments, and must also be held liable. The Union is likewise liable for conspiring to effectuate and benefit by this breach of trust.

Lewis took the union into another investment area, that of coal shipping. He met with coal-company presidents and railroad executives to start a new line, American Coal Shipping, Inc. The UMW took a one-third interest along with business enterprises, and thirty ancient Liberty ships were bought from the government to carry coal overseas. The new company quickly ran into union trouble of its own. Contracts were hastily signed, one of them with District 50 of the UMW, headed by John's brother, Denny. District 50, originally started by Lewis for organizing in all fields, was now acting like a maritime union to go with its other endeavors. Other AFL-CIO unions protested the contract with District 50, and picket lines went up. The company went to the National Labor Relations Board to secure injunctive relief against the jurisdictional picketing. John L. Lewis, the implacable foe of Taft-Hartley and the labor injunction, was on the board of directors of American Shipping. As an employer this time, he supported the move for an injunction, almost without a show of embarrassment.

Although the big-money-management phase of his career began with the bank, Lewis had earlier indulged in the use of Mine Workers' funds to deal with his entrepreneurial urges. Back in 1942, just before Philip Murray was sent into exile, he had chartered a corporation in Delaware, the legal seat of so many industrial giants in the United States. He called it Lewmurken, adopting the first three letters of his name, that of Murray, and of Thomas Kennedy, the secretary-treasurer. Its assets were UMW funds. Its business address was 900 Fifteenth Street, N. W., in Washington, the UMW headquarters. Its first big investment was the buying of 30 percent of the Rocky Mountain Fuel Company, a mining business that was once owned by Josephine Roche. It also loaned $1,451,104 to Rocky Mountain Fuel Company on a demand note. Even with the infusion of such an amount of union money, the Rocky Mountain Fuel Company went into receivership before the year was out. The note was carried year after year on the books in its full amount, with no chance that it would ever be repaid. Whether sentimentality, business judgment, or whatever motive moved Lewis to establish his dummy corporation to make loans of this type, it was still use of union-dues money without any apparent knowledge or awareness of the membership, all done at a time when the word of Lewis was never to be questioned on any matter.

Lewmurken made another loan too, in later years to the Freeport Coal Company of Morgantown, West Virginia. Freeport then leased its land to a nonunion operation known as Kingwood Mining, which then mined the coal in direct competition with UMW interests. This too made no apparent dent upon Lewis and his associates.

In addition to using union funds and Welfare Fund assets to make the transactions he desired, Lewis began to pay particular attention to the condition of the coal industry after World War II. He had been unusually conscious, for a union leader, of the industry's problems in the 1920's, partly because of their effect on the union and its members and partly because his belief in his own abilities strengthened his view that he could run the mines better than their owners, a likelihood that few knowledgeable people ever doubted.

Lewis's business sense recognized that coal could be dug with machines far better than with men. Mechanical loading equipment began to come into the mines in the early 1920's, although the industry's general chaos and the availability of manpower into Depression years prevented any massive spread. As could be expected, miners viewed the new equipment as a threat to their work. After the union's rebirth in early New Deal days, UMW conventions were filled with rank-and-file resolutions against the machine. The usual approach was to recommend a tax on the coal loaders to make them too costly to operate. In 1936, 1938, and again in 1940, delegates proposed taxes on equipment. Lewis gave them the usual quick burial accorded any proposal which he disfavored. He never wavered from his position that the union should accept mechanization and take from it what could be gained.

When coal output began to decline in 1948, Lewis told the UMW convention in October that he was going to do something about it. He was fearful of the throat cutting of Depression years, the closing of mines in selected areas, and price wars that would be disastrous in their effects on miners and their families. He bemoaned the lack of leadership in the coal industry. "They have sectional group leaders, each one thoroughly lacking confidence in the other, and it is impossible for the Mine Workers to find any stable agency on the side of the bituminous operators with whom we can discuss a national program, however conducive it would be to the welfare of the industry, both on the investment side and on the side of the mineworkers."

He was the man to remedy that deplorable situation. By 1949, when bargaining for new contracts began. Lewis met with three groups of mine operators. Negotiations continued into 1950; another strike brought a Taft-Hartley Act injunction and more contempt proceedings against the union. But a new contract, known as the National Bituminous Coal Wage Agreement of 1950, was forged, establishing a new Welfare and Retirement Fund, giving the union control over working time with its "able and willing" clause in the contract, and further solidifying UMW dominance over the industry.

From the 1950 struggle emerged a new national organization of the operators, known as the Bituminous Coal Operators Association, empowered to speak for as many as 262 employers, including the giants of the industry. True nationwide bargaining was possible at last. Lewis could sit down with Harry Moses, the BCOA representative, and "two-man" bargaining became the new technique that brought years of stable labor relations to the coal-mining industry.

Even by 1950, Lewis was labeled by *Fortune* Magazine as the best salesman the "machinery industry ever had." Nearly 60 percent of labor underground was used in loading and hauling coal before the advent of big machinery. Even by 1913, half the underground coal was machine cut, as the miner's pickax began to disappear. By 1953, the ax was no more. Machines that would both cut and load coal began to come into the mines. Mechanical conveyors and shuttle cars quadrupled in number between 1945 and 1959. The continuous-mining machine eliminated drilling and blasting. The steel claws of the continuous miner would tear the coal from its seam, scoop it up, load it, and move it out of the mine far more quickly and effectively, and at less cost, than could the miners who filled the underground pits in the late nineteenth and early twentieth centuries.

While the new mechanical miners made output easier, the coal market was still in disarray. Production was at 516,000,000 tons in 1950, but had fallen in 1958 to only 410,000,000. The fuel market was shifting during the postwar period, as crude oil, petroleum and natural gas began to heat American homes. From 1940 to 1964, the industrial market for coal dropped from 30.3 percent of the fuel energy consumed in the United States down to 23.1 percent, retail sales of coal dropped from 19.6 percent to 4.6 percent, and railroad purchases dropped from 9.8 percent to almost nothing in 1964. The ancient coal cars of our boyhood days had been totally replaced by the diesel engine.

The principal users of coal now were the electric utilities, as we have indicated. By 1964, coal production was on the rise again, although still below the 1950 figure.

The impact on the membership of the United Mine Workers was dramatic. When Lewis negotiated the famed 1950 agreement, there were some 416,000 men working as miners. By 1959, the last year he was president of the UMW, there were but 180,000 men at work, and five years later, in 1964, the number had dropped to 130,000 men. Average daily production, however, had increased to 12 tons by 1961 (it was only 4.5 tons in 1940) and up to 16.84 tons per day in 1964. (The comparisons with production in other countries are also astonishing. British miners were producing 1.2 tons per day, and 0.83 ton per day was the average output in Belgium, France and Austria. A Japanese digger had to work eighteen days to turn out as much coal as an American miner produced in one day.)

In a remarkable interview in late 1959, shortly before his retirement as president of the union, Lewis took great pride in the modernization of the coal industry. When Lewis was asked if his union cooperated with industry, he retorted: "The United Mine Workers not only cooperates with the operators on that—we invented the policy. We've encouraged the leading companies in the industry to resort to modernization in order to increase the living standards of the miner and improve his working conditions."

He spoke with detailed examples of increased productivity, with the infinite knowledge of any industrial magnate. He pointed to specific companies that had turned mechanization into profits, told of their dividends and stock splits, and how some of them hoped to increase output to 45 tons per day.

He also told of the attrition of manpower. "There are pensions for those above sixty years of age. The younger men go by the tens of thousands into other industries to get jobs. Some of the older men stay in the area and manage to get along with the help of relatives. . . . There is public assistance and Social Security assistance in some cases."

He praised the status of miners in glowing terms. "The miner who fifty-five years ago lived in poverty now lives like an ordinary citizen. He is a respectable member of the community. He lives in a modern house, with carpets and rugs. He has a bathroom, TV and every electrical gadget to make household work easier for his wife. His child goes to school. He can often afford to send him to college. No young man in a mining community now has to go into the mines to work without getting a high-school education, as formerly happened. . . . It's true there aren't as many miners. But those young men who have been absorbed in other industries are better off than working in a coal mine far underground."

Thus spoke the man who was then being described as the "savior" of the industry. His description of a miner's life in 1959 was an incredibly roseate view not exactly in accord with reality. Unquestionably, the increased wages and the achievements of the Welfare Fund had brought a new sense of economic welfare to coal miners. But the idyllic picture of a modern home with young men going off to college was hardly more than an imaginary dream. Even with the considerable advances that had been made, there was still a kind of dreary desolation in the mining towns throughout West Virginia and western Pennsylvania. Much of it came from the idle lives of the men who had been displaced. Many of them suffered from infirmities from the mines, from shattered backs to black lung; all of them bore the insecurities of men who saw machines do more and more of their work.

There was no program of retraining or rehabilitation for the coal miner who lost his job to a push-button machine. As we shall undertake to show in the next chapter, at the same time that men were losing their jobs there was a tightening of the Welfare Fund, with new rules and new restrictions and new cutbacks to make it harder for ex-miners to enjoy the benefits. The men who could no longer work in the mines were the older men with injuries, and it was they who were in greatest need of widening welfare benefits. The unpleasant truth is that these members of the United Mine Workers of America were human discards. They were simply ignored by their leaders. They were conveniently lost.

Yet, a most plausible argument can be made for the way of John L. Lewis. Some union leaders have opposed every new device that replaces men with machines. "Featherbedding" has become an ugly word in the American labor lexicon, and even federal law has tried, albeit unsuccessfully, to make it illegal. Labor unions fight for job opportunities for their members, often opposing rival brotherhoods with a vehemence and bitterness reserved for old industrial foes of the past, whenever a few jobs are in dispute. Lewis constantly, deliberately and knowingly curtailed job opportunities for the mine workers. His theory was the simple one that mechanization would increase production and workers could be better paid. Those who were ousted had to find another way. The industry's argument, of course, is that without the gains achieved through the help of Lewis, coal would not be competitive with other fuels and there would be even fewer jobs for coal miners at far poorer conditions than now exist. This is almost unanswerable.

Lewis's great concern for the welfare of the industry became manifest in another of his great enterprises, the National Coal Policy Conference. He brought together the operators, thirty-two railroads, seven major power companies and several large equipment manufacturers, along with the union, into an organization to meet regularly and deal with the industry's problems. Its chairman was, of course, John L. Lewis. "It makes quite a group," he said. "All of us are interested in improving the efficiency of the coal industry. All of us do what we can to contribute toward that improvement. It makes quite a formidable aggregation, all dedicated to seeking to promote a national coal policy that will recognize the importance of the coal industry to the nation's economy and accord it equality of privilege."

The National Coal Policy Conference, in its own way, was a splendid achievement. No other industry group in America, however, had ever had a union leader as its head. But the disturbing question was: While the Policy Conference was promoting the welfare of the industry, who was there to probe deeply, conscientiously and devotedly into the intrinsic welfare of coal miners, the men who made up the membership of the organization that was the ascendant managerial force in the industry?

This never-answered question caused the Conference to collapse in 1971. After Lewis retired, several industry executives served terms as chairmen. Tony Boyle, as UMW president, served twice as chairman; but without Lewis, the old leadership fire was missing. Pressures on Boyle within the UMW, attacks upon his "pro-industry" attitude, and his involvement in so many lawsuits caused him to pass the word to Consolidation Coal Company, the major power among the producers, that the union could no longer continue in the Conference. The withdrawal of the UMW was the cue for uneasy business enterprises to pursue their own ends.

There is another chapter in the union-management-cooperation story; it tells of the stream of antitrust suits that has filled the court calendars over the past decade. These ponderous legal struggles, difficult even for lawyers to unravel, proceeding through the federal court system into major contests in the United States Supreme Court, have involved deep issues in labor law and business law, as well. They have touched upon the sensitive areas of where lawful competition ends and "sweetheart" cooperation begins. They have been an almost foreseeable consequence of the policies of John L. Lewis.

Many of these cases arose out of the union's campaign to organize the eastern Kentucky and Tennessee coal fields. They were separate and distinct from the other legal actions brought as a result of the violent campaigns of terror. The thrust of the Sherman Act suits was that there had been a conspiracy by the UMW and the major coal producers to drive the small operators out of the business. All the remarks of John L. Lewis over the years gave credence to this theory. In 1959, Lewis spoke glowingly of the drive toward bigness in the industry. "The mergers of coal properties have produced better leadership on the side of industry. When we had eleven thousand producing entities in the coal industry, no one operator could speak for the industry as a whole, on legislation, on wages, on anything. They were all competitive enemies, and acted accordingly. Now the big companies give national leadership to the industry side."

Among the numerous suits, the union has suffered at least three devastating legal defeats, where findings of guilt have been made for antitrust conspiracies with coal operators. The Tennessee Consolidated Coal Company brought an action against the UMW and the West Kentucky Coal Company, claiming a plot to eliminate it from business. While part of the theory of the case revolved around the union's financial investments in West Kentucky, the major attack was on the Mine Workers' agreements with all of big industry to stamp out the small operators. West Kentucky escaped with a defense verdict, but the jury found against the union. A judgment of $1,498,000, plus interest and attorneys' fees was piled on the union treasury. This verdict was upheld by a United States Court of Appeals in 1969.

A year later, an even heavier judgment was imposed for the same pattern of conduct. The South-East Coal Company brought an action against the union and Consolidation Coal Company, one of the industry giants, for the same restraint-of-trade conspiracy. South-

East won an enormous verdict against both defendants, likewise upheld in 1970 on appeal. Again, the Supreme Court refused to hear the case. The United Mine Workers had to pay out of its treasury $3,783,178 plus interest on this one. Even by big-business standards, these are staggering sums of money to be assessed against any organization's assets; and for a labor union, they are almost catastrophic.

But the worst may yet be pending, as the Mine Workers took an even harder legal blow in 1971. The same determined lawyer, John A. Rowntree of Knoxville, Tennessee, who had acquired both an antitrust expertise and a long list of clients in his career of suing the United Mine Workers, won an even greater victory than his triumphs in the South-East and Tennessee Consolidated cases. One of his earlier trials in the United States District Court in eastern Tennessee involved sixteen smaller coal companies in an antitrust suit against the union. After a long trial without a jury, the district judge dismissed the action because of his legal view of the standard of proof required to hold the union guilty. He found that if the ordinary standard of preponderance of evidence had been required, he would have upheld plaintiff's claims in their combined action which sought a mere thirty million dollars. His decision was barely affirmed after long proceedings in the Court of Appeals, but it was overturned in 1971. The United States Supreme Court took the case, heard argument, and then ruled that the district judge was wrong. He should have found for plaintiffs on the evidence before him.

This case, known as *Ramsey v. United Mine Workers,* has now been returned to the lower federal courts for new findings, which will include more damages. Because of the number of companies involved and the legal prayer of thirty million dollars, even though exaggerated as most damage claims are, the union could be almost wiped out. Under the antitrust laws, whatever damages are found, they must be trebled. Even a finding of five million of actual damages, only one sixth of what is demanded, would require an assessment of fifteen million against the UMW treasury, a sum that might lead the union toward bankruptcy. This litigation is not likely to be concluded for several more years, when the ultimate judgments will have to be paid.

No labor union in the past quarter century has been hit with antitrust judgments except the United Mine Workers.

Yet even these judgments have their troubling aspects. For all the legal jargon about "conspiracy," what Lewis was essentially trying to do was impose uniform working conditions on the entire coal industry, large companies and small companies alike. The cry of the little men was that they could not afford to pay the same scale as the big operators, a common claim in every industry in America. Here is where the antitrust laws become fuzzy and difficult to disentangle. The Supreme Court has recognized that unions have a right to negotiate for uniform conditions. But it is only when they step over the line and agree with big management to use this weapon to wipe out the small producers that the law is violated.

This is often hard to detect, and the evidence against Lewis is none too convincing to one who has read every one of the voluminous antitrust opinions. But perhaps the most telling point is that Lewis's coziness with the operators, his devotion to their interests, his own belief in bigness, made the UMW a far easier target for judges and juries than some other union that may have lived more at arm's length with its industrial counterparts. Thus, the fruits of entrepreneurism turned up in the most prolonged series of antitrust judgments ever rendered in all of America's legal history.

The full impact of these judgments on the union and its membership even now, in 1972, has not yet become manifest. The internal wars of 1969, the Yablonski murder, the charges against Tony Boyle, the overwhelming number of other lawsuits have all tended to obscure the devastation wrought by the antitrust judgments. The events that produced them grew out of the policies of Lewis of concern for the welfare of management. Lewis retired at the end of 1959 and died in 1969, before the millions of dollars of adverse judgments were heaped upon the union. But the residue of his managerial policies will affect his union for a full decade after his burial. If their massed accumulation, along with all the verdicts that have been rendered and are yet to come, results in a judicial taking that wipes out all the union's assets and its treasury, the cruelest irony of all from the rule of Lewis would be imposed. The master of money would have dissipated it all.

Even though the prospect of bankruptcy once the coming judgments are paid is serious, it is not fatal to the institution. The treasury was almost gone before the 1933 rebirth; funds can be restored, although never quite as fast again, because there will never again be as many members of the United Mine Workers of America. The great business losses of the West Kentucky adventure and the Lewmurken shoddiness can be overcome, too. The human concerns will not go away, however.

For, not only has the loss of the millions been neglected, but the meaning of the policies that produced the devastation, both economic and human, has not yet been considered, either inside the union or out. What has entrepreneurism wrought, with its primary concern for the welfare of management rather than for that of men? Does cooperation with the employer, a helpfulness to his fortune, bring more benefits to the people who pay the dues? Or, should the employer be left to his own adventures, with gains for the members won by power and persuasiveness, the way Lewis won them by the great strikes? Does the adversary system the law knows so well work also in labor-management enterprise and in other endeavor? Or, could the coal industry have survived without a Lewis to help save it by his willingness to permit total mechanization and cast men aside? Can the gains for the remaining few be justified ahead of the miseries of the many who were cast out?

The losses of the money, the questionable use of the bank, the movement of millions into bad investments, the inordinate attention to the needs of the industry might all be forgiven if the devotion to entrepreneurism had not had its ultimate effect on the loyal men who paid the dues, who breathed the dust and pushed the mechanical buttons, and went underground, and endured the bleakness and desolation. For it was in the management of the Welfare and Retirement Fund, the noblest of all the UMW's enterprises, that concern for business overrode the concern for people. That too became a tragedy of the institution that had begun to exist for itself, like so many others created by mankind, rather than for the souls below for whom it was created. While the despotism and the violence leave their heavy vapors, the abuse of a dream is sometimes more of an infinite human desecration.

8. The Fabulous Fund

PIONEERING AND PASSIVITY

If relief of human misery is a noble goal of mankind, the creation of the miners' Welfare and Retirement Fund stands as a memorable achievement. It ministered to the broken bodies of coal miners, it brought hope to their wasted lives, it assuaged their pain, it turned life into a more meaningful venture for hundreds of thousands of men and their wives and children who had suffered with them in the past.

It was surely the foremost of all the successes of John Llewellyn Lewis. In a scale of human accomplishment, it must stand ahead of even the organizing of industrial America, the rebuilding of a shattered union, and the welding of a group of working people into the firmest force of solidarity ever to exist in our history. It stands above all the great efforts of Lewis because of its essential humanity, its alleviation of suffering, its kindling of light in the souls of torn and warped people. This judgment must remain, despite the sadness of later days of the Fund, despite the callousness that later crept into it, despite the afflictions of weary bureaucracy that brought it to humiliation in a courtroom and deposited bitterness among its beneficiaries.

1·

It was a product of the finest hours of John L. Lewis. He gave it his devotion and his abilities during the wartime strike era when his intuitive insights into reality were at their highest level. He began his campaign in 1945, before the end of World War II. Coal operators had always paid attention to their machinery. They oiled it, repaired it, replaced it, cared for it. The care and feeding of equipment was fundamental; men came and went and died. Human beings were entitled to the same treatment as machines, said Lewis. The time had come for the operators to pay attention to the body of man as well. The thought processes of industrial America had never grasped the point before; the Lewis demand was bold and startling.

There must be a trust fund established, said Lewis, to provide medical care, disability benefits, and pensions for coal miners. It must be financed by royalties on every ton of coal produced. This was the basic idea, simple, workable, and needing only the agreement of the operators to put it into effect. The human capacity for resistance to new ideas, especially from owners of coal mines, reacted with its usual consistency. They opposed it, they would never grant it, it would bankrupt the industry, it was not necessary.

There was a short strike in April, 1945, before the war was ended. Lewis demanded the royalty payments; the strike was settled without them. But his campaign had barely begun. In early 1946, he began to fill the pages of the *Mine Workers Journal* with picture stories of disaster, to demonstrate the need for what he wanted. There was a mine explosion in McCoy, Virginia, killing a dozen miners. The *Journal* ran a cover-picture story of a crying waif, half starved, mourning for his lost father, and captioned it, "One Reason for a Health and Welfare Fund." In the very next issue, two weeks later, the cover had a picture of an Alabama black miner without legs— lost in an accident—sitting with his wife and three small boys. The same pointed caption, "One Reason . . ." was again used. The drive was in full momentum.

When the annual strike began in 1946, the welfare program was one of the union's primary demands. The mines were again seized by the government; Secretary of the Interior Julius A. Krug was now the "operator," the man who could make an agreement. The true owners could say they never granted it; the government did. When Krug signed with Lewis, the agreement became historic. The Fund was created; it started with a nickel. Five cents on every ton of coal mined must be paid into a trust fund. The contract was executed in the White House. A new arch was formed.

Difficulty followed genesis, as in every new endeavor. The money had to be collected, banked, assigned, planned, administered. With the government in control of the mines, the money began to accumulate. Whether it could ever have been made to work among the chaos and multiplicity of mineowners is doubtful; the "socialism" of the sovereign gave it a start with at least a chance of success. It would be run by three trustees, one from the union, one from the operators, and a third who was to be "neutral," chosen by the two partisans. This is the typical American tripartite arrangement that has been an integral device in labor-management relations for decades. Lewis was the union trustee, of course, as he was for all the remaining days of his life.

The Fund made its first payments in early 1947. They came after a disaster. A mine blast in Centralia, Illinois, one of the most severe and tragic in the long bloody history of the pits, killed 111 men. Death-benefit checks for $1,000 were sent to ninety-nine families, the first financial relief of its kind ever given. Death-benefit payments were the most common payments in the early years of the Fund; there were always sufficient disasters to provide victims who needed the help.

When the mines were returned to their owners, a new contract was signed in 1947, increasing the royalty payments to ten cents a ton. Lewis had demanded a pension plan, and it was then written into the national agreement. The trustees were required by contract to deposit a portion of the royalty payments into a separate fund for pensions. The big gains were coming one by one now. Pensions for coal miners were almost a reality. But it required another enormous national effort by Lewis and the men, another national emergency, and more court proceedings, before they could begin.

The owners, after regaining their properties, had their first chance to name their own trustee. They designated a dour, elderly operator named Ezra Van Horn, a man as determined and unyielding as John L. Lewis, a man whose mere presence and attitudes could frustrate the Fund as effectively as if his orders had been written in the single word "sabotage." He fought with Lewis throughout the remaining months of the year on point after point. Early in 1948, the neutral trustee, Thomas E. Murray, torn between the struggle of two such indomitable wills, resigned.

This gave Van Horn every advantage he wanted. The agreement provided that the union trustee and the operator trustee would jointly select the neutral. Selection was now impossible, since Van Horn could veto any nomination by Lewis. There were no pensions for coal miners.

Lewis sent warning notices to some of the operators. He asked to meet with them to try to resolve the pension impasse. The answer was a curt refusal even to discuss the matter. Lewis warned them again of the seriousness of the dispute. There was no movement.

Then John L. Lewis wrote a letter.

It was to all the officers and all the members. It was the Lewis rhetoric at its most scathing. It was Lewis the uncontrollable national tiger, before the bank and before the loans and before the accommodations. His efforts to start the pension program "were without avail."

> The Coal Operators and their Trustee continue gleefully to violate the contract, and count each day a success when they can prevent expenditure of this money designed to alleviate the human misery in the coal industry. The destitution of the aged, the extremity of the sick and injured and the poverty of orphans and widows are things which concern them not.

If there was "glee" in the management suites, it was concealed behind the scowl of Van Horn. But Lewis touched the spirit of the men in the pits when he tolled the unconcern of the owners. They had shown no interest at all in putting the plan in operation.

> The winter is now gone. This office proposes to go forward in requiring the coal operators to honor their agreement. Your ears will soon be assailed by their outcries and wails of anguish. To relieve themselves, they need only to comply with the provisions of the Agreement which they solemnly executed in this office on July 8, 1947.

There was not a word in the document about a strike. He concluded in this manner: "Please discuss this matter in your local unions so that our membership may be fully advised. You will later hear more from this office on this subject."

When the letter arrived, coal miners began drifting to the top, almost as if a blackened seam-vine ran through the Appalachian mountainsides. After the letter's first day, production fell a quarter million tons of coal. On March 16, 1948, the day following, there was a million tons less coming out. On March 17, Wednesday, even less; the day following, there was another drop. Men were failing to come to work by the thousands, and by Thursday, March 18, the Bureau of Mines said that 224,371 coal miners were off the job. Lewis sat patiently in Washington, saying nothing.

President Truman acted quickly. Five days later, he created a board of inquiry under the new Taft-Hartley Act's authority to deal with national emergencies. The board invited Lewis to appear. He ignored the summons. The Department of Justice hurried to the United States District Court in Washington and secured an order to compel Lewis to attend as a witness. The board found a work stoppage, not undertaken individually by miners as Lewis claimed, but a concerted union effort.

Lewis wrote to the membership again. He denied any thought that he had suggested a work stoppage. He had merely reported to his minions. "Your actions in this regard . . . were your own, individually determined by you." Lewis had only asked them to discuss the problem. "As far as I know it is still the inherent right and privilege of American citizens to continue to exercise the right of free speech and freedom of assembly."

With bituminous coal production in the United States once again completely stopped, the government moved for a Taft-Hartley injunction on April 3, commanding the miners to return to work. Lewis conferred with no one but his lawyers. Miners paid little heed to the court order. A contempt citation against Lewis and the union quickly followed, with a hearing scheduled for April 14.

The old Republican party connections of John L. Lewis somehow arose among the same men in the 80th Congress who had passed the iniquitous "slave labor" Taft-Hartley Act so passionately denounced by Lewis. Speaker Joseph W. Martin, in an attempt to exercise majority Republican government in that year of Truman's "vulnerability," summoned Lewis and Van Horn to his office on Saturday, April 10, while lawyers struggled with their preparation for the scheduled court battle. Martin wanted to recommend an ideal trustee, Republican Senator H. Styles Bridges of New Hampshire. Van Horn agreed. A meeting with Bridges was arranged for Sunday, and on Monday Lewis sent two telegrams to the field. The first one told of the Bridges appointment and it said, "Your voluntary cessation of work should now be terminated and your protest ended." This instruction was to cost Lewis dearly in the litigation that followed.

Later that day, after another meeting with Senator Bridges, the second wire said, "Pensions granted. The agreement is now honored."

Lewis had won again, but even though miners immediately returned to work, the government went ahead with its contempt-of-court case, the second major attack upon Lewis and the UMW. Both were found guilty again; one million four hundred thousand dollars of UMW money was assessed in a fine; another $20,000 against Lewis personally. The price never seemed to bother them. The defendants argued that there never was a union-authorized strike; the Lewis telegram telling the men to return to work was enough for the courts to decide otherwise.

This was another chapter in the irony of authorized effort. Lewis literally begged the operators to meet with him when Van Horn stopped the pension plan. They refused. He warned, he foresaw "wails of anguish," he tried to work within the contract. Only when the men, his army of solidarity, stopped the production of coal did the government step in, did the Speaker of the House of Representatives, who perhaps considered himself the nominal head of government in that year of Republican 80th Congress euphoria, give his personal attention. But even after the problem had been temporarily solved, the law took its bite, exacting nearly a million and a half dollars from funds of the men who had to defy legal authority to get what they ostensibly already had under a legal contract. This too is a repetition of a thousandfold pattern in man's "legal" behavior.

But even then the operators had no intention of yielding on pensions for coal miners. Van Horn, overwhelmed by the regularity with which Senator Bridges voted with Lewis to start the program, filed a lawsuit against both of them. It came before District Court Judge T. Alan Goldsborough in Washington, who had twice imposed enormous contempt fines on Lewis and the union. Van Horn's case, backed by the operators, argued that all three trustees must vote unanimously before any action could be taken. If this succeeded, of course, pensions for coal miners would be almost hopeless. This time,

Judge Goldsborough stunned the operators. He told them in open court, "The Court doesn't think, gentlemen, that there is any justification in law or in sound reason for this petition, or complaint, as it should be called. The complaint, gentlemen, will have to be dismissed." Any retired miner who reached the age of sixty-two was now entitled to receive $100 a month. Even the elderly jurist who had been the Miners' nemesis in the courtroom could see that which failed to move the operators. On the pension and its $100 amount he told them, "It is just enough to keep them from being objects of charity in their old age; it is just enough to give them a little dignity; it is something to make them able to hold their heads up."

While the pension fight was in its winning process, the Fund continued to work at the medical-care side of miner life. Understanding of the Fund's essential purposes and operations is perhaps easier when one divides it in half. Even its two-pronged name is helpful—welfare and retirement. The retirement part, which means pensions, has its own separate field, separately administered and controlled. Money for its operation must be taken separately from the total receipts of the Fund, as the trustees decide. All else comes under the welfare side, but this is broken down into the particular parts of miner welfare. As we have indicated, it started with disaster benefits, but its major thrust was for medical care, which meant doctor bills and hospital bills.

The first approach on medical care came in 1946, when the government was still a party to the agreement. A Navy doctor, Rear Admiral Joel T. Boone, headed a survey team that produced a report on the deplorable health conditions that enveloped America's coal miners. Its guidelines were helpful in what followed. The union, in many areas, had contracted with doctors to treat coal miners, and even had checkoff payments from individual earnings to pay the bills. Every observer found incredible abuse in this system—poor care; doctor profiteering; little effort to attack the real suffering of disabled coal miners.

In 1948, the Fund hired its own medical director, Dr. Warren F. Draper, and divided the mine fields into ten areas. Committed young socially aware doctors were recruited to work on a salary basis, one to direct each medical area. Skilled administrators were hired as technical assistants in each area. The attack on poor health care for coal miners was undertaken with a new zeal, with a thoroughness and dedication never before known in American industrial or medical history.

The first important medical-care beneficiaries were the paraplegics. Fund doctors went into hillside cabins to look at torn and broken remains of disabled miners. Some were so twisted that their bodies were in an S-shape, unable to fit on a stretcher. Neighbors had to come in to pick up their beds and carry them down miles of mountain trails to highways where they could be evacuated. Many of them were placed on the first airplanes they had ever viewed on the ground, and flown to faraway hospitals for treatment. In June, 1948, for example, twelve paraplegics were taken to a Kaiser Permanente Hospital in Vallejo, California, at the Fund's expense for a program of rehabilitation. By mid-1949, the Fund was able to report that 431 men had been taken for hospitalization and care. Almost half of them were able to leave their beds and walk again. The healers had touched human lives.

The area doctors began to give new supervision and direction to treatment of miners in every section of the coal fields. As the new system of medical care began, physicians employed by the Fund began to attack the carelessness, the gouging, the sloppiness that had characterized the old system of "private" medical care. When one considers the enormous medical needs of the miners, the poor care they had been receiving, and their all-pervasive misery, one can have little patience with the old argument of "freedom of choice of doctors" versus "bureaucratic medicine."

The evils of the old system, thoroughly exposed in the Boone Report, were pointed out again in 1951, when the Fund doctors went into Kentucky to review the existing medical-care programs. While the Fund could pay hospital bills, even where the limited facilities could be used, basic medical treatment was still provided in doctors' offices and on house calls, which apparently were still being made in those days in southeastern Kentucky. Local doctors still had their contracts. Some of them covered several camps. Multiple-contract doctors would then hire young medical graduates at a low wage to do the work. The extras, for "shots," obstetrical care, and other add-ons, exceeded the contract income for some doctors. The investigators found one doctor who held eight contracts covering

2,000 miners and their families, and received $96,000 a year for the superficial treatment he gave.

The major effort at solution was the area hospital, with its comprehensive care. In 1951, the Fund established nonprofit corporations in Kentucky, West Virginia and Virginia to own and operate ten hospitals strategically located, six in Kentucky, three in West Virginia, one in the western corner of Virginia. An energetic building program was started, with thirty million dollars of Fund money poured into it.

On June 2, 1956, John L. Lewis came to one of the new institutions in Beckley, West Virginia, for a dedication ceremony for all ten hospitals. It was a shining brick and glass structure, with modern equipment, well-staffed, simply known as the "Miners' Hospital." It still stands today in the same gleaming fashion along U. S. Highway 19, still a memorial, still known as the Miners' Hospital, still ministering to the sick, despite the enormous changes of recent years. Inside the foyer of the hospital, almost the first object to catch the visitor's eye is a large photograph of John L. Lewis.

Medical treatment and hospital care made the miners' program the envy of American trade-unions, enthralled students of public health, became a showpiece for foreign visitors, and brought to the men and their families benefits that had never before existed. It won award after award—in 1951, from the President's Committee on Employment of the Physically Handicapped "for spurring the whole concept of real rehabilitation"; in 1954, from the same committee again; in 1956, the Albert Lasker Award, the highest in the public-health field, "for creating a model program of health services to a million and a half workers and their families in mining towns from Alabama to Alaska"; in 1957, from the National Rehabilitation Association, "for the development of advanced rehabilitation programs;" in 1960, from Goodwill Industries of America, "for its outstanding example of good will toward the handicapped in a major industry."

Albert Deutsch, the country's leading writer on medical care in those years, said in 1960:

> The concept of the regional hospital system was first put into wide-scale operation through the Miners Memorial Hospital Association chain. If it had made no other contribution, the UMWA Welfare

and Retirement Fund would have earned a significant page in American medical history through this trail-blazing act alone. Many medical planners view it as an impressive demonstration of a general pattern that could and should, with modifications based upon regional and economic differences, be adopted widely in the United States.

On the welfare side of the Fund's operations, disaster payments and disability benefits were the other staples. Death benefits went to widows and survivors. Disability payments of $40 per month were made to miners until the end of 1949, when, with the growth of the pension program, this was stopped. Rough, scrawled letters from grateful miners began to come in to the Fund. One note, from a Pennsylvania mining camp with the unlikely name of Scalp Level, said: "Received the checks from the Welfare Fund and only God, my wife and I know how welcome and how much we need that money. Before that we tried to get by on $20 a week with three small children, the two infants." An ancient disabled miner from West Virginia, with nine children, a broken back and broken legs, wrote: "And part of my children had to finish school this year without any shoes and part of the time they didn't have money for lunch. I have three babies that ought to have milk to drink and I can't buy it for them because I don't have the money. I have no other income only what I get from the Welfare Fund."

Royalty payments went up to 10 cents in 1947, were raised to 20 cents in 1948, up another 10 cents in 1950, and then were finally boosted to 40 cents per ton in 1952. This marked the high point; the payments remained the same throughout all the ensuing years, until the 1971 negotiations.

In 1960, when the Fund was operating at a reasonably high level of efficiency and productivity, it spent $143 million. Pensions formed the major expenditure, nearly $79 million. Hospital and medical care made up the other important part, as more than $60 million was paid out. Funeral expenses and widows' and survivors' benefits were now only a minor part of the expenditures; health care was basically the Welfare part and pensions made up the Retirement side of the Fund. A large bureaucracy in Washington administered its benefits; detailed rules and regulations governed its people. That fiscal year, it spent more than it took in. But it stood as the great success story of labor-union achievement in the decade and a half after World War

II. Its leaders were rhapsodic in their praise; thoughtful people every-where agreed. John Lewis said: "No pen can write, no tongue can tell, no vocabulary of language is large enough to express the many benefits that were made through the establishment of the Welfare and Retirement Fund."

The little gray lady who administered the Fund, Josephine Roche, stirred members of a Senate subcommittee in 1949 when she appeared to describe the destitution of coal miners and how the Fund had helped.

> No less shocking than the record of mine killings and deaths resulting from the hardships of mining existence is the record of those who linger on maimed, broken, disabled, daily tortured by their helplessness, their pain and the constant realization of the burden their dependents carry. A backlog of human misery has been rolled up through the decades by the destruction of human bodies, health, of human values, as well as human life.
>
> Excessively high rates for tuberculosis, silicosis, arthritis and many other chronic diseases prevail among miners. Unbelievably poor medical and hospital facilities—or none at all—have been the lot of the mining population for decades. The startling lack of adequate medical provision, of proper standards of medical and hospital care, of diagnostic and specialists' services has gone on year after year, each year adding to the vast numbers of disabled, ill and injured men who have had recourse only to public-charity pittances and charity hospital wards.

It was that backlog of human misery that the Fund attacked so brilliantly. It had cared for the sick and brought hope to the aged. It was a success story, American style. It had brought a touch of humanity to the most brutalizing industry ever to exist in America. Its blessings were bountiful; it verged on, although never quite achieved, the triumph of a dream.

2·

Then its troubles began.

The most critical one was money. But the energies and insight that might have been used to deal with it were wrapped up in the banking business, making loans and buying up the West Kentucky Coal Company. There was an enormous decline in employment in the coal industry, beginning in 1948, when the postwar mechanization began to take over. Each year, the labor force went down, down. In 1948, there were some 411,000 soft-coal miners working in the fields. By 1959, only eleven years later, the number of men at work was down to 150,000. This brought new hardships to mountain men in West Virginia, Kentucky and Pennsylvania, where needs for welfare were far greater. The unemployment of coal miners was a major part of the poverty in West Virginia that John F. Kennedy discovered so dramatically in 1960.

Coal production declined too, which brought less money to the Fund, since payments were made not on hours worked, as in most industries, but on tons of coal produced by signatory operators. In 1950, total production was at 516,000,000 tons, and by 1958, down to 410,000,000, much less in proportion to the decline in manpower. In 1950, when the Bituminous Coal Operators Association was formed, a new period of stability in labor relations began. The big nationwide strikes were at an end, not to recur again until the 1971 struggle. It was during this period of peace that the Fund, with its money problems, began to adopt a new administrative hardness that squeezed needy coal miners.

The three trustees of the Fund had enormous authority. While the labor contract with the industry created the supply of money, it provided only a broad statement of purpose. The trustees had the power to say who got the money, how it was to be spent, how it was to be invested, what benefits were to be paid. They would meet and make their own rules. They were the legislators, they were the executives, and they were the Supreme Court on any appeals from the rules they made. Coal miners were to receive only what the trustees were prepared to give them. Theoretically, the membership could make its demands known through its own trustee, who was John L. Lewis, and who told them almost nothing. Annual reports were published regularly in the *Mine Workers Journal,* better understood by lawyers, accountants, public-health professionals and actuaries than by coal miners who could not be expected to fathom the fine print and the dazzling figures. Their guardian at the exchequer should have been unusually alert to their needs; he was the great leader they trusted and loved.

The first serious cut in Fund benefits came in 1953. The original rules had stipulated that a miner was eligible for a pension if he had had at least twenty years' employment in the mines. In 1953 this requirement was amended so that an applicant's employment was recognized only if it had been accrued within thirty years of the date on which the pension was applied for. This change struck hard at two classes of men, the old-timers and the disabled. The old ones who had worked before 1923 and had been in and out of the mines couldn't count any of their earlier time. Some of the men who were hurt by this rule change didn't realize what it meant to them until years later.

A West Virginia miner named Odell Gwynn, who had worked twenty-eight years in the mines, was one of those who lost under the new rule. He had started at the age of fifteen. When the great UMW drive in 1933 swept through the mountains, he was one of the first to sign a union card. He was vice-president of his local union for four years, served on the grievance committee and was one of the stalwarts of the strike in 1946 that brought the Fund into existence.

In 1949, he was one of the common victims of a mine injury, at the age of forty-three, never to work again. He waited until his age entitled him to a pension and then applied in 1965. He could not understand the treatment he received. "They wouldn't even give me an application," he said. "They told me I'd been out of the mines too long." He couldn't qualify under the 1953 rules. Josephine Roche explained the 1953 change in terms of economy and then added a phrase that sounded far more like a cold-hearted banker than the proud, humanitarian lady who once beguiled Senators with a discourse on the humanity of the Fund. "It was felt that by 1953, the equities of the older miners, who had been active almost entirely before the fund was created . . . had been fully met." (In 1965 this rule was changed back to where it had been before the thirty-year period had been imposed; any twenty years in the mines were enough.)

There was another curtailment a year later in 1954. Cash benefits to some 30,000 disabled miners were stopped. Widows and children of dead miners were also cut off, and this took another 24,000 from the rolls, most of them elderly widows surviving in the mining towns. These were usually serious deprivations, cutting off money to the infirm and aged—money that could not be replaced; money on which they had formed a regular dependence. One might argue that it should never have been paid in the first place, since pensions and medical care were the prime goals of the Fund, but once its small sums were given, the taking away was a sheer act of cruelty in far-away Washington.

While wages went up during each contract term, royalty payments did not. With production decreasing, the Fund's annual flow of money went down, but hardly to danger levels. At the end of the 1961 fiscal year, benefit payments exceeded income by $17 million, but there was still almost $100 million in resources in the Fund accounts.

Another rule change in 1960 brought another serious cut. A brief notice in the UMW *Journal,* signed by Josephine Roche, went to all district and local union officers. "By Action of the Trustees," it said, regulations for hospital and medical care were changed. Miners who were out of work for one year were no longer to be covered. Even those who were still working, if in any mine whose owner had not signed the national wage agreement, were cut off. This blunderbuss action involved the Fund in many lawsuits, which led to embarrassment and eventual defeat, but not until 1969.

While the 1953 and 1954 cutbacks were shrugged off, the 1960 loss of health cards of coal miners was the beginning of the puncture of the dream. There were angry meetings in some mining towns in Pennsylvania and West Virginia. A few mines were picketed. But suspicion and distrust started—"from the day they took my health card," said one miner—and it eventually led to lawyers' offices and federal courtrooms.

The trustees won most of the early lawsuits, as the courts upheld their authority to make rules for running the Fund. Then, in 1968, the United States Court of Appeals in Washington held that judges could review the conduct of the trustees, but only if their actions were, in the familiar legal terms, "arbitrary and capricious," or, in the words of the nonlawyer, "unreasonable as hell." The 1960 rule was put on the line in a pension case, where a veteran UMW member had worked his last year in a nonunion mine before he applied for his pension. His courtroom testimony was graphically eloquent as to why he quit his job in a union mine and went elsewhere to work.

Q. They didn't lay you off?

A. No, the top got so bad I got scared and quit and I wasn't making too good nohow.

Q. How did you happen to work for L & G Coal Company after you found out they weren't under contract and you a member of the United Mine Workers?

A. Well, I tell you buddy, they wasn't nowhere to go hardly. Couldn't hardly find a job and I had a bunch of kids and I had to work.

He won his case. Federal Judge Alexander Holtzoff had no hesitation in making the legal finding of "unreasonable, arbitrary and capricious" against the Fund rule.

The unfairness of the requirement is patent in respect to a person, such as the plaintiff, who for many years worked in a signatory coal mine, but during the last year of his work in the industry was constrained by circumstances to accept employment in a nonunion mine. On the other hand, a person could have worked during his entire career in nonunion mines and yet receive a pension if he managed to secure employment in a union mine for a single year immediately preceding his retirement, although his participation in the creation of the Fund would be negligible. Such results are unfair and unreasonable and border on the absurd.

Such was administrative sensitivity among the Fund's hierarchy in those years.

In late December, 1960, the trustees made another announcement. Pensions were reduced from the $100 a month that had prevailed for many years down to $75 a month. (They later were increased to $115 in more prosperous seasons, until the Boyle coup in 1969, when they were raised to $150.)

While the trustees in Washington were making their restrictive new rules, the boys down at the creek branches were applying their own form of leverage. Applications for benefits were handled through UMW local unions in each mine locality, which had its practical effects. When the trustees sent down their application forms for pensions, there was a space for certification that the man who applied was currently a member of a particular local union and district.

There was no legal requirement that a man had to be a current member to obtain his pension, since many miners had stopped going underground before they reached eligible age, and when they left the mine they stopped paying dues. When local officials gave them the application form for a pension, there was often a demand for hundreds of dollars in back dues to "reinstate" their membership. The later manipulation of elderly miners on pensions was a major factor in the 1969 Boyle-Yablonski election campaign.

Federal Judge Gerhard Gesell, in his 1971 decree against the Fund, was indignant about this practice. "In continuing to use patently misleading forms which encouraged applicants to believe that a paid-up Union membership was a prerequisite to receiving benefits, the trustees were grossly negligent, to an extent that constitutes breach of trust. The trustees have apparently not acted decisively even to this date to terminate use of these misleading forms." Judge Gesell did it for them, issuing a broad injunction against continuation of this conduct.

Another invidious practice, begun in 1962, also met the condemnation of Judge Gesell. When some of the small, marginal operators fell behind in their royalty payments, the trustees revoked the health cards of their workers, "apparently on the theory that this action would lead the operators to pay up to avoid wildcat strikes. This practice was highly improper, for the benefits owed the miners as qualified beneficiaries could not, under the terms of the Fund, be canceled solely because their particular employer was in default on his royalty payments." This too was found a breach of trust. This program was stopped in 1966, after it had affected some seven thousand working miners, but before the massive lawsuit was brought against the fund.

By 1962, the hospitals which had opened with such hopes for new medical life in Appalachia became a financial burden to the slumping Fund. Josephine Roche, with the permission of Lewis, had made the hard decision to close the hospitals and retrench the medical-care program. Even before the public announcement, inevitable rumors began to sift into mining communities in eastern Kentucky in late 1962. To close the hospitals, leave them empty and desolate, discharge the young doctors who had committed themselves to a new kind of medical practice, turn the other workers back to the poverty of their communities, and stop the channels of care to miners and their families would have been an ignominious failure for the Fund and its goals. Yet the decision was made; the paper preparations were begun.

Then a series of events began to occur, as people began reacting to the circumstances. Strangers were drawn into the struggle to save the hospitals, from a mountain minister to the President of the United States.

The effort to save the hospitals had its beginning when Kentucky miners complained to a young Presbyterian minister about the rumors of closing. The pastor, anxious to help the people where he lived, but with little idea of what could be done, passed his concern through higher church channels until the issue came to the Board of National Missions of the United Presbyterian Church, in New York. There was no particular appeal to Presbyterians; the only concern was health care for coal miners in Kentucky. Robert Barrie, chairman of the Division of Health and Welfare of the Board of Missions, believed his church organization ought to do something. With the approval of Dr. Kenneth G. Neigh, the general secretary, he secured enough money to make an investigation. A New York hospital consultant, Dr. Eugene Rosenfeld, was hired to assemble a team, study the situation, and report back to the Board of Missions.

Dr. Rosenfeld and his team visited the hospitals and talked with doctors and miners. They met with Josephine Roche and Dr. Warren F. Draper, the Fund's medical chief. Miss Roche said there was no way the hospitals could be kept open. Five of them in Kentucky were already scheduled for an early closing.

An elaborate, complicated plan was put together. President John F. Kennedy, out of his concern for the poverty he saw in West Virginia in his 1960 campaign, had provided the political impetus for creation of an Area Redevelopment Administration within the Department of Commerce to provide funds to help depressed parts of Appalachia. There was also the possibility of some financial assistance from the Commonwealth of Kentucky. If federal and state money could be assembled to buy the hospitals, someone would have to provide the administrative leadership to establish a new management. This was the designated role for the Church Board, if its membership could be persuaded to approve.

Serious opposition within the Presbyterian Board began to develop; it was led by a Midwestern doctor who saw nothing but evil in the "socialized medicine" practiced in the mineworker hospitals. Members of the Board from around the country were called to New York to meet on April 26, 1963, and vote on whether the Church would undertake this voyage into altruism. Those who wanted to go ahead were counting their prospective votes the night before with considerable apprehension; opponents appeared to have the strength to stop any further work of Barrie and his consultants to save the hospitals of coal miners in far-off Kentucky who had so little relationship to the Presbyterian Church.

A dinner for the assembled members was scheduled the night before the vote. The late Whitney Young, head of the Urban League, was invited to speak to the Presbyterians on what he thought should be the role of the Church in dealing with the issues beginning to overwhelm the society. Young, totally unaware of the tension and difference among the members of the Board over the miners' hospitals, delivered an eloquent and moving dissertation on the obligation of true Christians to aid their fellow men, to show concern over the welfare of the less fortunate, and do more to emulate the deeds of the Galilean carpenter.

Reverend Dr. Neigh, who had spent great energy in backing Barrie in his struggle to inject the Church into the hospital campaign, was elated over the impact of Young's speech on the delegates. He turned to Dr. Rosenfeld, who had been invited to the dinner to hear Young, and said, "This does it. They will not dare vote it down tomorrow." And so it was that the Church Board voted to act, swayed by the eloquence of an urban black man who knew nothing of the contest over hospitals in mountain regions of Kentucky.

They proceeded through a nonprofit corporation, Appalachian Regional Hospitals. They enrolled leading citizens in each of the Kentucky communities to serve on local boards, to broaden the base of the hospitals to take in all those in need of medical care. With the hospital corporation established under the Church's leadership, serious negotiations were begun to buy the hospitals from the Welfare and Retirement Fund. There were weeks of hard bargaining with Miss Roche and her staff; the price, while far below the actual value of the properties, was still far above the reach of an empty shell of a nonprofit corporation without any money. Although they still looked hopefully to the federal government for a grant of Appalachian money, there was no binding commitment for anything.

Miss Roche, weary of the prolonged negotiations into 1963, told the Presbyterians and Dr. Rosenfeld that five Kentucky hospitals must be closed before there was any further drain on the Fund's resources. At the same time, there were serious rumblings from angered miners in the areas. The mood of Harlan County and similar communities was bitterness and destruction; there was open talk in the streets that if the hospitals were closed, the old weapon of angry coal miners, dynamite, would be used to turn them to rubble. The deadline approached; letters were prepared and addressed to every doctor and every staff worker in the hospitals telling them of their discharges and the closing of the institutions. The documents were scheduled for a Friday mailing; Miss Roche was asked to hold them until the following Monday; an emergency meeting was arranged on Sunday, June 9, 1963, at the Department of Commerce to make one last attempt to secure enough federal money.

The Undersecretary of Commerce was Franklin D. Roosevelt, Jr. His memories of the feuding of John L. Lewis with his father, of the bitterness between the two great men of such wills and such vanity, was apparent to those who assembled on that Sunday afternoon. Roosevelt had repeatedly made unflattering remarks about Lewis and Miss Roche and the UMW; he told Barrie and the Reverend Dr. Neigh and Dr. Rosenfeld that one million dollars was all the government would put into the program. The Welfare Fund had reduced its price to 6.5 million, so reasonable that it was painful to all who wanted the hospitals to survive. But the government largesse wasn't even close.

There was another participant in that Sunday meeting along with the various affected government personnel. Daniel P. Moynihan was then an Assistant Secretary in the Department of Labor, which also had an interest in health care for working people. He knew that John F. Kennedy was aboard the Presidential plane, Air Force One, returning from Hawaii, where he had attended a conference of United States mayors. Moynihan left the group to personally call the President to tell him the story of the hospital crisis.

President Kennedy acted immediately. He placed a call directly to

Roosevelt. Those in the room heard Roosevelt's response. "Yes, Mr. President. I understand, Mr. President."

The Undersecretary of Commerce then turned to the waiting group. President Kennedy had ordered that six million dollars of government money be made available for the purchase of the miners' hospitals. The Presbyterians had won. The discharge letters were never mailed. The hospitals were still open to receive the sick and injured.

And so they were saved. The energetic devotion of Robert Barrie in New York, fueled by others who performed out of personal concern, was the kind of human effort, often unsung, that leaves a mark on the lives of people. The hospitals were now open to more than coal miners; they served the broader community in their mountain neighborhoods. Miners continued to come to receive care. The Fund paid their bills, and those who were not miners financed their treatment in more conventional ways. The people still call them "Miners' Hospitals," and that they shall remain, as a monument to the goals, aims and efforts of the Fund in its days of growth and achievement.

It was in the decade of the 1960's that the Fund suffered its administrative hardening of the arteries. Its money problems had been severe around the time of the sale of the hospitals. Royalties during 1962 covered only 72 percent of all soft coal produced. Four years before, royalties were being paid on 80 percent of all the coal coming out of the ground. This meant there was more nonunion coal; many of the small operators who worked with UMW contracts simply didn't pay their bills. Local union officials, who were often on a first-name basis with the small producers, were sometimes willing to forget, if the payments would force the mine to close and would throw a few more men out of work. It was during this period that the UMW, certainly deeply concerned about its loss of membership, took on the Kentucky-Tennessee organizing campaign that produced so much bloodshed and disaster.

But the illness was for more penetrating than lack of dollars. In fact, a more thoughtful argument is that if there had been a vital, energetic direction of the Fund, the economic issues would never have been so difficult to overcome. By 1961, the coal industry had started its resurgence. The Tennessee Valley Authority was becoming an enormous customer. Utilities began to buy coal in greater quantities everywhere. Production was gaining each year by 15 million tons. From 1963 to 1968, annual output had gained 85 million tons. Major producers were smiling at their stockholders; profits were large, resplendent, and reasonably likely to keep growing. Yet royalties never rose. The union, as well as the Fund, was not keeping pace.

Direction of the Fund became almost an inner-chamber secret. John L. Lewis was the union trustee until the day of his death; Josephine Roche was there with him, holding the crucial vote in her hands, to do the will of Lewis. The employer trustee through those years, Henry G. Schmidt, represented the youth movement of the trio. He was as old as the century and retired at sixty-nine, shortly before the death of Lewis. Schmidt drew $35,000 from the Fund along with his $75,000 pay as chairman of the North American Coal Company; his disagreements with Lewis, if any, were far outweighed by his enthusiasm for the Fund's policies of buying utility stocks and the apparent comfort to which two incomes led.

The annual reports, loaded with the boredom of figures, contained all the information the beneficiaries could get in those years. Decisions were quietly made, wholly in accord with the will of the great man who dominated the Fund as he had always dominated the union. On one occasion, Josephine Roche had the temerity to question his decision to place Thomas Ryan, the Fund's comptroller, on the board of the Washington National Bank. When she took this up hesitantly with Lewis, he "just smiled," and Miss Roche let the matter drop. There was no longer any link to the coal miners in the field, no longer any apparent awareness of the feelings, the emotions, the desires of those the Fund was supposed to serve. It was as alienated as its faraway address in Washington, pursuing its mysterious machinations, always exerting pressure on those who were its own, the miners, making it difficult to collect benefits, "progressing" into cold efficiency.

Recourse to the law was almost inevitable. The forgotten men in West Virginia began to talk, to assemble, to consult lawyers. Their yearnings came at a propitious time in the legal developments of the decade, for there were young, energetic, socially conscious advocates to take up the fight for them. This new effort was far beyond the individual battles of miners to win their pension rights, which had produced so many cases against the Fund.

The time had come for an attack upon the central nexus of the Fund itself, against its trustees, against its policies, against its operation. A young attorney in Charleston, Paul Kaufman, worked at the West Virginia level. The central case leadership came from youthful Harry Huge, of the Washington firm of Arnold and Porter. A number of other public-interest lawyers gave their assistance, too.

The law was their only outlet, their only opportunity to correct the illnesses of the Fund. Long months of preparation went into the gathering of evidence, the joining of plaintiffs to bring the court action. There was one group of disabled miners who had been denied pensions—like Willie Ray Blankenship, of Hewett, West Virginia, whose name later formed part of the title of the case; Odell Gwynn, of Beckley, who had long yearned for his pension; Howard Linville, of Peyton, West Virginia; and many others. A second group came from widows of miners. A third platoon was formed from active UMW members who were concerned about their future benefits. The suit was filed in the United States District Court in Washington in the summer of 1969, shortly after the death of Lewis, and became known in the lawbooks as *Blankenship v. Boyle*. Boyle and other UMW officers were sued, as well as the union itself, the trustees, the Bituminous Coal Operators Association, the Washington National Bank, Barnum L. Colton and other bank directors, and the Fund itself.

The case came to trial early in 1971, before Judge Gerhard Gesell, one of the hardest-working and most scholarly federal judges in any jurisdiction. The trial itself ran for many weeks, was overburdened with voluminous documents as exhibits, and trudged slowly through many witnesses, most of them seeking to justify their roles in the complicated events of the past.

The major thrust of the case was an attack on the mismanagement of the Fund. The accumulation of unused money was a breach of the trustees' duty, said the complaint. A second count claimed a conspiracy between the union and the bank to divert the Fund's money into the bank for the benefit of the bank and the union. Another claim protested the old Fund policy of withholding health cards from miners whose employers were delinquent in their royalty payments. The use of misleading application forms to compel old miners to pay union dues was also attacked. The investment in utility stocks was another element in the complaint. It was charged that insufficient efforts were made to collect delinquent royalties, a count that was later dismissed by Judge Gesell. The increase in the pension fund in 1969, which had been maneuvered by Boyle, was also put into the case, even though it arose while the final preparations for filing were being made.

Judgment day was April 28, 1971; the Fund was found guilty. The ruling came on points of the law of trusts, dry, crusty, sometimes as flexible as the judge's own idea of right and wrong. A less demanding rule-maker than Judge Gesell, one whose managerial standards were far more proprietary, might easily have rationalized a verdict against the widows, the disabled, the almost-forgotten. But Gesell's ruling was backed with sound evidence, the overburdening documentation of the record, and a moral intensity about what should have been done, even in hindsight, that made it a monument in the law of labor-management trust funds. Again, the United Mine Workers, even though not willingly or happily, were leaving an enormous influence upon the industrial law of America.

While the verdict was rendered against the defendants who were in court, there was one absent wrongdoer whose history permeated the case. It was the dead patriarch, of course. It was his policy, his dominance, his will, his control, that ran the Fund, that committed the breaches of trust that had to be stopped. The witnesses all told the same story; they were doing the bidding of John L. Lewis over the years.

It was wrong, said Judge Gesell, to allow so much cash to accumulate without being used for the benefit of coal miners. In 1956, thirty million dollars, 23 percent of all the Fund's money, was unused. It dropped to fourteen million in the low year of 1961, but by 1966, when the industry was in full enjoyment of its new prosperity, the Fund had fifty million not in use. A year later, the idle cash rose to seventy-five million, an astonishing 44 percent of its total resources. This amounted to far more than mere errors in judgment, said the judge.

One must wonder how the thundering Lewis of the war years would have defended; with his combination of charm, scorn, eloquence, and certainty he would have made his impact. Josephine Roche was the only defender at the trial. Her story was an admission of failure.

"Mr. Lewis felt very strongly, sir, the necessity of having a good deal beyond what we could invest without raising the taxation problem, keeping it very much in a situation where we could get at it at once. He did not feel enthusiastic for a long time over tax-exempt securities such as municipals.

"I talked to him frequently about it personally, aside from the general discussions we had. And I finally in '67–'68 realized how strongly I probably had been mistaken myself on anything that had to do with minute fiscal things. And I said, you know, Tom Ryan we both have the utmost confidence in, and he feels we ought to get some of this money out, make it earn money. Now let's think again about municipals. And he did . . . And finally he definitely agreed in '68, he said, Yes, we better go ahead, go ahead.

"So it was really a long-delayed decision which really probably, and I know completely from the point of view of a financial expert, that there is no excuse perhaps for it at all. To us who had felt that need, too, but felt these others things so terribly imminent, it is not the brightest chapter that we have, but we did some other things that perhaps made up for it a little bit."

Then she sadly concluded, "The fiscal requirements certainly didn't justify what we had on deposit. I know that perfectly well."

There might have been a better argument that it was only poor judgment had there not been the tie-in with the bank. This was the element that overwhelmed the Fund's defenders and brought the judge's strongest condemnation of Lewis. "Lewis and Roche chose, without taking legal advice in the face of strong objection to the legality of their actions, to advance the interests of the union and the bank in disregard of the paramount interest of the beneficiaries who were entitled to receive the benefit of prudent investment of their funds."

He found a conspiracy by Lewis, Roche and the bank. Since Lewis was acting for the union, damages were to be assessed against the UMW.

The court likewise found violations by the trustees in the withholding of health cards from members when their employers became delinquent in royalty payments and in the misleading application forms which implied a requirement of full union membership for retired miners. It found misconduct in the 1969 pension increase.

The court ordered the removal of the aging Josephine Roche as a trustee of the Fund. Judge Gesell also disqualified Tony Boyle, who had succeeded Lewis, primarily because of his 1969 manipulation of the pension fund. The ruling imposed a future course of conduct upon the new trustees: investment and management primarily for the men who dug the coal.

The Fund, despite these adversities, has continued to function, still providing pensions and hospital and medical care for miners and their families. Its 1970 report, however, showed that it spent 28 million more than it received, despite the highest income in all its history. The Boyle-maneuvered pension increase accounted for almost all of the deficit. Dire predictions of bankruptcy followed—from critics, from investigators, from a Senate subcommittee. The 1971 report showed an even greater deficit, amounting to 38 million. More than 66,000 miners were receiving pensions, based upon twenty years' service and reaching the age of fifty-five. This age standard, one of the lowest in any plan, was particularly beneficial to coal miners with their hazards of existence, and again, must represent one of the Fund's major achievements.

The financial problems of the Fund were greatly alleviated by the 1971 increase in the royalty payments. With its new management, the new court-imposed standards, and the cleansing effect of the lawsuit, there is every likelihood that it will continue and perhaps even expand over the years, to benefit miners and their families, and accomplish some of the noble purposes for which it was founded.

3.

What caused the Fund to become so alienated, so unresponsive, that its beneficiaries were compelled to turn to the law to bring it back to their needs? Why did this most humanitarian of enterprises decline to the level of administering its routine chores and turning its back upon the heart-considerations of its constituency? Where lie insights of avoidance, what predictable furrows of human behavior are involved, what bitternesses ought to be expunged?

When any organization yields its right of decision to any one man, there is the likelihood, amounting almost to a law of human behavior, that mismanagement will occur. The statement itself has become almost a cliché; the only remarkable thing is that men can know and understand and parrot its truth but seldom recognize it during its ascendancy or even do anything about it. And when so remarkable a personality as John L. Lewis is the dominator, the difficulties of curtailing the monarch are all the more overwhelming.

Such incapacity to act can become legally costly, as the union discovered when Judge Gesell rendered his decision in the Fund case. Union lawyers offered the halfhearted defense that it was all the personal fault of John L. Lewis in the hope that liability would not be imposed upon the UMW itself. Gesell's answer, perhaps more tongue-in-cheek than naïve, full of legal soundness but practical nonsense, said that "the union could have designated another representative to act as trustee, had it been unwilling to accept the benefits of the course that Lewis had so obviously set." Its minions had long before forfeited the right to impose the membership's will upon the old man who clung to the trustee's job in the waning years of his life.

But it was not the late years of Lewis that befouled the Fund. When he turned toward money management, banking and power dealing shortly after it was established, the Fund began to drift away from the human-service goals that it could have fulfilled. Lewis's acceptance of automation in the mines brought economic misery to thousands of displaced and disabled miners; there was never any creative drive on the part of the Fund to make it up to them, to expand the Fund, to train, to teach, to respond. Along with the path to the dumping ground, there came the tight rules restrictions that made the Fund less flexible and less helpful to the men it might have saved.

To place all the blame on Lewis, of course, is only another avoidance of the responsibilities that men cannot escape if they desire to keep any control of their destinies. Coal miners acted no differently from French citizens before a conquering Bonaparte, or any other level of supposedly civilized people turning over their decision-making function to strong personages, whether in a state or a corporate body or any other institutionalized group. Apparently, a repetition of such patterns is inevitable; a stoppage at happening time is almost impossible. Unless men learn to adopt such built-in checks and balances as the genius of Madison and his contemporaries produced, they will surely be deprived by the Lewis-type geniuses that bring them so much on the one hand and leave them with such failures on the other.

Thus, one may reflect upon the sad and almost stereotyped conclusion that the despotism of Lewis was the great undoing of the Fund. Along with it came an administrative inertia that perhaps bedevils any such structure without a house ombudsman. These happenings must thus be recorded, their lessons hopefully learned. The probabilities that they will not be repeated encourage us little.

9. The Most Dangerous Game

AWARENESS AT LAST

1•

Coal mining kills people—by the day, by the week, by the year. It kills them with massive explosions that wipe out their lives in great numbers. It chews them to pieces by ones and twos when roofs fall in, equipment breaks, or coal cars crash in the dark. And then it chokes them to death, filling the breathing apparatus of a man's body with dust, leaving its tortured victims to die an early but sometimes merciful death.

It has claimed its human casualties as long as men have pulled black rocks from below the ground. No other occupation of mankind has been so relentless, so predictably fatal, so destructive of life. The high cat-walker, whether atop a skyscraper or on a Verrazano Bridge, may live almost as dangerously, but his is not so common a calling. And he has an open and totally free choice of livelihoods. No tradition of family, no prison of mountain glen, no sheeplike acquiescence holds him to the urge to climb into the sky and risk death by a fall. And when he does his work, he leaves a monument behind—if not in the building's contribution to "civilization," then in the beauty of a soaring bridge. The miner leaves nothing; what he produces is burned into ashes.

But even the man who walks the great heights lives a safer life than a coal miner. His sponsors protect him with equipment and a custodial desire to preserve his life. Once he accepts the challenge of his calling, it is largely his own mistakes that will cost him his life. And if he should die, it will most likely be alone. And while he lives, there is an excitement that surrounds his soul, a prideful superiority over mere mortal beings who could never achieve his daring ascendancy. And in addition, there is the reality that he dies so seldom.

But the coal miner dies so often. The equipment he takes with him is not to protect his life, but to pull out more coal. His overlords have shown through all the history of his digging an almost total unconcern about preserving his being. Decades of acceptance have taught him the brooding expectancy of death, and he has given his willing compliance. And when errors in human judgment are made by one man in the mines, it is often that many men die with him. There is no excitement in his life except the knowledge of daily danger, for his dungeon is too dark. While the bridge builder goes up, the coal miner goes down—and the contrast is all-pervasive.

Yet death goes on, as it has in America for all the recorded time of coal mining. In a century of keeping records, 120,000 men, an average of a hundred human beings every month for a hundred years, have died violent deaths in coal mines. When mining was in its primitive stages, men were killed in small numbers in many localized tragedies. As the mines grew in size, so did the capacity to wipe out human life.

The first great mass explosion, never exceeded in fatalities, came in December, 1907, in Monongah, West Virginia. A mine blast wiped out 361 men in one tragedy. Mining engineers went into all the major coal fields to observe conditions and learn what they could about forestalling disasters in the future. They identified almost all the major causes of death. They recommended sound standards for prevention. Their thoughtful analyses stand today, seldom observed and seldom even considered by those never fully concerned.

There were usually outcries after every disaster. As early as 1886, when a severe explosion killed many men in Newburg, West Virginia, protests by prominent citizens led to an act of the legislature to try to improve mine safety in the state. In late 1940, after 276 men were killed in a single series of blasts, Congress moved the next year to pass the first federal Coal Mine Inspection and Investigation Act. It was weak, ineffective, general in nature, careful not to disturb the industry too much, and almost meaningless in the cold, dark world of mine danger. There was another federal law in 1952, and the "best of all" safety laws in 1970.

The tragedies kept occurring—Centralia, Illinois, March 25, 1947, 111 miners killed in a single explosion; West Frankfort, Illinois, December 21, 1951, 119 miners dead; West Frankfort again, February 4, 1957, only 37 killed this time; Bishop, Virginia, October 27, 1958, 22 men killed; Carmichaels, Pennsylvania, December 6, 1962, 37 in one blast; Dola, West Virginia, April 25, 1963, 22 men dead; Farmington, West Virginia, November 20, 1968, 78 miners wiped out; Hyden, Kentucky, December 30, 1970, 38 men killed.

A single factor was present in every one of the large explosions, from Monongah to Farmington to the 1970 Kentucky disaster. They all occurred in cold weather, never in the summer. Cold dry air dehumidified the mine. When coal dust is set in motion, methane gas, the deadly explosive itself, is liberated. For decades, miners would warn of the dangers of cold weather, the explosive season. The UMW *Journal* carried its warnings, too, of the approach of the dangerous months. In Farmington, West Virginia, on November 19, 1968, a cold front had passed over the state and barometric pressure had dropped. The next day the mine blew up.

Over and over again, human behavior produced the same repetitious charade. Cold-weather explosions bringing death and tragedy. Official handwringing. Often, new laws. Then the same monotonous statements, like those of Assistant Secretary of the Interior Jay Cordell Moore, who flew from Washington to the Farmington disaster to add his bit of conventional wisdom, "Unfortunately, we don't understand why these things happen."

Yet the Bureau of Mines, in a 1960 almanac of mine disasters, had reported that as long ago as 1886, it was known that suspended coal dust in mines had violently explosive characteristics. The engineers who searched for causes in 1909 published their findings of the dangers of dust. Year after repetitious year, men ignored what was so apparent—from 1963 to the date of the Farmington tragedy, all twenty-four inspections by the Bureau of Mines had revealed substandard rock dusting. This was the fundamental preventive, using crushed limestone to "wet down" the dust. But nothing was done about the transgressions—not even after seventy-eight men had been killed.

The big blasts attract the attention, make the front pages, raise cries of concern and pity, and sometimes produce laws that have not yet worked. But the day-to-day destruction of human life has gone on year after year, killing miners and leaving broken and twisted bodies for those who survive. There is the roof fall—the deadly cave-in of the top of the tunnel above the working miner—that takes its toll every year. Small explosions wipe out other miners. Defective machines that cause accidents destroy still other men. These are the daily events that cause wives to send their men off to mines each day always wondering whether they will return alive.

By the end of 1940, the big accidents and the daily destruction had been killing miners at an average of better than two thousand a year for thirty years. When the Coal Mine Inspection and Investigation Act was passed in response to the series of tragedies, the death rate began to fall somewhat. The Bureau of Mines reported in 1947, for example, that 908 men had been killed that year in underground accidents. The great Centralia explosion had accounted for 111, but the consistent killer was always "falls of roof or face," in which 464 miners were killed. Haulage, referring to accidents while moving the coal out of the ground, accounted for 195 other dead men. Death from explosives wiped out 21, electrocution claimed another 24, defective machinery killed 24 men, and others died in that omnipresent category in every statistical compilation, "miscellaneous."

In 1948, the same general situation continued. Fewer men had died, when the totals were added, but there had been no major explosion like Centralia that year. "Falls of roof or face" killed 484 men, more than in 1947. Haulage, explosives, machinery and electricity accounted for approximately the same number of fatalities as in the previous year.

By 1969, after the Farmington tragedy and when the nation was again entertaining mild concern about the safety of coal miners, death was still writing its inexorable statistics. There were not nearly so many coal miners then as in 1947 and 1948, but the percentage of men dying was about the same. The old constant, falls of roof, killed nearly half of the men who died underground in 1969. Haulage too took its usual toll, along with the same causes of electricity, machinery, and explosives that featured the government reports of more than twenty years previously. In 1970, there was a slight increase in mine fatalities, even apart from the December blast in Kentucky that killed thirty-eight men. Roof falls and haulage had their familiar places in the tragic body counts that turned dead miners into statistics.

In November 1971, when the national strike of miners was ended, eight men went to their deaths in the very first week they were back at work. The "haulage"-type accident in Farmington, for example, claimed an experienced miner who had worked for months trying to recover bodies from the 1968 blast. Benny B. Tippner, fifty-five years old, was a front-end motorman on the small underground electric locomotive that hauled coal over the tracks in Consolidated No. 9, where the explosion had happened. His train was pulling eighteen cars, carrying twenty tons of coal each, over the main-line tracks down in the mine.

As the engine pulled up an incline on its way out, it began to slip on the tracks that had become slimy from disuse during the strike. There were brakes on the front-end locomotive and brakes on a pusher engine in the rear, but none of the heavily loaded cars had brakes. Their weight pulled the train rapidly backward, down, down, faster and faster, until an eventual derailment and crash occurred. The rear motorman jumped when the train ran wild and his life was saved.

Tippner kept fighting up front to control the runaway. He wound up under his own locomotive, crushed to death, another victim, another statistic, another sacrifice to the monumental carelessness that pervades work in coal mines. An official of the Bureau of Mines called it "overloading for the condition of the track."

There could have been precautions. Perhaps there should have been an effort to clean the slime off the rails. But there was a simpler and easier solution—fewer cars. But no one apparently cared about that, and Tippner joined the other casualties of deadly No. 9. Some who do care about the lives of men underground have urged that brakes be installed on mine cars, just as they are on railroad boxcars, but that would "cost too much."

The figures on death are so overpowering that little attention is paid to the constant maiming and injuries that disable miners on other days. In 1968 alone, more than 3,500 miners in West Virginia were injured at their work. The grim figures year after year, all over the United States in the coal mines, are that for every death, there are from forty to fifty injuries. This proportion has remained almost constant for twenty years, as predictable as the turning leaves on the calendar. Legs and arms are torn from men, backs and spinal columns are crushed, and blows fall upon their heads. The common public reaction is silence.

All the mines are dangerous, from the giant underground cities to the tiny dogholes of eastern Kentucky. In the small ones, no one bothers much about safety, in the eagerness to pull out the coal. In the big mines, like the Maple Creek Mine on the Monongahela River in southwestern Pennsylvania, the sweep of the caverns carries its own perils. United States Steel Corporation owns that mine, which was called a "captive" mine in the days of the great Lewis organizational drives. It lies in one of the richest coal beds in the world, in a seam of solid coal that runs for hundreds of square miles under the earth. The huge continuous mining machine that voraciously eats into the seam can continue its pace in the Maple Creek mine alone for another forty to fifty years without exhausting it.

The big mine has tunnels that sometimes reach out for fifteen or twenty miles underground. Track must be laid, and wires must be put down. And every foot of the distance requires a concern for the roof overhead, with the great weight of the earth above it imposing its reminder of death for the men who dare to go so far. And the farther the tunnel stretches, the greater the risks for the men who venture out in the cavern. The cold and the blackness add to the danger, especially the dark. The miner can see only what his headlamp hits upon; there is no peripheral vision, no space awareness that accompanies the surface man with his lantern at night. A danger signal may go unnoticed in the darkness and may cost a man his life.

How a big mine, the "good" mine, the "safe" mine, can kill people was shown in March, 1971, when two elderly miners, Richard Randolph, sixty-three, and Charles Gibson, sixty-four, with more than seventy years' mine experience between them, were killed. They worked for the Buckeye Coal Company, in Nemacolin, Pennsylvania, deep in the great Pittsburgh seam. Buckeye Coal is a division of Youngstown Sheet & Tube, another "captive" mine, turning out almost a million and a half tons per year for the steel mills.

The Pittsburgh seam contains a high concentration of methane gas, which makes it inherently dangerous without the other perils of mining. But the management at Nemacolin apparently ignored sound safety precautions, as the mine's record indicated from 1970 to the time of the tragedy that killed Randolph and Gibson.

In May, 1970, a fire broke out in the mine during a night maintenance shift. Fortunately, only a few men were around, and they escaped. A roof fall had knocked out a section of 300-volt DC overhead tram wire on to a steel rail, and the resulting arc fired off coal dust that hung in the air. Federal inspectors found that wires were strung so loosely and tracks laid so sloppily that sagging wires could hang low enough to electrocute passing miners. There was no system at all to prevent overloading of electrical current or short-circuit protection.

Three times in the year before Randolph and Gibson were killed, the mine was actually closed by federal inspectors. In a series of checks from December, 1968, they found 214 health and safety violations. Yes, 214 separate health and safety violations in a two-year period!

This is some of what they found: Insufficient air flow, which is vitally important in the Pittsburgh seam, because pockets of methane gas can develop rapidly in working areas; improperly spliced cables; inadequate rock dusting; dangerous accumulations of loose coal dust, a fire hazard as much as gas. They found a fan which had been placed improperly and was recirculating stale, gassy air back into the mine for the men to breathe. They uncovered seventy-five feet of uninsulated cable lying next to the steel rails on which supplying cars were hauled in and out of the mine.

The incredible roll call goes on. On another inspection, they found a 600-foot length of live high-voltage line on the floor of the mine, in contact with pipelines and sections of track. After a visit in late 1969, inspector Richard Reid reported that an escapeway from Tunnel 118, where the men later died, was "obstructed with standing water and mud." An escapeway from another section nearby was "obstructed with roof falls at two locations." A third escapeway was not marked with direction signs. Several times, inspectors warned the company about oil-soaked coal dust beginning to concentrate in "dangerous quantities" around machinery.

These repeated violations finally brought a "proposed" assessment of fines from the Bureau of Mines in early 1971. The total cost to Buckeye, even if ever paid, was only $9,700, far less than the profit from a single day's production. One fine for "imminent danger" was $2,000, and two others, for "unwarrantable failure," were only $1,000 each. Fifty-seven other fines of $100 each, the minimum allowed under the law, were thrown in. The Company filed its protest, a neatly packaged presentation of one inch of paper. It was in the mail to the Bureau of Mines on March 26, 1971, the day an air compressor leaking oil caught fire in Section 118 of the mine.

Eighteen men fled the fire, but Randolph and Gibson never made it. Rescue teams came in during the day and drilled holes into the section. Microphones were lowered into the holes in the hope of picking up a sound of human life. The men outside heard only the crackle of burning coal. Air samples showed fatal concentrations of carbon monoxide. A thermometer lowered into the seam recorded a temperature of 380 degrees, a sample of literal hell enveloping the bodies of men who could not possibly be alive.

Five days later, officials reached the morbid but necessary conclusion that all hope was lost, and they ordered that the seam be flooded to put out the fire. There followed the usual cryptic announcement: "It is not possible at this time to estimate how long it will take to extinguish the fire. It is hoped, however, that when the fire is out, the bodies of the trapped miners will be recovered."

This two-man tragedy, so small, so insignificant to a nation inured to battlefield slaughters, automobile carnage, hand-gun homicides in the cities, and a century of acceptance of death in coal mines, aroused little attention or comment. "Too bad." "Sorry about that." Buckeye Coal Company could continue its business as usual, even if ever so slightly concerned about the incredible safety conditions it fostered day after day despite the unusual presence of inspectors who reported the violations.

These were the conditions that were killing miners at Nemacolin and in West Virginia and in Kentucky. It was production that counted—get out the coal—not the lives of the men who worked in the death traps. The mechanized equipment had to be kept running. Too much time and effort on safety would cut down on the tonnage figures that meant profit.

Knowledgeable students of mine safety have known for a long time that the primary cause of the tragic toll has always been management's rush for production, with corner-cutting at every opportunity. As one industry expert put it: "If you space the roof bolts farther apart, you'll be able to keep up with the continuous-miner more easily, you won't have to buy as many bolts or bolting machines, and you can get by with hiring one man to do the bolting even though it would be safer to have two. And if the roof falls, chances are the miner will get blamed for spacing the bolts too far apart. Especially if he's dead, and can't answer back."

The same observer made a similar analogy on the handling of

cables. An entire shift could be shut down if a cable had to be replaced on a loading machine. Therefore, the answer was usually to put in another temporary splice. If there were a dozen other splices in the cable, the answer could always be that there had been no tragedies yet. Roof falls and haulage accidents and defective equipment keep on killing miners.

Industry leaders keep making their persistent points about the economic costs of mine safety. Congressman Ken Hechler of West Virginia, who became deeply devoted to the safety of miners in his state after the Farmington tragedy, received a lecture on the industry's position from Herbert Jones, president of the Amherst Coal Company, who wrote that to have a growth industry, certain economic considerations must be satisfied.

"Coal prices are increasing," said Mr. Jones, "because of added costs in mining brought on by the impact of increased safety regulations, stricter mining laws, and higher workmen's-compensation costs."

Such attention to safety, of course, was detrimental to the growth of the industry because it was too expensive. The implication was clear; the old hard-nosed line that safety cost too much was rephrased in the more sophisticated term, "inhibition of a growth industry." These certain economic considerations had been with coal mining throughout its bloody history.

To avoid the cost of safer conditions in the mines, the owners have told a simple story, repeated a thousand times. Coal mining is so dangerous that nothing can be done about it. They have fostered the idea, promoted it, and nurtured its acceptance like tablets inscribed from Mount Sinai. It was easy to propagate during the industrial ethic of the late nineteenth century and almost as easy to continue in the first part of this one. After every mine tragedy, it finds its willing spokesmen. After the Farmington explosion in late 1968, the honorable governor of West Virginia, Hulett C. Smith, doubtless without any urging at all from mineowners, intoned his echo in this way: "We must recognize that this is a hazardous business, and what has occurred here is one of the hazards of being a miner."

At the same time, John Roberts, the public relations head of Consolidated Coal Company, the employer, offered this gem to the world: "This is something we have to live with."

And so it goes on and on. Dr. Elbert F. Osborn, the new head of the Bureau of Mines, made his contribution after the late 1970 disaster in Kentucky: "I think we can almost expect one of these a year." Osborn had something else to say, too: "We've had two pretty good years." His reference was to the time span between the Consolidated blast and the Hyden explosion—two pretty good years, in which 406 men had been killed and in which 15,575 had suffered injuries. Although he may not have meant it that way, Osborn's comments sound quite callous.

As long as the man in charge of the government's program for United States coal mines continued to expect a tragedy a year, as long as he continued to believe that 406 dead men marked a fine level of performance, as long as such thoughtless attitudes continued to dominate the federal service, then coal miners would surely keep on dying in the same senseless pattern as always.

2·

Why would a man work in a coal mine?

What would move a human being to spend his productive life in cold, pitiless darkness? How could he endure the stupor of it, with its clogging dust that would destroy the functioning of his body? How could he face the knowledge that an explosion could occur on any day he went below, and would cause his tunnels to collapse upon him or seal his path to escape or consume the precious oxygen, depriving him of the breath to survive? Or a fire, or a fall, or errant electricity, or tumbling cars that could crush him against a wall of rock or coal?

How could a man give his life to this? His fathers taught him of its peril, yet he followed them into it. He knew from all the tragedies that he witnessed from boyhood awareness to adult sorrow that it was the most dangerous undertaking of any in the universe. He knew that it would almost surely kill him, in one way or another. He knew he would leave a woman and the children he had begotten to exist in an even more mournful misery than that which surrounded his life.

Yet he would do it, almost as if chains shackled him to his valley. There were no rewards—only the dollars they gave him for his pay. These pieces of silver could never compensate for the offering of his body. And even then, the miner had to fight harder, so it appeared, to get the same amounts of money that went to other workmen for far less hazardous labor. There was nothing else; no sunshine, no flowers, no music, no comfort, no learning.

And worst of all, there was no hope. Even a miner who might advance to the position of a company foreman could expect to die in the same tunnels with the men who did the basic work. The line of Alexander Pope, "Hope springs eternal in the human breast," became an aphorism of society because of its universal truth—for all except coal miners. All the digger could hope for was a survival to the day following that would bring no more to his life than the danger of his current hours.

Was there some omnipresent death wish that sent him underground each day to breathe the dust, blacken his face and eyes and hair and hands, work in a dungeon, and endure the chance of a catastrophe that was almost certain to come at some unexpected hour?

Or did some malevolent habit hang over his soul, binding him to an indenture from which only death or maiming could free him?

There has been a kind of prison that has entombed coal miners— one made of nature's tricks, whether it be classed as environment, geography, or mountain regions that were named Appalachia. The mountains contained the coal; their slopes and their contours contained the people to do the work of digging the coal. They became a literal barrier to keep the people from the outside world. It was this thrust of the earth that became the formless prison, even though without walls or warden, that dominated their lives so much that few of them ever learned how to leave it.

There are many physical barriers that impress restraints upon the lives of people. Rivers and railroad tracks and highways all exert enormous influences, but none, surely, so formidable as the hillsides in the coal industry. Mountains breed their own kind of insularity, developing even their own culture and their own forms of speech. They inbreed a kind of ignorance too, that makes the world beyond a strange and forbidding land not to be entered easily. Fathers and their sons, and their sons after them, go to work in the coal mines, and thus it has been in all the days of their lives.

The terrible insecurity of life in a new land sent the immigrant to the coal mines in decades past. In the great coal fields away from Appalachia, such as the deposits in central and southern Illinois, where mountain barriers were not nearly so formidable, Eastern and Southern Europeans went to work alongside sons of earlier arrivals from the British Isles. An old friend whose great-grandfather came from Scotland to work in the mines of southern Illinois has told of the hold of the pits on all his family.

"Powder blew up in the face of my grandfather," he said. "He spent twenty-five years of his life in a hospital bed. My father's brother was crushed to death in a rock fall. My father started as soon as he was big enough to work. He died at the age of forty-three, clogged with so much dust that his heart could no longer move the blood around in his body. By the time I was sixteen, I knew that I was going to work in the mines, too. That is all we knew, all we understood. There was nothing else for any man to do in our part of Illinois."

Two events saved this man from the mines. The news of the Centralia blast in 1947 overwhelmed his small mining town. He went with three other miners' sons to the scene, and stood there for three days while bodies were brought topside. The screaming and wailing of widows when the name of the victim was called out haunts him to this day. This, with all the other knowledge that his young life had acquired, escalated his fear quotient to the point of internal questioning of his lot. The second event was military service that took him to far parts of the world and taught him there were other universes than southern Illinois and its coal mines. When he returned, he went away quickly to find a job in greener and happier precincts, to break at last the generation chain of the coal mines.

"My father swore every summer of his life that he would never go underground again," he said. "The mines in Illinois used to close in the summer, and the entire family would pick peaches. When the whistle on the tipple blew in September, my father was the first man there. There could be no hungry mouths at our table that winter or any other winter, and he did this until it killed him."

John L. Lewis told the Congress after the Centralia explosion in 1947 that young men were beginning to escape the mines.

> A young man who grows up in a mining community now in most states cannot enter the mines under various state laws and regulations until he is seventeen or eighteen years of age. As a result, he secures some education, and he does not have to go to work in the

mines, as his father did who perhaps lived through a lifetime of abuse in the mines under the conditions imposed by the operators and under the callous disregard of the public for the mineworkers' conditions—his father has advised him to find his vocation in life elsewhere, and that new blood which in the past has contributed so much to the upbuilding of our industry and making it the most productive industry in the world is no longer available for our mines.

But the old ones continued to go on until their lives were either crushed or exhausted. The sons who stayed with them clung to the closeness of the family unit. The fear of the unknown world outside the mountain regions, the end of the educational process, the clasp of the familiar kept them as coal miners.

Men do become inured to hazards. Men who continually hope hour after hour, day after day, that nothing will happen, they will not be killed, finally persuade themselves that they are not going to be killed and they have a driving incentive not to lose the work because of the requirements at home, and they continue to accept the hazard and take a chance.

Lewis told this to the Congress, too, in 1947.

Thus men continued to mine coal and continued to die. Any world other than that of coal mining was never apparent to them before World War II. They, like so many other masses of people with an infinite capacity for enduring danger and poverty and misery and darkness, kept on going underground because it was all they knew that the world could provide for them. The decline of manpower needs in the 1950's made it unimportant for a time that few new men were going into coal mining. Their ages became older and older, but the mountain walls contained enough of them to keep the coal moving.

And the explosions went on and roofs continued to cave in and haulage accidents continued to crush their bodies and the dust enveloped their beings as always. And in this repetitive annihilation of human life, there was always the question of what they could do to stop it, and what their efforts at joining together in an organization could accomplish.

Would it ever end?

3.

The law has always been society's way of trying to solve most of the problems that have erupted throughout the growth of the republic. Death in coal mines has been subject to the law's attention for three quarters of a century. Every coal-mining state has safety laws and protective laws on its statute books. The federal government has legislated on the subject time after time. The Congress wrote a law in 1969, the Federal Coal Mine Health and Safety Act, that was thought to be a model act even by the severest critics of the hazards of coal mining.

Yet the law has failed. It is difficult to conceive any other area of regulated life where statutes and regulations and legal machinery have produced so little effect on the lives of people. The aged and often iniquitous societal cliché that laws will not work when people are either opposed to them or don't care about them may have its strongest underwriting in the story of coal mining.

It began in the federal sphere in 1910, when Congress created the Bureau of Mines. The new government agency soon became the in-house advocate of the industry, captured by the lords whom it was supposed to oversee even more quickly than most government regulatory bodies succumb. It functioned for many years as a research section for the industry, spending taxpayer dollars to try to discover new production methods the companies could adopt. The operators might easily have done for themselves what "socialized" research handed to them. If a new method helped make a mine shaft safer, like the adoption of roof bolts, it was largely coincidental.

An effort to do something about safety, rather than production, on the federal level did not occur until 1941. It came, of course, only after a series of explosions had temporarily shocked a nation not yet consumed by Pearl Harbor. Congress passed the Coal Mine Inspection and Investigation Act, which tentatively, hesitatingly, and half-heartedly opened the mine doors to federal agents. An inspector could go in if he had the owner's permission. And if he received permission, all he could do was give "advice." Since production had to go on, what advice was given could be conveniently ignored and life could go on as usual. And death.

The West Frankfort explosion in 1951 produced a revision of the safety law. It was called the Mine Safety Act, and this time it allowed inspectors to go in without permission. When President Truman signed the bill, he called attention to many serious omissions that still showed the tender solicitude for the economics of the industry. Underground machinery, no matter how unsafe, as long as it was being used in 1952, could be retained by the owners. It was obviously too expensive to bring in new, safe equipment. Mines were classified in two categories, "gassy" and "nongassy." The "nongassy" mine received all the breaks in loose safety standards; the law was tougher for "gassy" mines. The difficulty was that 85 percent of all mines qualified as nongassy.

Just as men had to die before anyone paid attention enough to produce federal laws in 1941 and 1952, it was the Farmington death count that led to the enactment of the 1969 statute. The new law gave greater authority to the Bureau of Mines to close down unsafe collieries. Fines could be imposed for violations. Tougher safety standards were prescribed, and they were the most realistic ever passed. For the first time, it dealt with the problem of coal dust, setting forth measurable allowances. It took cognizance of the prevalence of black-lung disease from dust and provided for benefits for miners.

Then the disintegration began. President Nixon uncomfortably and hesitatingly signed the bill in 1969. Since enforcement was still the responsibility of the Bureau of Mines, the director's job became of even greater importance to the industry. John F. O'Leary, a holdover from the Johnson administration, who was known as knowledgeable and tough, was fired. "He was the one man at the Bureau who knew the law and had the backbone to stand by it," said Congressman Hechler.

At a time when it was vital for the Bureau to have the leadership to begin its job of enforcement, there was no director for two months. Then, a mining engineer from Virginia Polytechnic Institute, J. Richard Lucas, was nominated. He was so blatantly proindustry and demonstrably unconcerned about safety that his selection became a political embarassment and had to be withdrawn. More time dragged past mid-1970 before Dr. Osborn, the present director, was brought to the office.

The job of "chief enforcer" in the Bureau was later given to an unknown Iowa lawyer whose major asset appeared to be his undeviating old-line Republicanism. Edward D. Failor, from Dubuque, a former municipal judge, party fund raiser, lobbyist for Iowa coin laundries, and an early enthusiast for Barry Goldwater in 1964, was named as an assistant to Osborn in charge of seeing that the law was obeyed. When questioned about his qualifications for such a job, he talked about "administration" and "motivating" people. His knowledge of coal mining appeared from his previous background to be an unspoiled zero.

Confronted with the new law, the Bureau of Mines undertook to adopt an inspection manual in good government style for its field men. This manual must have "top priority," it was said in October, 1969. In April, 1970, there was a statement that it was "almost complete," and would be out within ninety days. By May, 1971, more than a year later, there were still no manual, no guidelines, no instructions for inspectors, for better or for worse.

In early 1970, a memorandum went out from the Bureau to its inspectors telling them to telephone Washington for approval before closing any mine for safety violations. This directive remained in effect until the news leaked out and protests in Congress caused its withdrawal. Field men surely had the message by then.

Senator Harrison Williams of New Jersey, discouraged with the Bureau's work, asked another government agency, the General Accounting Office, to investigate. The G.A.O.'s report, released in June, 1971, not only was a scathing indictment of another federal force, but dramatized the failure of law and bureaucracy to work when there was no spirit behind it.

More coal miners died during the first fourteen months after the law had been passed than in the same comparable period before the model statute was enacted! In addition, in 1970, there were 10,575 nonfatal injuries among only 133,000 miners.

The General Accounting Office studied Bureau of Mines field offices that were responsible for supervising 80 percent of the nation's underground mines. In the first fourteen months of the law, the Bureau had made only 31 percent of its required safety inspections and only 1 percent of its required health inspections. While the Bureau was short of trained manpower, the G.A.O. found this excuse unacceptable.

It was "extremely lenient, confusing, uncertain and inequitable" about enforcing the law. It had done little to compel owners to comply with requirements for roof control, ventilation, and emergency action when fans failed. It had ignored six criteria of the law for assessing fines. Repeated violations were ignored. There was no requirement of dust-sampling programs. The conduct of the Bureau of Mines was a disaster.

The Bureau had little incentive to do its job as long as government leadership above it had shown its gross unconcern. The President had originally threatened to veto the act itself. The firing of O'Leary, the lack of urgency about finding a successor, and the nomination of Lucas, who was an affront to miners, were matched by the designation of Republican functionaries to serve on a "safety advisory committee." One such nominee was a former airline stewardess, whose familiarity with coal mining was at least as good as that of Edward D. Failor, who was going to use "administration" and "motivation" to get his job done.

Mineowners complained about the harshness of the law. Several of them filed suit alleging the act's unfairness, and were favored with an early federal court injunction stopping enforcement. Many of its provisions will have to survive legal challenges, and it may be several years before any coordinated, workable enforcement procedure will go into effect. But those who know legal procedures understand very well that the law itself can be made to work once the frustrations of legal attacks have been settled, just as the Welfare Fund itself, the National Labor Relations Act, the various civil-rights laws, and other remedial legislation finally settled down to accomplishment after the early litigating years were survived.

The failure of the law to make coal mines reasonably safe is not an abdication of the process. In fact, it is likely that law is the only mechanism that can ever do the proper job, once it is allowed to work.

The fault, then, is not in the stars; nor is it something that we have to live with. Until there is a positive force in the world of coal mining that demands and insists upon mine safety, it will probably never proceed beyond its confusion, contradiction, ineffectiveness and impotence that leave us, in the words of many critics, with nothing less than a "national scandal."

Where was the institution of the United Mine Workers of America as a positive force? Is the union of the men who mine the coal the structure, the positive force, that ought to do what must be done for those who suffer? This is perhaps our most realistic and important inquiry, but before we turn to it, another destroyer of the people who work must be taken into account. It is black lung, hideous enough to catch attention, dramatic enough to make people concerned, important enough to move the forces that controlled the lives of the human bodies and souls who mined the coal.

4·

"At work you are covered with dust. It's in your hair, your clothes and your skin. The rims of your eyes are coated with it. It gets between your teeth and you swallow it. You suck so much of it into your lungs that until you die you never stop spitting up coal dust. Sometimes you cough so hard that you wonder if you have a lung left. Slowly you notice you are getting short of breath when you walk up a hill. Finally, just walking across the room at home is an effort."

This is what a doctor said. It came from Dr. Lorin E. Kerr, Director of Occupational Health for the United Mine Workers, who learned about coal dust from spending most of his professional life studying miners.

"In the mornings, I get up I can't hardly get my breath. And you know when you come out in the morning, I have had it in my head felt big as a washing tub, and spit up balls of black stuff as big as your fist pretty near. I just have to sit down and wait, and sometimes I gasp for my breath. When you get up you start to cough. Right now I'm short of breath, right now."

This was what one working miner said in 1971 when interviewed by a television correspondent.

Then there was an old miners' song, put together at least as early as 1913, which said:

I used to be a drill man . . .
till it got the best of me
It killed two fellow workers
here at old Parlee

And now I've eaten so much dust,
Lord, that it is killing me.

There was an official line about coal dust that endured for decades. It was good for miners. It was a healthy influence. It helped combat silicosis, so went the version that was sold to the public. Silicosis came from dust from rocks which were pulled out underground to get at the coal. It was the only recognized, or "official," disease in the mines for decades. For many years, up until its tenth edition in 1959, Cecil's *Textbook of Medicine,* a well-known general treatise, maintained that coal dust helped the miner, because it cut the rock dust that produced silicosis.

In 1969, the honorable Medical Society of Cabell County, West Virginia, took up the coal-dust controversy on behalf of the owners of coal mines. They too said it could be healthy for miners. "A consensus of medical authority," their resolution said, "considers simple uncomplicated and uninfected coal workers' pneumoconiosis a condition compatible with reasonable health and not associated with significant disabling diseases."

Dr. Kerr, in his moments of medical freedom not confined by UMW doctrine, made his reference to the doctors who were so beholden to business interests that they ignored what every coal miner knew. "The failure to take earlier action constitutes what may be labeled in the future as the greatest disgrace in the history of American medicine." This may not be exaggeration at all, but pure reality.

Somewhere, it picked up the popular name "black lung." The medical term had a more alarming sound, coal workers' pneumoconiosis, a word that is a struggle to even utter. Not many people were going to become concerned over an affliction when they couldn't even pronounce it. Somebody thankfully shortened the term to C.W.P., but that too was relatively meaningless until the dramatic use of the words "black lung" came into the fight to protect the lives of miners.

Doctors in England recognized the disease in the 1930's, and by 1943, British law recognized C.W.P. as an occupational disease. Other European mining communities showed their concern too, and by 1963 nine million dollars a year was going into research on how to combat the dreaded affliction. In that same year, the United States

Public Health Service had its first grant of only $100,000 for study purposes. But even by 1952 the state of Alabama, never considered one of the country's enlightened legislative areas, made pneumoconiosis a compensable disease. However, in 1950, the Public Health Service had released figures that showed that miners were five times more likely to die of a lung disease than men employed in other industries. By 1956, when Dr. Lorin Kerr began to write articles on the subject, he found it extremely difficult to find any medical journal that would publish them.

What is black lung?

Black lung, or coal workers' pneumoconiosis, is an incurable lung disease brought on by breathing coal dust. This simple statement from concerned doctors was published in the *Health Rights News,* October, 1971, and went on to say: "At first, self-cleansing devices (such as hairs in the nose and other passageways) soon get clogged with dust and break down under the heavy strain and the coal dust begins to collect in the small air sacs in the walls of the lungs. Eventually the walls of the lungs collapse and the air spaces are joined together and in the process many of the small blood vessels in the walls of the lungs are totally destroyed."

The disease itself is incurable. Damaged lungs can never be repaired. But it kills in other ways, too. When it creeps in, it is followed by shortness of breath, cough, sputum, wheezing and tightness around the chest. The more prominent the feeling of tightness, or of a band around the chest, say the doctors, the more chance there is of related heart disease. The more prominent the cough, sputum and wheezing, the more likely bronchitis is part of the problem. It also leads to emphysema, hypertension, enlarged heart and heart attacks. Some West Virginia doctors had been placing the blame for these conditions on cigarette smoking after it became a public villain. They had ignored the fact that, in many areas where miners suffered the most, fundamentalist religious sects to which many of them belonged forbade all smoking.

While coal dust had been a deadly enemy of the bodies of coal miners throughout all the underground years, its miseries accelerated during the mechanization of the mines. The giant machines that went into the tunnels, grinding and tearing coal out of the walls of the caverns, stirred up more and more coal dust. As coal production went higher and higher, so did production of the black powder that enveloped all the men who lived in it and breathed it and absorbed it into their bodies and thus got the incurable disease.

At the 1968 United Mine Workers convention in Denver, Dr. Kerr told the delegates:

> Coal workers' pneumoconiosis is the most important occupational dust disease occurring in the United States today . . . It is safe to conclude from all available information that in the United States at least 125,000 miners have coal workers' pneumoconiosis. Since 1930 it has constituted the greatest medical and social problem in all industry.

But no one appeared to be listening.

In every struggle to arouse the interest of people toward reform, whether political, social or industrial, there always seems to be a small band of gallant persons who see and feel and spread the word. Like the small group of Adamses and Paines that proclaimed the righteousness of the Colonial cause, and even like Lewis and the small crew around him that launched the CIO, a few men turned the tragedy of black lung into a campaign that aroused coal miners, taught unlettered mountain men how to become indigenous leaders, and awakened the sleeping membership of the United Mine Workers of America. The most notable heroes in the beginning were not miners, but doctors, who wiped out some of the shame of their profession with their new efforts.

A portly middle-aged West Virginia physician named I. M. Buff turned his natural talents for drama into the battle against black lung. He used the dread term constantly, not the thought-squashing meaningless word *pneumoconiosis*. He had been talking with miners for some time. All who did not understand the peril of black lung were the enemy; he knew how to criticize and condemn and attack; there were targets aplenty ripe for his thrusts.

Over in the pulmonary laboratory in the Appalachian Regional Hospital in Beckley, where John L. Lewis had once dedicated all the hospitals, there was a quieter, more scholarly physician accumulating more knowledge about black lung than almost anyone else in the country. Dr. Donald Rasmussen, whose red hair was closely clipped, in contrast to the most crimson beard this side of Leif Ericson, was deeply devoted to the health of coal miners. He and his thoughtful wife, Jeanne, who added her skills of writing and photography to the campaign, soon became formidable forces among West Virginia miners. A third doctor, Hawey Wells, Jr., son-in-law of Congressman Harley Staggers, was also concerned, and he had some of Dr. Buff's flair for drama. He once crumbled a piece of blackened lung in his hand before a group of miners and said, "You're crazy if you let them do this to you."

It was the Farmington explosion in November, 1968, that ignited a new concern for the safety and health of coal miners. Just as television brought some of the horrors of the Vietnam war into American living rooms, the picture story was told of the terrible destructiveness of human life and hope that followed the big blast at Consolidated No. 9. There were TV sets in miner's homes now; they were able to watch the scenes on the national networks; they could not fail to perceive that perhaps the time had come for them to act.

Dr. Buff, too, sensed the responsiveness of the miners. He recruited Dr. Wells and Dr. Rasmussen to join him in talking to miners all over the state. He began to attack the owners with new enthusiasm. The union, he said, was just as guilty. The Bureau of Mines was likewise culpable for ignoring for decades what should have been apparent. The three doctors were immediately condemned by medical authorities over the state, some of them uttering the ancient and ignorant phrases about the benefits of coal dust to miners.

In January, 1969, less than two months after Farmington, a group of miners in West Virginia formed the Black Lung Association. By the next month, a spontaneous wildcat strike had swept over West Virginia. Miners went to Charleston and demanded that the state legislature pass a black-lung law. In what students have called a legislative miracle, the lawmakers enacted the most enlightened workmen's-compensation provisions in the country.

When Congress passed the 1969 Coal Mine Health and Safety Act, it wrote in a provision on black lung. The disease became compensable under the Social Security laws, entitling disabled miners to federal funds. Administrative and legal problems have brought controversy to this program, but federal recognition of the need to pay disabled men has been written into law. The work of three West Virginia doctors had led directly to an act of Congress.

Equally important, the law now prescribes limits for the accumulation of dust. Average concentrations of respirable dust now may not exceed 3.0 milligrams per cubic meter of air. In 1973 that limit goes even lower, to 2.0 milligrams per cubic meter.

There is genuine hope now that after all the decades of misery, black lung can be controlled. Australia attacked the disease twenty-five years ago and today has almost no black lung among its coal miners. Great Britain has had an enlightened program for many years, with particular emphasis on protecting the individual miner. Every year, English and Welsh miners are given medical checkups. If any evidence of lung disease begins to appear, the miner is immediately withdrawn from the dust area and placed on a job somewhere else in the industry. Once disabled, a sound pension program protects him thereafter. Germany and Czechoslovakia have made enormous progress against black lung since they first took action against it, years before the slumbering American interests recognized its existence.

And finally, new research methods now under study are attacking the dust itself. There is the possibility of preconditioning the coal seam to keep down dust. The use of foams and high-velocity water jets presents possibilities. There is even consideration of new cutting machines that will raise less dust. Remote-control mining equipment to keep men out of the dustiest regions is also under experimentation.

But the most important impact of black lung has been in the political area, not in the medical. It became the primary catalytic agent for the awakening of a people. The Farmington blast stirred them, and the senseless killing of their numbers that went on and on added to their resolve. But it was around black lung that they began to organize, to discover leadership qualities in simple people who had never spoken before, to begin the remaking of the great institution to which they all belonged.

> I don't suppose you have ever laid down in a mine tunnel with your face in a half-inch of water and pulled your shirt up over your head, expecting to die the next minute from an explosion you heard coming toward you. I have, and when God performed a miracle and stopped that explosion before I died, I think it gave me some understanding of these things, and I think I can understand what these men were thinking about and how they suffered in that Centralia

mine when they were waiting to die from the gas, because there was no oxygen in there—the explosion had consumed the oxygen; there was nothing there to help them, and they were dying, and they wrote notes to their children and their wives. I think I know some of the things they said to each other.

And as God gives me strength, I am going to be true to those men who died, and those who are going to die before this is corrected, and raise up my voice in justice to the living and in justice to the memory of the dead, to ask a surcease to this bloodletting. . . .

Thus spoke John L. Lewis to a House Labor subcommittee in 1947, during its hearings after the Centralia explosion. Lewis had come to Congress to complain about the failure of Secretary of the Interior Julius Krug to enforce government safety standards. The Centralia tragedy came during a period when the government was running the mines with Krug as the nominal chief operator. Lewis sadly discovered that government control meant little more than private ownership when safety interfered with production.

What made the 1947 Illinois death count even more poignant was that four officers of Mine Workers Local 52 had pleaded with the governor the year before to save their lives. The men who worked in the mine were frightened because state inspectors paid no attention to repeated violations of the laws of Illinois on mine safety. The four top officers of the local signed a letter to Governor Dwight Green asking him to "please make the Department of Mines and Minerals enforce the laws . . . before we have a dust explosion at this mine like just happened to Kentucky and West Virginia."

Their final line to their governor was "Please save our lives."

Three of the four men who signed that letter in March, 1946, were killed in March, 1947, when the mine blew up.

John L. Lewis did raise his voice, time after time. The men who worked in many mines, like the doomed souls in Local 52, raised their voices too. Lewis won dramatic points as he assailed Secretary Krug, the mineowners, and the state inspectors (there were no federal investigators in those days). Again, with some of his most penetrating wisdom, Lewis told the nation why miners continued to die.

These disasters occur with impunity, and each time there is a disaster in the industry the newspaper columns are filled with stories of probes, investigations, experts being rushed to the scene of the disaster, rescuers at work—rescuers for the dead! An endless repetition. The public is sorry for the victims, and people on the street say, "Oh, isn't it too bad!" And it ends there, and nothing is done, and the widows wait, and the orphans grow up in poverty and in ignorance and in deprivation of opportunity, because someone found it cheaper to kill their fathers than to protect them, and the public was too busy with its own affairs to care very long, or to do anything about it.

The union was alone through all the decades up to the end of World War II in its efforts to make coal mines more responsive to human life. At the time the union first achieved some recognition of strength in the early part of the century, safety legislation was purely a state function. When young Lewis went to Springfield as a union lobbyist in 1915, he was placing his talent where it was most likely to have an effect. Most of the mining states had perfunctory laws on the books, with limited personnel to enforce them. Mining companies had reasonably easy times with the small-town business interests that came to statehouses to write the laws. There was very little chance that strong measures could be passed. There was even less to fear from mine inspectors. In Illinois, as the union discovered in 1947, state mining agents were too busy soliciting political contributions from the big coal companies to make any serious effort at safety enforcement.

The union's efforts in the state capitals accomplished little more than to keep the issue of mine safety as a recurring conversation piece around town. As long as the public accepted the long-established propaganda line that coal mines were so inherently dangerous that men who were foolhardy enough to go underground should expect to be killed, there was little that would be produced by any group of lawmakers.

If the law, or the body politic, could not be counted on for assistance, there was left only the traditional trade-union method of "self-help." Each mine had its own safety committee among the men, who could meet with the managers and demand correction of obvious hazards. This was an advisory group, not an enforcement agency. If the mineowner ignored the safety committee, the only recourse was to turn him in to a state man, if he ever came around, or a federal man, if he ever came around. Not much was accomplished with governmental police forces, as the grim toll of the years testifies.

There was one other intrinsic trade-union weapon, the strike. When people rise to act in concert with a determined purpose, whether it is storming the Bastille or miners demanding more for their bushels in Daniel Weaver's time or black citizens arising in the South, grievances have to be great. Ordinary molds of behavior can be shattered only when the level of toleration has been exceeded. Miners over the years learned to tolerate an enormous amount. There was always the pressure to keep earning money, the hope that tomorrow would bring no greater danger, the thought that someone else would be the victim. There was, finally, the obedience syndrome, the compulsion to follow the wishes of the father, the boss, the mine manager. All of these exerted their influences on men to keep digging, even in the face of the crudest violations, just as they kept working in Centralia until they died.

But coal miners, among all American workers, knew the effectiveness of the strike weapon. They had turned it off and on to near perfection in the tense years of the 1940's. But to strike for human safety, when conditions varied from mine to mine, when diggers in the Pittsburgh seam had no personal awareness of the daily conditions in Logan and Mingo in West Virginia or even in the deep Illinois tunnels, required national leadership. It was never put into action.

The one man who could have turned the strike weapon into a safety device placed his reliance instead upon legislation. He came back again in 1952 to thunder at Congress after more miners were blown up in West Frankfort. He went to the scene and went underground. The spectacle of John L. Lewis coming from down under, dressed in miner's clothes, hard hat and head lamp pushed back, broad face covered with coal grime, was a memorable newspaper picture of that year. He again went before the Congress to demand safety legislation, and this led to the 1952 statute.

His presentation, as usual, was moving, dramatic, scornful, effective. A federal inspection report had found thirty-one violations of the Safety Code, twenty-one of them uncorrected from previous visits. He wanted Congress to give federal inspectors authority to close unsafe mines. When the colloquy before the Senate Committee on Labor and Public Welfare shifted to what the miners could do about unsafe mines, Lewis turned it into an attack on the Taft-Hartley Act. He told the committee that Congress would have to repeal that law in order to allow the union to do its own policing.

There had been occasional wildcat strikes by men who refused to work in dangerous mines. Lewis told the committee of the lawsuits filed against the union and of the discharges of safety-committee men, and he referred scathingly to newspaper editorials which advised the union to withdraw the men from unsafe mines. The editors overlooked the economic and legal penalties involved, said Lewis, and exaggerated the powers of the safety committees.

Unfortunately, Lewis missed the whole point. Whether his great intuitive insight into reality had begun to wane, or whether his goal to keep the mines in production or his intense dislike for the Taft-Hartley Act dulled his generalship, he overlooked the fact that it was basically a matter of contract. When the union had signed a contract with a no-strike clause and miners thereafter walked to the top over safety, they were in breach of the agreement, and the union could be sued. When a safety-committee man led his fellow workers out of the mine over obvious hazards, he could be discharged because his action was a breach of the agreement not to strike.

A few years later, Lewis did write into UMW contracts certain rights over the issue of safety. The Federal Mine Safety Code of 1953, for example, was made by agreement a part of the contract. This part of the document required operators to comply with the Safety Codes when federal inspectors found violations. But the inevitable loopholes crept in. If the company "felt" that compliance would cause irreparable damage, it could appeal to the Joint Industry Safety Committee made up of two men from management and two from the union. Unless the Committee backed up the safety regulations, the employer was relatively free to ignore the matter.

A safety committee at each mine was recognized by the contract. "In those special instances where the committee believes an immediate danger exists and the committee recommends that the management remove all mine workers from the unsafe area, the operator is required to follow the recommendation of the committee." This was a reasonably sound clause; if the safety committee acted arbitrarily and capriciously, its members could be removed by the employer.

The union could then contest any removal as improper. But the realities were that very little happened. Mine safety committees seldom took the step. The zeal for making mines safe ebbed away.

That Lewis could have done more is certain. Yet no one could doubt his desire to protect the miners, his compassion for their families, his mourning of their deaths. He cared deeply about mine safety; other goals diluted his concern.

Once the 1952 act was passed and signed by President Truman, even with its deficiencies, the United Mine Workers of America and its members did little more to improve safety conditions in the mines. The official newspaper, the *Journal,* continued the same news-awareness campaigns that it had always run. It offered safety instructions in many issues. It continued to print facts about hazardous conditions. It ran series of photographs of federal mine inspectors, with directions to the men to study the pictures so they would know their inspectors. Its safety campaigns were sound, repeated, relevant and serious, but in the end they had no greater force than other newspaper admonitions.

A second imposing weakness of the institution was perhaps even more incomprehensible than its failure to stand for stronger protection of the right to strike over safety conditions. Its safety department in its Washington headquarters consisted of but one man.

When human life was so important in any congregation of people, the fact that the union never had but one individual to act on this issue is startling inattention. The safety director could visit parts of the country and make speeches. He could occasionally talk with friendly legislators in Washington. He could help prepare the safety news that appeared in the *Journal.* He could talk with local mine committees to learn what hazards were threatening life on particular days.

But one person could hardly do a job that required a battalion. Unquestionably, there could have been full-time safety-staff people in each district headquarters. There could have been roving UMW inspectors, recruited from the ranks of working miners, to act as the union's own police force, making unannounced visits to coal mines. There could have been a dozen other energetic devices if the institution had devoted the interest to human safety that the issue demanded.

If the solution to unsafe mines was to shut them down, the Welfare and Retirement Fund would have suffered for lack of royalty payments. No production, no money to the Fund. Lewis's great concern over saving the industry in the 1950's was directed toward production and more production, as he constantly boasted of the capacity of the American mines to produce so many tons as compared with the lower figures of the far safer European mines.

In the last decade of his leadership, his strident attacks on the industry for placing production above human life ceased. Age or innate satisfaction or fatigue or management-directed views, or any number of other factors, may have prevented him from continuing to "raise up my voice in justice to the living and in justice to the memory of the dead, to ask a surcease to this bloodletting."

If the old lion was unable to do it, neither were the men whose lives were affected by the dangers. They had long ago yielded to the man in Washington their will to make decisions. The local committees were watched by UMW men in the district offices, all appointed by and responsible to Lewis. In addition, during the 1950's, Lewis told them repeatedly he would not tolerate wildcat strikes; he said the contracts must be honored; he threatened retaliation upon those miscreants who protested; he allowed company discipline to have its effects. Although Lewis viewed his position not as a safety issue but as a production factor, its effect was to almost totally destroy the will of men at the local mines to resist unsafe conditions.

During the short tenure of Thomas Kennedy as president after Lewis retired, and throughout the Boyle years until 1969, the union's efforts in the safety area were perfunctory. There were occasional appearances before Congressional committees to make requests for mild changes in the federal law. But on the mine fronts, where companies continued to ignore fundamentals of life protection, there was little effort outside of the regular accounts in the *Journal*.

It was in this milieu of softness and comfort that Tony Boyle made the remarks at Farmington in late 1968 that began to arouse the sleeping membership. "This happens to be in my judgment one of the better companies to work with as far as cooperation and safety are concerned," he said in defense of Consolidated No. 9 after the November blast that killed 78 men.

In all the years, there had never been a critical word raised about

the union's role until public gadfly Ralph Nader began to pay attention to mine safety. Nader sent a message to a West Virginia rally
in January, 1969, during the first round of the black-lung campaign.
His style of analytical attack touched upon each point of the union's
failures over the years.

Union contracts failed to provide for compensation for death and
injuries in the mines. There was no program of employer-paid insurance, as is so common in many industries. There was no more than
the royalty payments to the Welfare and Retirement Fund.

There had been no effort whatever to improve legislation at the
state levels, said Nader. The UMW no longer provided the customary testimony before legislative committees to support bills that
might have brought improvements, even if there was an overlap between federal and state laws. On the federal scene, the union had
made no progress at all since the 1952 law. There had been but one
revision of the federal Safety Code in over fifteen years. Nader also
spoke scornfully of the one-man Mine Safety Division in UMW headquarters. Then he criticized the 1968 union contract for its absence
of dust-prevention procedures, for lack of compensation when mines
were shut down for safety reasons, and for the absence of any requirement for simple toilet facilities for miners.

When the Year of Revolt came, in 1969, the fears and concerns
of the men about safety began to move them to a new kind of par-
ticipatory effort. The black-lung campaign in West Virginia, the
effort of Jock Yablonski to run for president of the union, and the
launching of court litigation against the institution were the major
efforts of a people beginning to stir to fill the vacuum of leadership
that had descended upon their union.

The Black Lung Association in West Virginia provided the central
thrust of the movement toward better safety and health. Its success
in persuading the West Virginia legislature to amend its workmen's-
compensation laws taught miners that people standing together could
get some things done. They began to form more Black Lung chapters
throughout the mountain regions. They started their own publication,
the *Black Lung Bulletin,* mailing it out from Charleston each month.
Roughly drawn cartoons from unlettered men began to appear,
carrying a message of sincerity and concern. Volunteers went out
to organize new chapters. New leaders began to emerge, men

who had never before stood up and spoken to their fellows. Black Lung leaders organized their own march on Washington to visit legislators and ask for improvement and enforcement of federal laws. Fun-raising devices, both new and old-fashioned, were utilized. In the *Bulletin* of May, 1971, there was this announcement:

> A Gospel Sing will be held at Breaks Interstate Park on Saturday May 29th. The singing sponsored by the Black Lung Association will begin at 12:00 noon, and will raise funds for our trip to Washington, June 6th. The following groups have agreed to participate: Clinch Valley Gospel Singers; the Cook Duet; Able's Valley Four; Buffalo Holiness Singers; Pineville Sacred Singers and Rev. Joe Freeman. All are urged to attend. Bring a box supper.

And they came in great numbers, to hear the old gospel favorites that were known in every mountain home, to eat fried chicken and potato salad, to talk with each other, to release badly needed dollars from their meager budgets to pay for the chartered buses. A new unity and a new brotherhood were beginning to grow among them.

They were no longer willing to ignore the welfare of their bodies and their persons down in coal mines. They were a new movement inside the old institution, seeking to revitalize it, seeking to make it responsive to the needs of the men who paid the bills. Coal dust and hazardous conditions were as much their enemy now as the employers.

But the most difficult force of all to combat was the echelon of officials of their own organization. From Tony Boyle as president down to appointed district officials and international union staff men, there was resistance to the new awareness. Boyle and his followers began the expected reaction of any power-holding group under attack—oppose, counter, fight back, seek to eliminate, destroy those who would threaten their own terms. They had all the weapons of incumbency, including the treasury and the cadre of salaried Hessians to do their bidding.

Thus, the kind of periodic civil war that besets any institution that falls into decay and despotism began to seize the United Mine Workers of America.

10. Aggrandizement, Plunder and Power

THE CORRUPTION OF THE KINGDOM

When John L. Lewis retired as president of the United Mine Workers in 1960, there was a quiet transition to the only logical successor. Thomas Kennedy had been the vice-president since the time of Philip Murray's expulsion, and he had served as secretary-treasurer before that. While Kennedy's consistent loyalty to Lewis was the cardinal factor in his survival and succession, he was not without ability. He was articulate, wise in the ways of the industry, skilled in negotiation. He possessed considerable stature in the union, and there was never any dispute about the fact that he was entitled to succeed Lewis.

Tom Kennedy was seventy-two and in ill health when he became president of the organization. The important office to be filled was the vice-presidency that he had vacated, for here was the waiting station for future union presidents. The executive board used its power of appointment, doing the will of Lewis, as usual, and accepted the old man's designation. William Anthony "Tony" Boyle, on the headquarters staff since 1947 as administrative assistant to Lewis, was the new vice-president and heir apparent. Boyle had been brought by Lewis from Montana and had made his mark, too, as a good and faithful servant.

Lewis went to the 1960 Cincinnati convention months after his official retirement, to accept the accolades of a lifetime. When he appeared on the rostrum the second day, coal miners stood and cheered for twenty minutes. He came to their testimonial banquet to rise and say, "I'm leaving you with the greatest union that ever existed—with a functioning organization, in the hands of officers who have a lifetime in the mining industry."

Kennedy's infirmities soon left much of the day-to-day operation of the union to Boyle. Kennedy died in early 1963, after three uneventful years as president, and Boyle at the age of fifty-eight took the office for which he had been apparently groomed. He carried with him the prestige of being the choice of Lewis. He knew all the functioning of the office from his experience around it. He knew its power and its perquisites.

He knew how John L. Lewis had dominated the organization; how the decisions of Lewis were never to be questioned; how virtually every officer and representative, except for the isolated few who were elected, owed his job to the president; how a membership was accustomed to adulation of its leader; how his mentor had adopted a concern for the economic welfare of the industry as a means of providing jobs and money for coal miners; how the office offered money and authority and a recognition that he had never before achieved.

The controls, the checks and balances, the restraints of rules and law that men have learned to place over their institutions were simply absent. There was a vacuum, a kind of carte blanche, a plum for the taking, a vast cornucopia for exploitation. The man with absolute authority had a treasury, an insulated fortress to occupy, an army of appointed legions responsible only to him, a hegemony that a medieval king could envy. Of course, there were forms of democracy in the constitution, and there was the law, but they were unused and meaningless.

It undoubtedly would have required a man of unusual integrity to eschew the temptation. Since John L. Lewis had built it and had obtained his satisfactions of soul from his own sense of personal worth and power, he had no need to exploit or plunder. But Tony Boyle was a far different human being, more mortal, more insecure, more frightened of the realities around him. He undertook to behave as the more cynical among us might expect the ordinary man to act in such a situation, to take what no one would resist. There was aggrandizement of self to assuage his insecurity. There was plunder with ease for his personal satisfaction. There was power to control and repel any who might lust for his throne. Tony Boyle established a course of conduct that almost any man of his caliber might have undertaken.

1·

Installing the portrait of the leader has become an accustomed American event. Corporate board rooms are adorned with paintings of grim-whiskered founders. Even appellate judges in older years sat for the government-paid artist. Pictures of presidents hang in every federal office building throughout the land. As quickly as Lyndon B. Johnson yielded the White House in early 1969 to Richard M. Nixon, the official pictures of the Democratic holder went down, and the new visage of the Republican successor went up. Labor leaders have adopted the style, too, as executive-board rooms in numerous union buildings carry either portraits or expensive enlarged photographs of the chief executive.

Great sums of miners' dues money were used to photograph Tony Boyle and other officers around him. These large new pictures were sent out to every UMW local union to be placed on the headquarters walls. One photographer, Chase Studios, Ltd., found a lucrative and repetitive business in turning out the likenesses of the new hierarchy. In 1963, the UMW paid Chase $2,346, but billings for 1964 rose to $26,477. This seemed a mere preparation for 1966, when the union paid Chase some $66,734. In 1968, Chase did almost as well, collecting $54,093 from the union. Another photographer, Charles J. Fox, shared in the proceeds, receiving $25,000 in the same period. Smaller payments to other photographers ran the total picture bill to nearly $200,000 of UMW money in six years solely for pictures of officers, primarily Tony Boyle. Smaller unions struggling for dollars to pay organizers and sustain strikers for better working conditions might readily feel envious at such sums of photography money. No working coal miner could ever doubt what Tony Boyle looked like; he could be refreshed by up-to-date new likenesses with regularity, as long as his dues could pay for the privilege.

Boyle's first convention as president came in 1964, before the referendum that was to elect the officeholder that fall. There was no visible opposition with any degree of strength, but printers and sign makers were kept busy with Boyle banners and placards to be carried on the convention floor. At appropriate times, delegates would wave their signs, heavily imprinted with the huge word, "Boyle," usually carrying the new president's picture as well. For those who did not have the opportunity to see the signs and the pictures at the convention, the *Mine Workers' Journal* was filled with scenes of the gathering, all prominently displaying the name and likeness of the president. Since rank-and-file delegates from the coal fields could hardly be expected to produce such a show, the planning, preparation and payment were all arranged by paid staff men, all appointees of the beneficiary of their adulation.

Since convention delegates are ordinarily leaders in the local ranks who can influence rank-and-file voters back home, they were worth special attention. Demonstrations for Boyle, stirred with music from bands transported to the scene, could make powerful impressions. The union brought four bands from various coal communities to Florida for the 1964 convention. The total bill for bands alone was slightly in excess of $300,000, with payments running from $70,000 to $82,000 for each group. In 1968, two bands went to the Denver convention, with almost $100,000 paid to each.

Each delegate in 1968 was presented with expensive "Boyle" gifts. An electric clock with the picture of Tony Boyle was handed to each person. A cigarette lighter was also given out, with the picture of Boyle drawn in the metal. There was a pen for each person, also, with the name of Tony Boyle. For clocks, lighters, and pens, some $87,000 in UMW dues money was paid out. It is not unusual for unions to provide small gifts for convention delegates; ordinarily, the union's insignia or emblem is on the present; what is unusual, in addition to the cost, is to display the picture and name of the union president so prominently as if it were a personal gift from him.

The most distressing display of Boyle-mania, however, came in the *United Mine Workers Journal*. This publication, issued twice a month, went to every member of the union. In the years when John L. Lewis was the patriarch, there were many stories and pictures of the union president, but seldom exaggerated in number and prominence beyond the role Lewis played. The diligent researcher can turn the pages of many back issues to find minor mention of Lewis in numerous *Journals*, even though the editor became his personal publicity agent. Stories and pictures of Boyle filled almost every issue. The early 1969 editions, months before the election campaign began, show almost nothing but Tony Boyle. The March 1,

1969, issue had Boyle's picture on the cover page, where Lewis had seldom appeared. The March 15 issue too had Boyle's picture on the first page, with a prominent story about him on the third page. Almost the entire issue was devoted to statements of Boyle on positions he had taken.

The next issue, April 1, had Boyle on the cover for the third successive time. The April 15 issue referred to Boyle, Vice-President George Titler and Secretary-Treasurer John Owens as the "Big Three." The May 1 edition had Boyle on the cover again, with his picture on page after page. In the May 15 edition there were, as well as the usual cover shot, seven pictures of Boyle at one rally. Even in the issue that was devoted to the death of Lewis, June 15, 1969, there was a prominent picture on the third page showing Lewis congratulating Boyle in 1960 when Boyle was named as vice-president.

The devotion to Boyle displayed by the *Journal* was attacked in the 1969 election campaign by rival candidate Jock Yablonski. Federal Judge John Pratt, in enjoining the newspaper from continuing as a campaign instrument for Boyle, made this finding of fact: "Examination of five recent editions of the *Journal* . . . includes 166 references to defendant Boyle, most of them in boldface type, as well as 16 pictures of defendant Boyle." The total number of references to rival Yablonski: none.

The obsequiousness to Boyle had perhaps reached even a different level in organization-style journalism the previous year after the 1968 national contract had been reached. A headline in the October 15, 1968, issue called it "The Boyle Wage Contract." The news story began with this line: "The President Boyle National Bituminous Coal Wage Agreement of 1968 . . ."

One wonders where lies self-respect in all this?

2·

There is often a revolving kind of self-escalation when unchecked officers begin to assert their authority over "their" organization. The self-homage leads toward the easy rationalization that one merits such acclaim. With such importance and such greatness, one should be able to provide for oneself from the treasury commensurate with what is "right." The Boyle regime had no difficulty at all in exploiting the monetary emoluments of its new power.

There were family members to be rewarded, perhaps not as ostentatiously as Bonaparte passed European crowns to his brothers and compatriots, but in the same anointed manner. Boyle's daughter, Antoinette, had become a lawyer back in Montana. It was easy enough to make her a staff attorney and allow her to keep her own private practice in the West. There were few miners in Montana and almost no union activity that would require a lawyer on the job. She would receive the same salary as the UMW's staff General Counsel in Washington, $40,000 per year. Edward L. Carey, the pugnacious, aggressive head of the legal department, at least worked very hard for his $40,000 salary. In reality, the $40,000 paid each year to Antoinette Boyle appeared more like a gift to Tony's daughter out of dues money of coal miners.

Brother R. J. Boyle was appointed as president of District 27 in Billings, Montana, but his salary was only $25,000 per year. District 27 covered Montana, Alaska, North and South Dakota, and part of northern Wyoming, not exactly active coal country. Dick Boyle was probably only slightly busier on UMW business than lawyer Antoinette.

The family of Secretary-Treasurer John Owens lived well off the union payroll, but at least put in working time to justify it. Son Willard was a lawyer, on the Washington staff at $40,000 per annum. Another son, R. C. Owens, became the appointed secretary-treasurer of District 6 at a salary of $25,000.

Bills for foreign travel began to accumulate. Tony Boyle went to Vienna in 1963 and to London in 1965. Brother Dick made the London trip also. These excursions cost the union more than $15,000. While many trade-union leaders make trips abroad to international conferences, most of them are in connection with official assignments through the AFL-CIO, to which the UMW does not belong. Costs and expenses are ordinarily within the reasonable range of the purposes of the trip. The UMW paid heavily for the Boyle trips—gross excesses characterized so much of what was done out of the Mine Workers treasury.

There were Cadillacs and hotel suites, too. Rooms were maintained for John Owens at the Sheraton-Carlton Hotel in Washington at an annual cost of nearly $11,000, year after year, from 1963 to more recent times. In a six-year period, almost $70,000 of union money went into the maintenance of Owens's suite at the Sheraton-Carlton. While able defenders can rationalize almost any expenditure, a justification of such largesse under any fair standard of spending organization money, be it of a labor union or even a business corporation, would indeed be difficult. This item, too, is one of the issues in the massive mismanagement suit filed by Jock Yablonski before his death.

The nepotism, the luxurious voyages, the limousines, and the good living at an expensive hotel were the small emoluments of the office. Perhaps even in an era of reasonably loose standards, not much would be made of them, and if there were not far more serious breaches, perhaps nothing at all. There was one massive raid on the treasury, however, that could be classified as pure plunder. It was a rich new private pension for Boyle and Owens. It was done in secret, without informing the membership, or even the executive board so beholden to Boyle. It was done with the stealth of the midnight jewel thief.

When pensions were originally provided for UMW officials, as they should be for all union employees, payments were made out of the general fund. In 1960, a trust fund was established—which was also a better way of doing business—which provided for full pay for life for those who had served ten years or more. Such generosity was in strong contrast to the small coal-miners' pensions, which were undergoing reductions in those years. After the Internal Revenue Service had disapproved certain parts of the 1960 pension program, Tony Boyle took action to amend the program to provide an elite plan for "Resident International Officers." The only persons who qualified were Boyle, John Owens, and the retired John L. Lewis. There is at this time no evidence that Lewis was involved in any way; he may not even have known about it; his lifetime pension was secure.

Boyle and Owens then transferred $650,000 out of the union's treasury into a special Agency Account to finance their own private pension plan. The executive board was not even told about it. The manner in which UMW records have been kept over the years made it easy for the transfer to go unnoticed. This too has now become a legal issue in the contest over the handling of the union's money.

3.

Enjoyment of the prerogatives could best be insured if the office-holder could maintain unquestioned control over the organization. Just as the rationalizations of "right" and "authority" justified the financial blessings, it was easy to argue that such enlightened leadership was entitled to be free of political insecurity in order that the organization could continue to have the benefits of such endowed capacities. In a world where dollars counted far more than ideals, goals or values, there was money, richly available, that could be used to keep the lower lieutenants actively enlisted in the campaigns of self-preservation. The checkbook was a handy substitute for the glowering command of John L. Lewis.

The district officers, representatives and organizers were appointed by Boyle and were thus subject to the most fundamental control. Generous distribution of money to local officials and those active in the affairs of the union at the lowest levels would sweeten their sense of harmony toward the top officers in Washington. The 1964 convention, the first major event after Boyle became president, was moved to Bal Harbour, Florida, far from the usual near-to-coal-fields location of Cincinnati, where miners from western Pennsylvania, West Virginia, Kentucky, Ohio, and even southern Illinois could conveniently come. The convention provided the opportunity to bestow Boyle's generosity upon rank-and-filers out of the UMW treasury in a manner to make them remember the financial rewards for a long time to come.

The key device was payment for service and expenses on a convention committee. President Boyle appointed the delegates who served on the committees. There was an Appeals and Grievances Committee, consisting of fifty-two men. Each was paid $1,457 for his "work" on this committee at the convention. Appeals and grievances? Not even one.

There was a Scale Committee, with fifty-five men receiving Boyle appointments. Each person drew $1,493 for his week's attendance. The committee took all scale resolutions and quickly referred them to the National Scale and Policy Committee, which met in contract years. One half hour would be a generous time allotment for the services rendered. The roll call went on and on. Some of the committees did perform minor functions, none of which seriously interfered with a delegate's freedom. The Rules and Order of Business Committee of forty-eight men, receiving their generous weekly allowance, adopted the same rules as prevailed in 1960 with one deletion and one minor change. The Committee on Officers' Reports, consisting of sixty-seven men drawing $1,454 each, spent only one evening in session. Even those who failed to show up were paid for their work.

The same situation occurred in 1968, when the next UMW convention assembled in Denver. The constitution, a document which most unions try to observe, covered travel pay by requiring the union to provide one fare for each local union with ten to five hundred members. As a further safeguard, it required delegates to "furnish receipts for fare paid." The constitution was ignored. Receipts were not required. Hundreds of unauthorized travel bills were paid to delegates in greater numbers than local union strength would allow, based upon degrees of loyalty to the Boyle administration. In addition, payments for travel were greatly in excess of the actual cost. Regular round-trip fare from Knoxville, Tennessee, the nearest airport for delegates from the District 19 area, to Denver, with a change of planes at Memphis, amounted to $180. Each traveler was awarded $494. From Pittsburgh, air fare was $166, yet, delegates from that section were given $350 each. The total excess payments amounted to a staggering sum of money handed out to men who came to cheer for Tony Boyle.

The constitution was a meaningless document in another important area of money. Article X, Section 1 provided for standards of payment for officers, executive-board members, tellers and auditors. Then, Section 2 stated: "The salaries of other employees shall be fixed by the International Executive Board." But salaries of other employees were fixed by Tony Boyle, as he decreed. The executive board, even though filled with his appointees, was never told, nor even given an opportunity to use its rubber stamp.

One of the major manipulative devices for not only stacking convention delegates, but maintaining additional political control was the use of the bogus local union. Again, the UMW constitution was forgotten and unenforced. It required a local union, to keep its active status, to have at least ten men working in or around a coal mine. When Secretary-Treasurer John Owens supplied a list of local unions to the Senate Labor subcommittee in 1970, his own records admitted that at least 566 local unions had fewer than ten active miners. These locals were allowed to send delegates to the conventions. If no one was available to go, and this was usually the case, a delegate from some other area could be supplied, like a purchased supernumerary. This too was constitutionally prohibited, but no one cared enough to raise the issue. The friendly outside chosen delegate could then be placed on a favored committee, receive his pay and expenses for such service, and cast his ballots as his preceptors decreed. This was part of a system loudly defended by Tony Boyle as "more democratic" than the United States Congress.

The defunct bogus locals were useful in many other ways. They could collect dues from old miners on pensions, a system that was found illegal in the 1971 ruling in the Welfare and Retirement Fund case. Any paper work that was required could be handled by an appointed staff man out of the district office. Some of them retained treasuries from the days when a busy mine kept members at work. Local 4917 in western Pennsylvania, for example, had $21,000 of idle money left over from previous days. Money in many of the ghost-town locals had accumulated in various amounts with no one to manage it but the staff men in the various district headquarters. But the locals continued to exist, not only for convention and financial purposes, but to play a substantial role in the 1969 international election where elderly miners, still buoyed with memories of John L. Lewis, could be shepherded in to vote the straight administration ticket.

Another important financial device to solidify headquarters control was the technique of "loans" to districts. Money could be poured into any area that needed strengthening, for whatever reason. John L. Lewis had started the practice of loaning money out to favored districts, and Boyle used this method repeatedly. In 1967, for example, District 19 in Middlesboro, always a source of strength for Boyle, was provided with $384,290. For District 6 in Ohio, where rebellious miners had begun to ask questions and press for change, only $5,000 could be loaned. District 30, adjoining District 19 in Kentucky, was handed $273,000. In 1968, District 19 received another $340,000 and District 30 was rewarded with $264,000. Total loans to all districts in each of those years exceeded $1.6 million.

Obtaining a loan from headquarters was apparently as easy as the asking, as long as friendly relations persisted. District officers would ask for money; the purpose was stated as "organization" or "administration" or "union expenses." That was all there was to it; no other explanation was placed on paper. Boyle would send a memorandum to Secretary-Treasurer John Owens to draw a check in the requested amount, payable to the district. Some checks were deposited in the district's own bank account. Others were cashed by district officials directly; the green silent money was carried out to the street for whatever disbursement was appropriate.

In the election year of 1969, loans were increased with particular emphasis on those districts where there was enemy strength. District 6, for example, received $115,000. District 19, which was totally in the Boyle camp, was reduced to $183,000. District 5, the home area of Jock Yablonski, whose headquarters was completely controlled by Boyle men, had its quota of money doubled.

Money can be manipulated when there are no records to show where it went. Almost every labor organization of which any knowledgeable student of the field is aware keeps accurate, detailed records of its receipts and expenditures. Indeed, federal law requires it, as well as making it compulsory to report to its membership. One international union even goes so far as to publish in quarterly printed reports an itemization of every single check drawn on its treasury, to whom paid, and for what purpose.

The United Mine Workers of America did not keep records as did other labor unions. Massive generalizations, such as "expenses," "organizing expense," "officers expense," with large sums listed thereafter, would reveal almost nothing to any interested person. A loan to a district could be funneled into checks for "organizing expense," converted to cash, and used for any purpose. As equally strange as the lack of proper record keeping, which was an open and obvious violation of federal law, is that no one objected or challenged this practice until 1970, when government investigators were taking hard looks at UMW conduct in many areas.

The government finally brought suit that year in the United States District Court in Washington merely to compel the organization to keep proper records in accordance with the requirements of law. After hearing testimony, Judge William B. Bryant made a series of devastating findings: the UMW had failed to keep proper records of loans to the districts, amounts repaid, if any, and arrangements for repayment (of which there were apparently none); the UMW had failed to keep proper records of money spent at the 1968 Denver convention, "a great portion of which was paid out in cash"; the UMW failed to keep records of "disbursements for organizing, mine safety work, lobbying, and other miscellaneous disbursements." He said further:

> Specifically, the evidence demonstrated that in many instances the defendant and its districts failed to maintain and keep supporting documents reflecting the date, purpose and specific amount of the disbursement, frequently in cash, and in many instances failed to obtain receipts from the ultimate recipients of funds disbursed by the defendant and its districts.

The payoff in cash, with no records, was the primary channel for any desired manipulation of money.

The court entered a 1971 decree compelling the union to keep proper records, follow the law, and conduct its affairs as did practically every other labor organization in the United States.

The government's investigation touched briefly on how money was used in the 1969 election campaign to defeat Jock Yablonski. In District 19, payments of $19,970 were made to twenty-three men and labeled "organizing expense." There was never a scrap of paper to justify the expenditure of one penny. There was likewise no evidence of any organizing efforts. In District 12 in Illinois, an executive-board member named Kenneth Ballard received a reimbursement and mileage for five days when he was in a hospital. In District 31, in West Virginia, seven checks totaling $9,700 were made payable to a bank, presented, and cashed, without any documentation whatever. In District 5, misuse of funds by Michael Budzanoski and John Seddon, the Boyle-loyalists there who fought Yablonski in his home territory, led to their criminal convictions. In District 2, in central Pennsylvania, seven men were added to the payroll as organizers after the Yablonski candidacy was declared; there was no organizing work going on, no vouchers or receipts or proof of any activity at all. The misuse of money, lack of proper records, and opportunities for abuse were apparent whenever a government agent inquired.

With such unrestrained use of union money, opponents could be seduced with jobs and lucrative opportunities. In 1966, a miner named Joe Ladesic easily secured enough nominations to run for secretary-treasurer of District 5 against John Seddon. District 5 was one of the few districts in the entire union where direct elections were held. Ladesic then declined the nomination, was added to the district payroll, and has happily carried out "special" assignments since that time. In 1969, in District 2, Owen Slagle had announced his support for the Yablonski candidacy. He was then appointed by Boyle as president of the district and promptly shifted his support. John Lease, another announced Yablonski supporter, was at the same time appointed as secretary-treasurer of the district at a substantial salary. In Ohio, William Howard had regularly criticized UMW officials for four years, had filed charges against them, and had worked closely with rebel forces. In 1969, he was appointed a "representative," was added to the payroll of District 6 and received $11,866 in payments for less than a year, ostensibly for exerting his influence as a newly converted Boyle partisan.

The free use of "control" money led easily into tactics of smashing whatever opposition attempted to appear. Boyle's first convention, in 1964, in Bal Harbour, was highlighted by his squad of supporters from District 19, where union money had so freely flowed, and where delegates were rewarded with payment for committee jobs. The men from District 19 wore white miner's helmets, with the words, "Tony Boyle, District 19," stenciled on them. Many of them were ushers, messengers or sergeants at arms. Early in the convention, there was a protest against voice votes, since wives, friends and other nondelegates helped fill the floor. This was shouted down, and Boyle commented, "I don't think we have to worry too much about votes."

A few rebellious miners tried to talk. Steve Kochis, who was preparing to run for president against Boyle that year, went to a microphone. He was pushed away by a man with a blackjack. John Stofea of New Eagle, Pennsylvania, went to a microphone to protest and was pummeled to the floor. White hats from District 19 surrounded him, punched him and took him from the hall. Three District 19 men stood by each microphone thereafter, ready to patrol any dissidence that might spring up.

The convention was "peaceful" thereafter, as was the 1968 Denver gathering. The faithful, fully rewarded, carefully screened supporters rose up with a resolution to elect Tony Boyle as president of their union for life. Encouraged by the free flow of Mine Worker money, they brought up another proposal to double his $50,000 annual salary. The king, confident of his security, with no rival even in his imagination, graciously declined both honors. The self-adulation, the available money to handle any "emergency," and the strength of all his chosen subordinates was apparently never to end.

4·

The cooperation with coal management that Boyle had observed during his years of work under John L. Lewis was an easy method of running the union's affairs, relatively free of strife and discord. Boyle proudly told a Senate subcommittee in 1969: "The UMWA will not abridge the rights of mine operators in running the mines. We follow the judgment of the coal operators, right or wrong."

Boyle continued Lewis's program of participating in the National Coal Policy Conference, where he met regularly with leaders among the mine operators. Each year the UMW paid $75,000 toward the expenses of this organization. Participation in it was ostensibly to aid miners through promotion of the industry, which would provide more jobs and benefits.

But the "Boyle" contract of 1968, despite the industry's prosperity, had no increase in the 40-cents-per-ton royalty payments to the Welfare and Retirement Fund, despite sixteen years of no change whatever. There was only a wage improvement. As critic Ralph Nader noted, "Union leaders could not even negotiate the placement of chemical toilets in the mines so that the men could relieve themselves in a decent and sanitary manner."

The "cooperation" theme helped solve another difficult problem for the organization down in District 19's bloody country of southeastern Kentucky and northern Tennessee. There was a better way to "organize" the small mines that had resisted the union scale for so long a time. Tony Boyle had been involved for several years in the troubles of that part of the union's territory; he would lend his personal attention to the problem. The solution was a signature combined with a wink.

Union organizers came in to have peaceful "facts of life" talks with small mineowners. "Sign the contract and pay what you can" was the approach in 1963 and 1964. Miners paid monthly dues of $5.25 to the union, the wage scale was ignored, and royalty payments were usually forgotten. One owner told a newspaper reporter that after a strike and after being told the realities, he signed his first contract. "I am paying maybe fifteen–sixteen dollars a day, and I am keeping two sets of books. I have had no labor trouble since." Many other owners followed the same practice.

Mine operators were eager to do their part in playing the game. Kentucky was a fertile state for dummy corporations. These paper enterprises could sign union contracts but never mine coal. Herman Dotson, a Pikeville attorney, told the *Wall Street Journal* in 1965 how it worked. "I have set up ten or fifteen little companies myself," he said. The dummy company would pay what it could in royalty payments and never worry too much if it fell behind. "If the Welfare Fund should ever seek recovery of unpaid debts there would be no immediate target for suit except a corporate shell or perhaps just a name," said Dotson. "If the pension fund should try to brush past the phantom signatory operator to get the real employer's assets, its lawyers would have to explain in court why a UMW official signed a contract with a coal company that never mined a ton."

In Pike County, Kentucky, the small operators banded together to form their own organization, known as Coal Associates. There were ambushes, rifle barrages and occasional dynamitings even in 1965 for those errant companies who did not go along. Coal Associates could help with union contracts, royalty payments and labor peace.

Tony Boyle was brought personally into the program when a Kentucky county prosecutor took the witness stand under oath in a trial before a National Labor Relations Board examiner. Thomas B. Ratliff, in addition to his job as attorney for the 35th Kentucky Judicial District, was also president of the Ratliff Elkhorn Coal Company. Boyle came personally to Pikeville to meet with him. Boyle offered him one million dollars from the National Bank of Washington to build a processing plant for his coal company, so testified Ratliff. Ratliff in return was to sign up all the recalcitrant operators in the area under the same helpful conditions.

"I told him I could not repay," said Ratliff. "I was told not to worry about that. It could be arranged also to send engineers from a Bluefield, West Virginia, construction company to draw up the plans."

Ratliff went on to testify how Carson Hibbetts, the appointed head of District 28, across the line in Virginia, came over to help negotiate with other operators the same kind of arrangement that was in effect with Coal Associates. "Hibbetts told me," said Ratliff, "that as to wages they would not interfere at all. It was a matter to be settled between the men and the individual coal operators."

This story, reported by only one publication in 1965, aroused no apparent interest about an organization that John L. Lewis had called the "greatest union in the world," an institution that was still existing, both from within and without, on the presumed glory that its great leader had brought it.

There was an immense deception about this, not only to the union members who had to struggle to fix their own wages with their own employers, but toward the larger operators as well. The union could proudly claim that it had solved the problem of the nonunion mines, that competitive costs had been equalized (when they were not), that royalty payments were being made to the Welfare and Retirement Fund, and that the standards set by the Bituminous Coal Operators Association and the UMW would be followed everywhere. The "sweeping-under" rug covered the entire kingdom.

On the national level, the union devoted its efforts in the years before 1970 to protecting the coal industry against the dreaded encroachment of atomic energy for generating electricity. Its lobbyists in Washington joined every effort of the operators to try to prevent the use of nuclear generation of electric power.

Atomic energy, like the oil burners of an earlier generation, was conceived as a monstrous threat to the coal industry. The UMW worked alongside the operators to use all its Congressional influence to stop any progress toward the use of atomic power by the electric utilities. The primary coal market was in jeopardy, was the theory. Less coal, less work for miners, was the justification.

The important question, however, was, as always, whether there was true fidelity to the membership. Leaving aside the buggy-whip argument of whether coal ought to be produced at all if atomic en-

ergy could more easily spin the electricity generators, and granting
the organization the advocate's right to fight for jobs for its members,
the issue becomes one of degree in asserting a position. Just as a few
portraits or a few trips or a few presents or a few self-praises might
be assimilated in the grist of an organization's over-all efforts, a help-
ing hand to the industry could be understood. It was the excess that
constituted the evil. Boyle and his cohorts turned all such endeavors
into absurdities. They moved from adversaries into wholesale
partners.

Thus, the harmonies of such arm-linking with industry necessarily
weakened the will to oppose when they met across the table at contract time. The daily concern with the welfare of the coal operators
made it easy not to press for mine-safety enforcement. The preoccu-
pation with fighting atomic energy on Capitol Hill left no time to effectively press for better statutory standards for protecting the lives
of coal miners. Once the theory of employer protection was fully accepted, its logical extension led to a conclusion that any bargaining
benefit might be harmful to the patron's welfare.

The concern for the problems of industry, the following of "the
judgment of the coal operators, right or wrong," was a concomitant
of a leadership ethic that had moved far from the feelings and needs
of men back in the collieries. It was entirely consistent with an attitude that the union's money was a plaything for power manipulation,
that its official journal was for the self-promotion of the men who
held the positions of authority, that its funds were for personal use
and enjoyment whenever the opportunity arose, and that its membership should be satisfied with the few additional dollars at contract
time that an inflationary economy would likely have brought them
even without representation at the bargaining table. Coal miners no
longer had an advocate.

5.

As in all history's repetitious stories of man's wrongdoing and re-
sultant movements against the evil, it was inevitable that men would
begin to question, to show concern, to oppose the excesses and the
outrages. It began, as such movements do, in scattered sporadic epi-

sodes and then entered a long period of sustained, slow acceleration. It culminated in the disastrous election of 1969, the murder of Jock Yablonski, and the use of the law to try to curb and reform the errants and the corrupters.

As early as 1963, miners began to agitate for improvements in their contracts. Boyle's first negotiation in 1964 with the industry produced the same $2-a-day wage increase that Lewis had obtained during his past three sessions. Boyle made his expected announcement: "the best contract ever negotiated by the United Mine Workers." It still had no paid holidays, a benefit enjoyed under almost every other union contract in the United States. Its seniority provisions, important to older miners, contained so many company-drawn exceptions that it could be used in almost any manner pleasing to the operators.

Wildcat strikes returned to the coal fields. Miners in Pennsylvania, West Virginia and Ohio simply stayed away from work for days, while they complained about their new agreement. The futility of their position was obvious enough to send them back after about a week, but the first evidence of discontent was present.

There were walkouts again in 1965, this time over safety conditions. At one time, 11,000 miners were out of the pits. Six miners had been fired in Moundsville, West Virginia, one of them Karl Kafton, who was later to play a role in the Yablonski campaign and the rebel movement. Miners accused the national leadership of a sellout; they organized a fund to fight for their jobs; a faction in Kentucky began to publish a monthly newsletter that attacked Boyle and his supporters.

Across the river to the west, in Ohio, in the mining town of Bellaire, several working miners met in 1964 in the home of Russell Whitlatch, who had been active in rebuilding the union in 1933 when the great Lewis drive began. Whitlatch, a short, round, gray-haired man, had been a delegate to many UMW conventions; he was one of the few with the courage to take the floor to question even the policies of John L. Lewis. He was respected as a wise counselor; he had once turned down a staff job he believed was offered only to silence him.

Karl Kafton, a large, fiery, determined, fast-talking miner, who has become one of the leaders in the rebel movement, when asked how it all began, pointed to Whitlatch and said, "It started in his living room."

Miners met there after working hours to talk about their union and what they could do to make it more responsive to the people who were its members. It was the smallest of beginnings, but both Kafton and Whitlatch were among those in 1969 who urged Jock Yablonski to run for president against Tony Boyle.

Kafton remembered something else that had come from the wisdom of miner Whitlatch, a ghoulish expression of his brand of intuitive insight into reality. At a September, 1971, rally of Miners for Democracy, in St. Clairsville, Ohio, Kafton was reminiscing about the Yablonski campaign that had ended so disastrously. "We were talking about Jock one day that summer," he remarked. "Russ Whitlatch suddenly turned to me and said, 'They will kill that man.'"

11. Reaction to Challenge

THE KILLING OF JOCK YABLONSKI

1·

It is almost axiomatic that those who run organizations with displays of dictatorial power are totally intolerant of criticism. The complainer must be crushed; his motives are base, low and vile; he is out to destroy the institution itself; he is an "outsider," a "foreign agent"; the leader who demolishes such opposition is truly serving his people. In his years of ascendancy, John L. Lewis used variations of these techniques with masterful skill, although in his late years, when he was able to assume the more Olympian role of senior statesman, he was more tolerant of occasional heretical mutterings. Tony Boyle was never able to achieve such status; any foe of his was akin to an enemy of mankind.

In his first election in 1964, Boyle had no reason to expect serious opposition. He had been in office only a short time; the image of John L. Lewis dominated the union, and he was the heir of Lewis. Yet the 1964 convention in Florida was little more than a massive campaign rally for Boyle, with its bands, banners, strong-arm men from District 19, and well-paid sycophants. His eventual opponent, Steve Kochis, was unknown, with no following, no money, no chance whatever.

Kochis could qualify for nomination because under the UMW constitution, the vote of only five local unions was needed to place his name on the ballot. Before his next election, Boyle had this rule changed to increase this number to fifty. The election itself was reasonably quiet, although there were charges in later years of ballot-box stuffing and use of union staff men as round-up men for votes for Boyle. To capitalize further on the Lewis name, Boyle picked one of John L.'s unsung brothers, Ray Lewis, to run for vice-president on his slate. Lewis was later forced to resign when he questioned some of Boyle's policies. The reported count in the January 15, 1965, *Journal* showed Boyle with 96,084 and Kochis with only 19,894. The breakdown of votes by local unions was never published.

Kochis, perhaps pleased that he had received nearly 20,000 votes without any visible campaign, continued to agitate as a lonely rebel voice. On Labor Day, 1967, he went to a miners' meeting in Wheeling, West Virginia, where Boyle was speaking, to advertise himself further. There were Boyle supporters present from District 19, far from the Wheeling area. Kochis was jumped and beaten by a group of men. He identified one of them as Silous Huddleston, who in 1970 was indicted for the Yablonski murder.

The public criticism of Boyle was first noticed after his remarks following the Farmington blast. Those who reacted keenly to that tragedy saw little similar concern from the Boyle leadership—only meaningless lip service. As the health-and-safety issue began to grow in West Virginia, those who were supporting it not only discovered a lack of real support from UMW staff men, but encountered downright hostility. The primary reason was undoubtedly the tender human ego; since the union was the only true spokesman for miners, anyone else was suspect and could not be credited; efforts of others could detract from the work of the staff men on the job, or worse yet, draw attention to their somnolent nonperformance.

Ralph Nader became interested in mine safety and was able to command attention. His letter to the miners who rallied in Charleston, West Virginia, on January 26, 1969, in their black-lung movement, was an outright attack on Boyle. "The record is overwhelming that Mr. Tony Boyle has neglected his responsibility to protect coal miners." After specifying the areas of Boyle's failure, Nader bluntly said: "You may conclude that he is no longer worthy of being your leader, that you need new leadership that will fight for your rights and not snuggle up close to the coal operators and forget about the men who are paying the dues and paying the price."

Congressman Ken Hechler of West Virginia, although previously friendly to the UMW leardership, had by then become equally disenchanted. He too attended the Charleston rally, as a friend of the miners who were his constituents. Waving a large slab of bologna in the air, he had the temerity to use it to illustrate the sincerity of the UMW's conduct on health and safety.

The *Journal,* with the consistency of a controlled organ to support those who commanded, soon attacked Nader and Hechler in a front-page editorial.

> The American labor movement has a shorter and more concise term for such troublemakers. We call them finks. A fink is a spy, a strikebreaker, an informer and a stool pigeon among other things. In our book persons who accuse the United Mine Workers and its dedicated International President W. A. Boyle of not doing their jobs in behalf of the health and safety of coal miners are finks.

When Boyle appeared before the Senate subcommittee on February 27, 1969, as a witness on the newly introduced mine-safety bill, he devoted as much of his time to denouncing his critics as to supporting the proposed legislation. He filled his remarks with characterizations of "overnight experts," "instant experts who rant and rave about the country," "modern-day prophets of doom," "ballyhooers," "cheap demogogues," "professional fakers."

Belligerence poured out of Boyle. Congressman Hechler, who had spoken only on behalf of coal miners, was now a pariah. In West Virginia, said Boyle, men who had suffered for twenty and thirty years with black lung had been agitated "by others, by outsiders, to speak, to lead a fight against this union, and lead a fight against anyone for their own political expediency."

"And we will correct that. Don't think we won't. We are not forgetting it overnight. And they won't say, like they did yesterday, that the baloney, and I am talking about one of your Congressmen who has never been in a coal mine, who said that, 'The baloney can go for Tony Boyle, up there.' " Boyle went on and on with his criticism of Hechler, and then said, "I will tell him when I meet up with him. Don't think I won't."

The chairman of the subcommittee, Senator Harrison Williams of New Jersey, who had listened patiently to Boyle's tirade, tried to shift the subject. Boyle ignored him and turned on the only other open critic of his conduct. "I will meet these other overnight experts too who never saw a coal mine, and know everything.

"I want to say this. He wanted to know who these experts are. These experts who are running around, who are not dry behind the ears yet, who know all the answers to automobiles, they know all the answers to the Food and Drug Administration bills. . . . I will tell him, too, when I see him, physically, mentally, in the alley, or anywhere he wants to see me."

George Titler, who had been named as vice-president when Boyle forced Ray Lewis to retire, shortly after the 1964 election, started his attacks on Hechler. He wrote his former ally on June 20, 1969. "I am getting tired of reading your lies in the newspapers. You are apparently some kin to Herr Goebbels, who believed that if a lie was told often enough people would eventually believe it.

"You and your two cronies, Drew Pearson and the instant expert, 'The Pied Piper of Lebanon' are what Harry Truman said about Drew Pearson, except you are also a prismatic liar." Ralph Nader had become the Pied Piper of Lebanon. Titler went on to write, "You and your cronies have been telling lies and half-truths continuously about the Welfare and Retirement Fund, about safety and about 'black lung,' in hopes of destroying the confidence of the coal miners in their officers. . . . In fact you are a 'monkey searching for a flea.' . . . You insult the intelligence of the miners with your distortions. You are a square peg in a round hole. I resent your trying to scab me out of my job."

The possessiveness about their jobs, their "ownership" of the union, their right as the only persons to act for coal miners was soon to face the only test that mattered—the election of 1969. After the four-year terms instituted by John L. Lewis, and after Boyle stood for his first election in 1964, he introduced another change in the UMW constitution. The terms of office were lengthened to five years, the maximum permitted under law. Early in 1969, there was some indication that Steve Kochis might try to run again. Another relatively unknown miner, Elijah Wolford, had said he would stand for election. Boyle's plans for another easy steamroller were altered when a formidable foe arose from his own ranks.

Joseph "Jock" Yablonski was one of the few elected officials of the union. He came from District 5 in the Pittsburgh area, one of the districts still possessing the right to vote for their officers. He was the district's member on the international executive board. He was well known in the UMW. He had even delivered the keynote speech at the 1968 Denver convention, proudly telling of the union's achievements, praising the leadership of Boyle. But he was also deeply aware of how the union was operated. His decision to break with the administration and stand for office has been told elsewhere in numerous reports. He had the support of Ralph Nader, Congressman Hechler and many of the dissident groups inside the union.

A lawyer came to his aid, too. Joseph L. Rauh, Jr., who had battled for many legal and political causes in Washington, who had won many significant cases in the United States Supreme Court, was widely known for his integrity, for his persistent aggressiveness in fighting for what he believed. To many lawyers who know his accomplishments, there is no more able legal-political lawyer in the United States than Rauh. When he signed on to represent Yablonski in the campaign, Rauh could surely never have imagined the amount of litigation that would require its way into the courts.

Yablonski had another legal ally, too, his son Chip. Young Joseph A. Yablonski was one of two lawyer sons of the Pennsylvania miner. He had learned about the union from his father and had been schooled in labor law as an attorney for the National Labor Relations Board in Washington. He left his job there, joined with Rauh, and began an investment in effort, time and learning that was to become the saddest and most significant in his life.

Yablonski, as a former supporter of Boyle, had been appointed to direct the union's lobbying organization in Washington, Labor's Non-Partisan League. After Yablonski announced his candidacy for president of the UMW on May 29, 1969, he was promptly fired from his job by Boyle. Rauh just as promptly filed suit to seek to enjoin the discharge on the grounds that it was an obvious reprisal for Yablonski's political activity in the union. As a part of the legal action, Boyle was summoned for a deposition, which is a full cross-examination under oath before trial by opposing lawyers in a case. This is a common legal tool, provided under law, which almost every trial lawyer uses in preparation for an eventual showdown in the courtroom.

Rauh began to question Boyle as to whether he had ever before discharged any person without at least one prior warning. This was an important issue in the case because Boyle's defense was based upon Yablonski's inefficiency or inability to do the job, even though he was considered to be one of the most able men in the entire UMW.

> Q. (By Rauh) How long ago was the last case where you re-moved somebody without a warning?
> A. I didn't remove anyone in the terms that you want to put it without a warning. Mr. Yablonski was on notice, plenty of notice. He gave his own warning on May 29.

This was apparent to Rauh. Yablonski had given his own warning by announcing his candidacy against Boyle, an act that could not be tolerated from anyone in the union hierarchy. Then Rauh persisted further.

> Q. I didn't understand that. What did you mean by that?
> A. You know what I mean by it, Mr. Rauh. You are not trying to be naïve with me as an attorney, are you? You sat at the press conference and guided him through the press conference as to what to say and what not to say and when to say it and when not to say it, at a closed press conference down at the Mayflower Hotel the day after he had been in my office for four hours. He was in my office on the 28th day of May, and on the 29th day of May you sat at a table with him advising him and counseling him for the press as to what to release and what not to release.
> And after release of, I don't know, 29 pages or whatever it was of a press release, Mr. Yablonski certainly knew then from that, with all of his experience that he claims he has in this organization, that he was in violation of the constitution.
> Q. What was the violation of the constitution on May 29?
> A. Because he wasn't carrying out the policies of the international organization or its convention.
> Q. In what way?
> A. By the statements that are in that 29 pages, or whatever it is, release that I presume you put together, by that statement which in itself—which speaks for itself—is in violation of the principles and policies enunciated by the organization down through the years since 1890.

Yablonski's offense, of course, had been to state his reasons why he was running for president of the union, and the program he offered. This, to Boyle, was the "violation of the constitution," the warning that Yablonski gave himself, the notice which was apparent that he would be fired immediately from his union job. The old adage was applicable again, he who tries to assassinate the emperor dare not miss.

2·

Yablonski's first task was that of being nominated. Under the UMW constitution, local unions would vote for nominees, and the member obtaining the highest vote at a union meeting was named as that body's choice. Under the constitutional change after Boyle's last election, a candidate needed the vote of fifty local unions to qualify for the election itself. Since there were more than twelve hundred such groups in the entire organization (the exact number always appears to be unknown, even to John Owens, the secretary-treasurer, who has charge of the records), this appeared relatively easy. Nomination by a great number would be an impressive showing of strength, helpful to any campaign.

The difficulty was that every local union was within a particular UMW district, and every district office was completely controlled by the UMWA president. Although the United States had filed suit as far back as 1964 to compel the union to return democratic autonomy to the districts, the case had slumbered quietly on the court docket in Washington. (A decision came in 1972, finding the ancient practice illegal.) The filing of the suit did not deter the union; in 1969, Boyle even took away the authority of one of the anthracite districts to elect its officers, installing his own men in a merger of idle territories. In the remaining districts where elections had been held—such as District 5, where Yablonski lived—the officeholders were dependent upon Boyle's support. The device of "loans" and the appointment of staff men to do the work that would bring the necessary support at voting time were enough to guarantee obedience.

The staff men were the contact with coal miners, visiting the pits and the membership. Their jobs required them to know when the meetings were held, where they were held, who was likely to come, the kind of business that would reach the local floor, and particularly, the trustworthiness of the men who held the local union offices, most of whom were elected in the active locals. They knew where Boyle was unpopular, where the rebels were, how the locals could be swayed. There was no one to oppose them, since Yablonski had no staff, little money, none of the knowledge of the daily functioning of the locals outside his own territory. Their job, like agents of any bureau, was to stop the nomination of Jock Yablonski.

Where they could control the local meetings, they exerted their force over the nominations. It could start by failing to send notice of nominations, even though the law required it, or by keeping them as secret as possible. A surprise nomination could be controlled, as John Aiello demonstrated in Local 7113 in West Virginia. He was an appointed staff man on the payroll in District 17, and was also financial secretary of Local 7113. At the union's regular meeting on Sunday, July 6, even before the nomination period had started, Aiello was given the chair to make a sudden announcement that nominations would be held. He then nominated Boyle. A surprised miner from the floor tried to nominate Yablonski, but Aiello ruled it out of order. Nominations were closed, he said, and that was the end of it in Local 7113.

The day before in Local 9603, in Ragland, West Virginia, one Rusty Runyon, who had just been added to the District 17 staff, successfully nominated Boyle when only a dozen of more than two hundred local union members were present.

The surprise nominations began to occur throughout the coal fields. In case after case, it was the staff men on the district payroll who came to conduct them. On July 16, when thirty members attended the meeting of Local 1687, William Reddington, executive-board member from District 25, was present. An effort to close nominations after Boyle's name was brought to the floor was stopped by Yablonski supporters in the audience. There was a demand for a secret ballot, as the law required. Reddington took over the meeting, said there would be a voice vote, and without counting the contrary shouts, announced that Boyle had won. This too occurred numerous times.

Two international staff men went to Girardville, Pennsylvania, on July 19 to control the meeting of Local 1577. During the afternoon, John Karlavage, a prominent Boyle staff campaigner, telephoned a man named Al Albert, who had spoken for Yablonski, and told him to stay away from the meeting scheduled at 6 P.M. William Rogers, who had come with Karlavage, offered Julius Savitsky five dollars to vote for Boyle, and then raised it to ten dollars when Savitsky refused. A group of Yablonski men outside moved into the hall when their watches read six o'clock. There was a clock on the wall inside which said 6:10 P.M. A small group had held the meeting, under the fast clock, had nominated Boyle, and had quickly declared the nominations closed.

Karlavage, in his home area of Shenandoah, Pennsylvania, had taken another staff man, Boley Overa, to break up a Yablonski rally on Sunday, June 29, as the campaign was getting started. Approximately fifty men were brought together, paid twenty dollars each for their work, and handed printed placards bearing the words, "Our UMWA team, President W. A. Boyle, Vice-President George Pitler" —who was so well known to them that his name was spelled incorrectly—"and Secretary-Treasurer John Owens." They were led down the street in unison toward the high-school auditorium, which had been reserved for a speech by Elmer Brown, who was running as Yablonski's vice-presidential candidate.

As the crowd marched into the auditorium, shouting for Boyle, Overa rushed to the stage, while Karlavage stood in the rear, motioning to those who had come to get out. When the noise and shouting continued, the Yablonski supporters had to adjourn the meeting.

The Shenandoah *Evening Herald,* the city's daily newspaper, expressed its editorial outrage. It captioned its comment, "A Disgraceful Performance." The editor was particularly astonished at the role of John Karlavage in the affair. He was an eminent citizen of the community. He was president of the Shenandoah Borough Council. He was president of the Locust Mountain Board of Trustees. He would never tolerate such tactics in his civic work; why did he lend himself to such measures in the union that he represented?

But John Karlavage, like other UMW staff men in other parts of the coal fields, who also may have been eminent citizens in their communities, was dealing with a threat to his livelihood. The strange comment of Titler in his letter to Hechler that the Congressman was trying to "scab him out of his job" had generated a similar reaction among all the men who depended upon Tony Boyle. But there was something more than loyalty to the purse. Karlavage had settled into the comfort of his work over the years; the staff men met together and drank together and loaded their favorites on the committees at convention time; they had become enmeshed into an administration as much as the political stalwart who defends his party's conduct while in office. The attacks of the public press, of the Naders and the Hechlers, and now the effort of Jock Yablonski to say that what all of them had done was wrong, touched deep reservoirs of human defensiveness.

It was easy enough to shower scorn on the little band of elderly miners and "malcontents" who wanted to listen to Elmer Brown on that Sunday afternoon in the Shenandoah High School auditorium. All the Yablonski people had become enemies, to be routed and trampled. It had become a kind of little war, and rules and laws and fair play no longer counted. The lexicon of intramural political combat took hold; the others were "bastards" and "sons of bitches" and "finks" and every other epithet that could be used. They were entitled to nothing; the more they were condemned, the more they deserved to be treated as outcasts and renegades; it became easy for men to begin to hate other men.

The conduct of John Karlavage was neither strange nor unusual, nor different from that of all the other conservators of a cause, whether they were company guards or state militia or Big Bill Hutchesons or coal operators. For him and other representatives who combined to try to maintain what had become their way of life, there was even an added reason to loathe Yablonski. He had been one of them; he had uttered all the familiar phrases of adulation; he had told them at Denver only the year before how great was their organization, how talented was their leader. He was a "traitor," a "backstabber," "holier than thou," more evil than Judas Iscariot.

Any tactic that could be invented was sure to be used; any sledge hammer of power that could be wielded was justifiable; any guile, any trickery, any distortion, yes, any lie, all could be rationalized to suppress and defeat those who were now enemies. If their meetings could not be prevented and if their votes had to be counted, there was no reason not to destroy their credentials and prevent them from forwarding nomination papers to Washington.

In District 28, in western Virginia, the acting president, Ray Thornbury, sent out a call for all local presidents and recording secretaries to come to headquarters. One of the staff men, Earl Brown, stood before them openly and, in his most blunt Virginia language, told them to hold back all Yablonski nomination forms until after August 9, the date when nominations closed. If the papers failed to arrive, the votes would never be counted. Then Brown gave each man the official "information" sheet on Yablonski, as scurrilous as Boyle's staff writers in Washington could concoct. Brown then gave each person a written directive, signed by Thornbury, to post the anti-Yablonski material on the bulletin board of each local union.

Ray Hutcheson, president of Local 1374 in Oakwood, Virginia, had spoken out for Yablonski. Thornbury and Brown talked to him repeatedly about the error of his ways. Then Thornbury told him to turn the nomination form over to him and he, Thornbury, "would take care of it." After Local 1374 voted to nominate Yablonski, Thornbury told Hutcheson and three other officers that they would go to Pittsburgh to District 5 headquarters to hear more of the "truth" about Yablonski. All costs of the two-day trip, including travel, food, hotel, time lost from work, would be paid out of the District 28 treasury.

This unconcealed excursion led to a federal indictment of Thornbury. He was charged in February, 1971, with converting union funds for personal political purposes, was tried and found guilty.

Two leading Boyle supporters in Yablonski's District 5 were also caught using union money to promote their leader's campaign. Michael Budzanoski, president of District 5, and John Seddon, secretary-treasurer, were indicted in 1970. At their trial in May, 1971, two District 5 board members testified that Budzanoski had received a "loan" of $10,000 from Boyle as early as February, 1969, before they knew Yablonski would run. He and Seddon ordered staff men to fill out false expense vouchers and pay the money back to the Boyle campaign fund. Both men admitted on the witness stand they had received the false vouchers, but came up with the excuse that the money was supposed to be used for a "fall organizing campaign." The jury wasted little time in coming in with a verdict of guilty against both of them.

There was another useful technique—to eliminate local unions wherever possible. All the hundreds of small, inactive local unions, the bogus locals, located throughout the UMW, had the right to vote to nominate a candidate. In District 5, where Yablonski could expect to get many nominating votes, Boyle by edict lifted the charters of all local unions with fewer than twenty members. In no other district was this done. In other areas, also where particular local unions showed enough Yablonski sentiment to be free of direction from staff men, the method could be used. Out in Minonk, Illinois, Local 247 had been kept in existence for eighteen years after the town's mine had closed, but when it was learned that the men there would vote for Yablonski, its charter was lifted.

The health-and-safety issue could be exploited, too. Boyle called for a rally on July 13, 1969, at Welch, West Virginia, at union expense. Chartered buses brought miners to the meeting to hear the three top officers. Signs and placards supporting Boyle were displayed on the buses. There was radio advertising for the rally, paid out of the UMW treasury. When the men assembled to hear Boyle talk about "health and safety," paid staff men fanned through the gathering to hand out literature and plug for their boss.

While the Welch rally was held, Yablonski scheduled meetings with miners in Matewan and Beckley, West Virginia, on the same day. UMW staff men came to his rallies with tape recorders and notebooks. They wrote down the names of those who came. The word was passed that the names would not be forgotten in district headquarters for all the days to come.

Yablonski himself was the victim of a widely publicized physical attack in Springfield, Ill., on June 28. As a meeting with miners was coming to a close in a hotel room, a man in the crowd rushed forward, hit Yablonski a severe blow, and knocked him unconscious. His doctors called it a karate chop on the back of his neck by an expert. The apologists' stories were that an angered miner went berserk because of Yablonski's criticisms and blindly lashed out at his jaw.

Yablonski's first effort to get his message to the voters led to the first of the many lawsuits that were eventually filed. He asked Boyle to have the union mail his campaign literature, as the express terms of Sec. 401(c) of the Landrum-Griffin Act provide. Boyle's house lawyer, Edward L. Carey, ruled that Yablonski was not a "bona fide" candidate, on the theory that since he had not yet been nominated, he was not entitled to protection of the law. Carey was far too able a lawyer not to know better; professional judgment is subject to the same distortions that convinced staff men that their conduct too was appropriate. A quick move by Attorney Rauh in the United States District Court in Washington brought the obvious ruling that the union must mail out Yablonski's material.

All the efforts to prevent Yablonski's nomination failed. By August 9, 1969, when the time expired, ninety-six local unions had voted him as their nominee. His name went on the UMW ballot for the referendum in December to oppose Tony Boyle for president of the organization.

3.

The tactics of the nomination period continued into the election campaign itself. Joe Rauh had written to Secretary of Labor George Schultz on July 9, 1969, again on July 18, and again on July 25, detailing specific violations of the law and asking the Secretary's intervention to stop Boyle's tactics at that early stage. Each request was turned down. Even though Yablonski had been nominated, Rauh wrote again on August 13, asking for some supervision of the upcoming election. "The successful struggle for the nomination will be rendered meaningless if these wholesale violations of law are allowed to continue," Rauh said. He also pointed out that "the immense long-run political advantages that they have acquired by their illegal activities . . . are affecting the outcome of the December 9, 1969 election." This plea too went unheeded.

Yablonski asked Boyle to agree to having the election run by either the Honest Ballot Association or the American Arbitration Association. This too was rejected.

Sheer circumstance intervened that summer to give Boyle his biggest campaign opportunity. All three trustees of the Welfare and Retirement Fund were involved. Aging Josephine Roche fell and broke her hip early in June. She spent the month in the hospital. Henry Schmidt, the employer trustee, had resigned, and a successor named George L. Judy, who proved to be weak and compliant, was named to replace him. Judy went to the Alexandria, Virginia, home of John L. Lewis on June 4 for a brief installation ceremony. Lewis, drifting into the immobility of his advanced years, had not left his house in months.

On June 11, 1969, John L. Lewis died.

As soon as the appropriate mourning period had passed, Boyle was named to succeed Lewis as chairman of the board of trustees of the Fund. Boyle called a meeting with Judy for June 24. Josephine Roche, the "neutral" member, and presumably the most important trustee, was not even notified. Boyle lied to Judy, as Judge Gerhard Gesell found, when he implied that he had Roche's vote. Judy, aware that his vote was meaningless if Roche supported Boyle, then agreed to Boyle's plan to raise the pension from $115 to $150 each month, the greatest increase in the history of the Fund. Boyle, who probably would never have obtained Roche's approval, took Judy's vote by falsehood to complete the maneuver that became the most important factor in his election campaign. While this was held to be shameless violation of the law, it could never be undone by the Yablonski forces.

There were some 292 local unions in the UMW made up entirely of pensioned coal miners. Their votes were tallied as 7,617 for Boyle and only 549 for Yablonski, a 93 percent bonanza for the man who engineered the pension increase. Throughout the union, there were an estimated 70,000 ballots cast by pensioned miners. If Boyle won 90 percent of them, as appeared realistic, this was solely the reason for his successful vote count of 35,000 more than Yablonski. A majority of the men who still worked in coal mines apparently voted for the challenger, despite all the power of the incumbent machine.

Loans in greater amounts went out to the districts. New men were added to the payroll, as "dust committeemen" and "organizers." One dust committeeman told an investigating Senate subcommittee that he "was never told what his duties were as a dust committeeman; he never entered any mines to check for dust conditions; he was instructed by the district president to distribute election materials for Boyle and to set up a Boyle campaign headquarters; he was also instructed to attend the meetings of three local unions and to have any discussion relating to Yablonski ruled out of order."

Boyle had his own private campaign fund, too. The staff men whose jobs depended upon his return were told to come forward. "Donations" of five hundred to one thousand dollars were expected from every one of them. Since Boyle had taken the illegal authority to raise their salaries, they could expect an increase in pay to adequately compensate them for their generosity. And in that way, too, the membership could have the further privilege of paying for the return of the leader they needed so much.

During the series of court actions that Yablonski brought during the campaign, he learned of plans for printing the election ballots. While there was a projected membership list of 193,000, the order went out to print 275,000 ballots, more than enough for any clandestine stuffing opportunities. More than 224,000 of them went in the mail before Lawyer Rauh could obtain a protective court order. During a hearing before Federal Judge George L. Hart, the judge said that officers of the UMW "pay attention to the Constitution when they want to and when they don't they don't."

Approximately a week before the balloting, Rauh appealed once again to Secretary of Labor Schultz for protection. He detailed another series of violations of the law. "That they intend to steal the election a week from tomorrow has been shown over and over again in these pages. We ask you to start an investigation at once so that evidence of these illegal actions will be obtained before the trail is cold . . ." He closed by expressing the hope, which was so forlorn, that action could be taken to "give the long-suffering miners their first fair election in fifty years." The answer he received was a "deeply concerned" letter from the Secretary on December 6, 1969, concluding "that the Department of Labor should not intervene in the election of officers at this time."

Boyle's team was fully prepared on election day. In western Virginia, in Local 7025, the president stood before the group before the balloting and said, "I don't want a single Yablonski vote in this local." Miners were led to tables, ballots were placed in front of them in view of local officers, and they were shown how to mark them for Boyle. Pensioned miners were brought to the polls in buses, handed sample ballots, and told how to vote. Yablonski observers were sometimes physically ejected and sometimes kept out of the polling places for hours. Tellers openly marked ballots for Boyle. Some ballot boxes were taken into back rooms in the custody of Boyle supporters. Hundreds of detailed violations were reported by the Yablonski observers who were able to function.

Down in District 19, where there was no Yablonski campaign, no poll watchers, no supporters, there was only an open field for the

Boyle forces. As early as 8 P.M. on election night, the returns from District 19 were in. They showed: Boyle, 3,725; Yablonski, 87.

The official count showed Boyle with 81,056, Yablonski with 45,872. District 6 in Ohio, District 17 in West Virginia's black-lung country, and District 25 in northeast Pennsylvania had voted majorities for Yablonski. In District 5, his home area, the Boyle concentration won by a small margin. There were heavy votes for Yablonski in the other West Virginia districts, but not enough. District 30 in Pikeville, Kentucky, next to District 19, brought in a 5,433-to-860 vote for Boyle. In faraway areas like Oklahoma, Kansas, Utah and Nova Scotia, where there was no Yablonski campaign at all, the results were almost as disastrous as on the hostile Kentucky ground. The organization's machine was just as unbeatable as it was in the days when the men under the control of John L. Lewis overwhelmed the idealistic effort of John Brophy.

But there was something different now. The years had brought an evolution in the law that affected labor unions, just as the law had expanded its protection in civil rights, race relations, courtroom procedures, and other rules that guided individual man. The knights of the kingdom seemed unaware; the law had meant little to them; they were accustomed to ignoring it.

Yablonski and his sons and lawyer Joe Rauh had compiled their roll call of the violations. Under the Landrum-Griffin Act, which had regulated union elections since 1959, they had first to complain to the UMW, delivering their appeal for electoral justice directly to Tony Boyle, who had supervised the transgressions. The next step was to the Secretary of Labor, who was the only party authorized to bring suit to set aside an election. After the killing of Yablonski and while public indignation was high, the Secretary filed his complaint in the United States District Court in Washington to try to invalidate Boyle's victory and ask for a new referendum.

The case came to trial in late 1971 before Judge William B. Bryant, who had heard an earlier proceeding on the UMW's failure to keep records required by law. Mike Trbovich, acting for the old Yablonski coalition, moved to intervene and participate. When this was rejected, lawyer Rauh, still winning case after case, went to the United States Supreme Court and triumphed again. He won the right to join in the trial; the lackluster government effort was now lighted with new determination.

The judgment was rendered on May 1, 1972. Violations of the law were "flagrant" and "gross" on point after point, said the judge. The *Mine Workers Journal* was a campaign tool for Boyle. Union funds were improperly spent in behalf of Boyle. Staff salaries were increased to allow the paid representatives to plow the money back into the campaign chest. The Miners' Committee for Boyle had received $142,710 in contributions from 229 persons, "virtually all of whom were on the union payroll in 1969," Judge Bryant found. There was a head tax; international executive board members and district officers "gave" $1,000; staff representatives paid $500. One of the latter, Charles Culp, testified at the trial that his district president bluntly told him to pay up or get off the payroll.

The hiding of the locations of the polls, the reprisal against Yablonski for running, the use of union money in district after district, the use of district offices as election headquarters for Boyle, the lack of a secret ballot, campaigning within the polling area, interference with Yablonski observers—all these were findings of the judge out of a massive panoply of wrongdoing.

A new election would be held. Next time, government agents would conduct the polling, administer all the details, and count the ballots. Under the law, Tony Boyle could stay in office until the new voting was completed and a government certification issued. The time of his last hurrah was approaching.

Jock Yablonski had started the process with his protest immediately after the 1969 results had been announced. He wrote his last union letter to the election officials of the UMW.

"Tellers, stand up before it's too late. I too once submitted to the discipline of Tony Boyle. But I shall die an honest man because I finally rejected that discipline."

4·

Silous Huddleston, the president of UMW Local 3228, was known as a tough man around LaFollette, Tennessee, where he had lived for many years. He had operated a café in the town after World War II, had robbed one of his own customers, and had drawn a three-year prison term for such man-bites-dog behavior. He worked in coal mines long enough to pick up symptoms of black lung and become a staunch supporter of the headquarters men in District 19. He went to the 1968 UMW convention in Denver as a delegate from Local 5885 across the nearby Kentucky line in Worley. It was an inactive, "pension" local, as was his own 3228. He too had one of the paid committee assignments.

Huddleston had a daughter, Annette, who appeared to have some of his callousness about life. She had gone off to Cleveland, Ohio, with children and her softer, more pliant second husband, Paul Gilly, who worked as a house painter and decorator with some small showing of talent. While Gilly had no record of criminal activity, he seemed thoroughly under the will of the firm views of Annette, who had become a tall, striking blonde since her departure from the mining and hill country.

Shortly after Jock Yablonski announced his candidacy for president of the United Mine Workers, it was decided to kill him, according to the later confession of Silous Huddleston. By July, Huddleston had talked with Annette and Paul Gilly, who was willing to carry out the deed. Gilly recruited two Cleveland hoodlums to help him, and the stalking of the victim began.

Paul Gilly went from Cleveland to LaFollette in October to meet with Huddleston and receive money and instructions. One of his recruits, Claude Vealey, was in an Ohio jail, and a part of the money Gilly received from Huddleston was used for bail money for Vealey. Along with James Phillips, who had agreed to help, Gilly and Vealey went to Washington, D.C., on October 23, 1969, then up to Scranton, Pennsylvania, and then to Clarksville, where Yablonski lived.

They drove around the Clarksville area on October 25 and then returned to Cleveland. On Friday, October 31, the three of them drove back to Clarksville. Early that evening, Gilly went into a bar, phoned Annette in Cleveland, and as soon as the call was completed, she called her father in LaFollette. After one half hour, Paul called Annette again to learn what Huddleston had said. The men returned to Cleveland that night.

On the next day, Saturday, Paul and Annette again called Huddleston in LaFollette to discuss their plans further. This required a personal meeting, as time was running out. On November 12, 1969, Paul and Annette Gilly took Vealey and Phillips with them to LaFollette and met with Silous Huddleston.

On November 20, 1969, when Yablonski was away campaigning,

Gilly, Vealey and Phillips went to Clarksville and entered his home to explore the house and its environs. When they returned to Cleveland, Phillips pulled out, having had enough of the stalking and planning. Apparently it was easy for Gilly to recruit a replacement who would participate in the murder for a few thousand dollars.

In late December, after the election, Gilly and Vealey went to Yablonski's home again, found him there, talked with him and departed. They were not emotionally ready to do the job. After they returned to Cleveland, there was another long-distance call to Silous Huddleston to report. Then, another trip to Clarksville on Christmas Day, a failure to act, and a return to Cleveland.

On December 30, 1969, with their new addition to the plot, young Aubran "Buddy" Martin, Gilly and Vealey returned to Pennsylvania to complete the task on which they had been working since July. The price for the job, to be split three ways, was $5,200, said Vealey. They arrived at night, slashed telephone wires, and entered the Yablonski home. Claude Vealey, who confessed to FBI agents shortly after his arrest in early 1970, told this version of the killings:

"I stood at Joseph Yablonski's bedroom door with the carbine; Paul Gilly was standing behind me. Buddy and I were to shoot simultaneously. Buddy opened the door to the bedroom and fired two shots into Margaret Yablonski, who was lying in bed.

"I aimed the carbine at the Yablonskis, who had awakened. Mrs. Yablonski laid in bed and was screaming and Mr. Yablonski was getting up. I tried to fire the carbine and it did not work. I thought the safety was on, pushed a button, but this was the magazine release and it fell to the floor.

"Paul Gilly took the weapon from me, picked up the clip from the floor, put it back in the weapon, fired one time at the Yablonskis, and tried to fire but the gun jammed. Buddy Martin came over, stepped just inside the door and fired four times, emptying his gun at the Yablonskis.

"After Buddy fired, the woman made no further sounds and I could hear Yablonski gurgling. I took the weapon from Buddy, the .38-caliber revolver, fully loaded it again, walked into the Yablonskis' bedroom and stood at the foot of the bed near the dresser and fired two shots at Joseph Yablonski.

"When I fired, Yablonski had fallen to a sitting position on the floor. Buddy came into the room and took some paper money, which was contained in a money clip, off the dresser and located at the foot of the bed. I later learned that there was $240 contained in the money clip, which we split three ways.

"I then walked into the daughter's room, saw that she was not moving in her bed, checked her dresser for any money and found none, and returned to where Buddy and Paul were. We went downstairs, put our shoes back on in the hallway, went out the same way we came in and returned to the car and drove out of Clarksville, Pa."

The bodies were found a few days later by Kenneth Yablonski. There were headlines, editorials, outrage, shock, grief. And there was fear too among the few who had backed Jock Yablonski and came to stand and weep in the snow at his funeral. There was a bitterness and a rage expressed by Mike Trbovich, who had his own wisdom about the *mores* of the men who ran his union. He muttered openly that the UMW had killed Yablonski.

A reporter covering the funeral asked him why he had said that.

"Why don't you ask Albert Pass?" Trbovich answered.

His retort in anger in January, 1970, meant almost nothing to the men who heard it. They did not know Albert Pass or who he was or where he worked or the strong hand he wielded in District 19 under Tony Boyle.

5·

The search began.

That the killers were clumsy amateurs was apparent from the clues left behind. Seasoned agents of the FBI made arrests within days after the funeral of Yablonski. Young James Phillips, who had dropped out, was quick to give a full story. Vealey and Martin and Paul Gilly were soon arrested and charged initially with a federal crime, that of interfering with the rights of a union member—by killing him.

The investigation, directed out of Cleveland because Gilly lived there, picked up evidence quickly, but lacked the connecting links to higher authority. Annette Gilly was soon charged, too. Elderly retired coal miners, coughing with the miseries of their underground labors, were subpoenaed from Tennessee and brought before the grand jury in Cleveland. Money had passed through many hands, but a hill-country code of silence was obeyed. Investigators were close to the proof they thought they needed, but there was never quite enough to break open the case.

Silous Huddleston was the fifth person to be indicted by the federal authorities, and he too was lodged in an Ohio jail. A grand jury was later convened in western Pennsylvania, and all five who had been arrested were indicted there for first-degree murder.

There were long legal delays as Pennsylvania prepared to put the conspirators on trial, one by one. The outrage had quieted, and there were long prison hours for the Gillys and Silous Huddleston. Vealey, who had talked to federal agents from the outset, was the first to come to court to enter his plea of guilty as charged and have his confession read in public.

A special prosecutor from Philadelphia, Richard Sprague, whose record of winning murder convictions established him as one of the country's most able criminal lawyers, was brought to small Washington County to try the accused killers. His zeal and professional skill overwhelmed the defense when Buddy Martin went to trial. The Gillys and Huddleston in their cells heard the news of the jury's verdict of guilty of murder in the first degree.

Paul Gilly was next. His lawyers had no defense. Sprague brought his witnesses to the stand to build another impregnable case. A new jury voted another first-degree conviction.

Annette Gilly had had enough. She wanted to preserve what might be left for her children. She was transported across the state to Philadelphia, accompanied by her lawyer, to tell Sprague about the involvement of men within the United Mine Workers of America.

Her plea of guilty was entered. Her signed statement was read in the same small Pennsylvania courthouse where her husband had been found guilty and sentenced to death. She told of how she worked with her father to carry out the planning of the crime. It was union-ordered and union-directed, she said. Much of it consisted of what she had been told; hearsay was not legal evidence in a courtroom. But she personally had gone with her father to the home of one UMW official where the crime had been discussed in her presence.

She named William J. Prater, one of the men on the District 19 staff. Prater was a seasoned veteran of the Middlesboro campaigns of the past and of the terrorism around Jellico, Tennessee. Prater was arrested on the old federal charge and brought to Pennsylvania. His murder indictment was to follow.

Sprague had been moving with the relentless pursuit of an Inspector Jouvert. The last of the original five, Silous Huddleston, was aging in disease and withering with the passage of time. An Eastern newspaper headline in April, 1972, foretold the next development in the story: "Huddleston, Near Death, Agrees to Yablonski Slaying Questioning."

The old man, too, succumbed to frustration and decay in his cell, forlorn and bereft of the aid that had been promised him. This was the story that Huddleston told in the course of his confession: He said he had been promised up to a million dollars if he got caught. "I haven't seen a nickel of it," his statement read. There was no longer the national unconcern with Mine Workers money; in underworld parlance, the "heat" was everywhere. The plotters were compelled to abandon Silous Huddleston and hope that his code of silence would go with him to his grave.

It started with Albert Pass, secretary-treasurer of District 19, Huddleston said. In the spring of 1969, before Yablonski announced his candidacy, Pass wanted to kill an unnamed man in Tenessee, who was an irritant to the authority of the district. Huddleston knew that his son-in-law Paul Gilly had been dealing in stolen guns in Cleveland. Paul could help import hired killers to do the job in Tennessee. William J. Prater, who had worked with Albert Pass through all the past bloody decades, was with Huddleston when Pass talked about the job he wanted done.

Yablonski announced his candidacy against Boyle in late May, 1969. A few days later, Prater called Huddleston. "Albert Pass wants to see us." They drove to Pass's home in Middlesboro. Pass came outside to their car in the driveway. The plans were changed. They could get the other man any time. He wanted them to kill Joseph Yablonski.

There were weeks of arrangements. The price was increased from the $5,000 on the head of the Tennessee man to $10,000 on Yablonski, because "he was very important." Prater told Huddleston he was raising the money. Paul Gilly brought two of the men from Ohio with him to Tennessee in mid-September to rob the home of a gun-collecting lawyer who represented the rival Southern Labor Union. After that crime, they met with Annette and Huddleston on top of a mountain near Jellico to discuss their further plans.

Huddleston reported it to Prater and they drove to Middlesboro to meet with Pass again. He gave Huddleston a back issue of the *Mine Workers Journal* that carried the picture of Jock Yablonski before he became the enemy. Pass drew an arrow pointing to the head of the man they wanted destroyed.

A few nights later, Bill Prater called Huddleston. The old man went to his home and met in the basement office where Prater conducted his UMW business. Prater handed a large brown envelope to Huddleston.

"There she is, ten thousand dollars," he said.

The two of them, using rags and wearing gloves, wiped both sides of the bills. Prater said that Albert wanted the money cleaned.

It was early October. Money was paid to Paul Gilly. The stalking of Yablonski began. There was frequent fumbling and discussions of ways to commit the crime, from the use of poison to the employment of the old faithful, dynamite. It had not been done in late November with the balloting only weeks away. Prater called Huddleston and told him Albert had called from Washington. He was on his way to Birmingham and would change planes at Knoxville. He wanted to see them at the airport.

Prater and Huddleston drove to the Knoxville airport.

The murder must be delayed for thirty days, or until after the election on December 9, 1969. When the expected "why" was asked, Pass said Yablonski wasn't going to win. It was apparent then; the power of the organization had the outcome thoroughly under control. "If Yablonski is killed now, people will think the union killed him to keep him from winning the election," Pass told them.

"Wait until after the election and we'll talk more about it," he said.

The election returns were as they had expected. A few days later, Prater came to Huddleston's home.

"Call your boys," he said. Albert had said the murder was on again. Move ahead with your plans.

And so it was done.

All of these charges were made in the confession of Silous Huddleston, read to the Court of Common Pleas of Washington County, Pennsylvania, by the FBI agent who received it. Huddleston changed his plea of not guilty to guilty of murder in the first degree.

Albert Pass was arrested the same day. He was not only the secretary-treasurer of District 19; he was a member of the executive board of the United Mine Workers of America. He had worked closely with Tony Boyle for many years. He was the highest-ranking international labor organization official ever to be indicted for a capital crime.

Did the complicity go even higher?

Sprague triumphantly proclaimed that it did, in a press conference the day after Huddleston's confession was enrolled in the court records. The hearsay and the speculation were still worthless in a court of law; the search was continuing.

The money was a major clue. Federal investigators came upon it early in 1970, just as Huddleston told them two years later. District 19 had a Research and Information Committee. "Loans" from Washington, as requested and as approved by Boyle, came directly into the district treasury under the authority of Albert Pass. The Committee paid money to old miner members for "organizing," even though there were no campaigns in Middlesboro country. Huddleston said the men had turned it over to Prater in cash. There was still the need for more evidence before new charges could be brought.

There was no longer any doubt: money from the dues of working coal miners had been paid to the killers of Jock Yablonski.

Whether or not Tony Boyle was involved is a matter of great personal concern to the Yablonski brothers and to the men who mine coal. It is a matter of great public concern to the nation.

But, no matter where the evidence leads or ends, or what happens to the man who was president of the institution in its days of corruption and dishonor, the killing of Jock Yablonski was almost an inevitable consequence of the code of behavior that had been adopted by the rulers of the kingdom.

There was an awareness of the bloodshed of the seasons. Their mightiest lord, John L. Lewis, had the iron command when murder and dynamite dominated the last years before his retirement. There was an ecclesiastical condonation of the use of the weapons of terror to eliminate those who were labeled the enemy. Even as innocents, there would have been a grisly parallel between the behavior of Lewis and Boyle and that of John D. Rockefeller, Jr., a half century earlier in Colorado. Rockefeller had allowed his managers to "handle the situation" before the massacre at Ludlow. Lewis and Boyle had long ago given the Kentucky-Tennessee men their licenses to handle their situations.

They were acclimated to murder and death. Talk in the villages of eastern Kentucky has always been of violence; it is their history, it is their ethic, it is their awareness. As it was a simple act to kill a difficult mineowner, so it was a simple act to kill a Jock Yablonski.

His heresy in running against Tony Boyle, their leader who reciprocated their protection, made him a candidate for destruction. It was ordered; it was planned; it was carried out in bloodshed and senseless slaughter.

It was the ultimate indiscretion; it exposed the oligarchy. It was the blood stain that could not be erased.

The downfall of the corrupters of the kingdom had begun.

12. What Might Be Done?

What might be done? . . .
If men were wise and loved each other.

1·

"The greatest union that had ever existed" was in a shambles. Its president had been convicted of a federal crime that, if not reversed on appeal, would disqualify him for union office. Three of its second-echelon officials had been convicted of federal crimes. Its defeated presidential candidate, his wife and his daughter had been brutally slain in their beds. The trustees of its renowned Welfare and Retirement Fund had been found guilty of forgetting its beneficiaries; they had breached their duty; they had used its money for improper purposes; there was a gross unfaithfulness. "The greatest union" was besieged with hostile lawsuits from its own members and from the federal government. It had been found guilty of unlawful cooperation with employers in a series of cases brought under the Sherman Anti-Trust Act, subjecting its treasury to the loss of millions of dollars.

Its men who worked underground were being killed and maimed in numbers comparable to those involved in tragedies of past bloody decades; it was charged with inaction, or worse, unconcern. Its members were in revolt; new converts to the rebel cause were joining as the months tolled on. The nation's information sources appeared to consider it as totally corrupt, just another disaster in the story of man's self-management.

There was a conclusion about it that was painful, semitragic, idol-shattering. The man whose memory they revered so much, their greatest leader, the titan who had won their greatest battles, had bequeathed them their disasters. The conduct and policies of John

Llewellyn Lewis had led directly to the miseries of the United Mine Workers of America in the decade of the 1970's. The organization of men that had so profoundly influenced their nation's domestic development had degenerated into an internal shame after their champion had departed.

His despotic control of the organization had emasculated decades of potential younger leadership. He had established an example of singular rule for his appointed successor to follow, and eventual revolt was the result. Tony Boyle assumed all the authority that was available for abuse, and he abused it. The word of Lewis had become law; the word of Boyle had become anathema. The majestic powers of Lewis were too ominous for ordinary men to emulate.

John L. Lewis had destroyed every element of democratic participation in the institution by the people who formed its membership. He had beguiled them in old conventions of the past when he told them it was "a question of whether you desire your organization to be the most effective instrumentality . . . or whether you prefer to sacrifice the efficiency of your organization for a little more academic freedom." The sacrifice was more than academic freedom; it was the soul of the organization.

When he had substituted the judgment of one man on using their millions instead of the collective wisdom of representative men, there was no one to resist. He could create corporations; he could buy a bank; he could loan their money to coal companies; he could waste it and lose it, and there was no one to try out in protest. He could manage the Fund that he had created; it would become his, not theirs; the law that required a tripartite governing of it would become meaningless, because he became all three parts. When he used its money to satisfy his own entrepreneurial urges, there was no other opinion that would be heard.

If John L. Lewis had lived, he would have been a personal defendant in the immense Welfare and Retirement Fund case in the District Court in Washington. As surely as the judgment was tolled, he would have been found personally liable, just as aged Josephine Roche was assessed with individual responsibility. He would have been ordered to pay out of his personal estate as much as was available back into the Fund itself. Only the expiration of his life spared him from that final judicial embarrassment.

His determination to save the coal industry had succeeded; it had neither saved nor brought meaningful joy to the laboring mountain souls who went underground to mine the grimy product. It had left them with their dangers, with continued explosions of gas, roof cave-ins, casualties of haulage, and more oppressively, the coal dust that had choked them to death. The political castration of the union's echelons of authority had wiped out the will to stand up for the miners, to try to save their bodies and their lungs, to resist the vora-cious drive for more and more production that Lewis himself had recognized was so vital to profits and prosperity for mineowners.

The violence he bequeathed to them left a bloody stain. It culmi-nated in the murder of the one man who had the courage to try to resist the political oligarchy. The killing occurred because it had be-come a pattern of permissible conduct in the operation of the organi-zation. The urges to beat and maim and dominate that reside in the male of our species were allowed to erupt in Kentucky and Tennes-see. His dominance authorized the thousands of dollars of loans that went directly to District 19 to pay for its bloody warfare; his prince-regent Boyle was a party to it along with him. His men used the bludgeon instead of the brief to carry out his will all the days of his command, from the fists that smashed Hapgood and Germer to the legions that fired upon hostile miners in Illinois to the convoys of terror that ravaged the roads and mines of Kentucky and Tennessee. To those who hope that somehow men may learn that killing our brothers is a rejection of humanity, the decades of violence are per-haps the most depressing chapter of all.

All of it was a part of the power of the man. His strength, his perspicacity, his will of unmalleable iron, his commanding presence, his articulation, his ability of leadership imbued him with the deter-mination to do what he wished; John L. Lewis was irresistible. Only Roosevelt and Hillman ever bested him; one had a far superior power of a nation at his command, the other the elusive glint of good fortune of a single moment. But even their triumphs were ephemeral.

His story was real-life proof of Lord Acton's great observation that "power corrupts, and absolute power corrupts absolutely."

The state of his union was what he had willed it.

2·

When governors of men or controllers of the destiny of people inflict wounds and injuries on their subjects, resistance becomes inevitable, as certain as any law of human conduct. It has occurred in every tribal story, every study of nations, every history of movements of people. The excesses of a British king aroused passions of leadership and resistance in American colonists. The indignity of human slavery produced cadres of concerned humanity that provided hidden escape stations for runaway slaves. The obscenities of Nazi occupations produced underground patriots willing to die for their own measure of self-respect. The heavyhandedness of the George Baers and countless thousands of other managers of production stimulated workingmen to band together and form labor unions.

There always seems to be a special breed among the resisters who yearn for a quality of justice. The oppressiveness of their rulers stirs them to action when their more complacent brothers silently endure. Experienced union organizers instinctively know this when they seek to win a new plant. They search for a particular kind of aware person, one who expresses the dissatisfaction of the shop over the grievances that go unredressed. These people of desire for betterment carry a spark inside them, almost like a boyish young Brophy of the past who spent his first nickels for pamphlets. Many of them stand above their peers in qualities of compassion and courage, of willingness to sacrifice, of concern for the welfare of their brothers. From their ranks emerge many of the contributors to man's progress. They produce their heroes and sustain their casualties, as John Brophy was a lesser casualty in his time and Jock Yablonski a greater casualty a generation later. Their ranks likewise contain the recurrent human complements of the Judas, the Brutus, the Benedict Arnold, the informer, the vacillators like those whose first support for Yablonski was quickly won away by temptations of Boyle dollars.

Coal miners too followed the patterns of history's warriors of opposition. Their resistance began with the uneasiness of a man like Russell Whitlatch, whose integrity was not for sale, with the aroused anger of a mercurial Karl Kafton, who protested the wrongs he saw about him, with the sad awareness of the disabled West Virginia miners that their wants could never be fulfilled. The Farmington explosion aroused all their realizations that their institution had lost its way. They put together a campaign. They found a leader from the ranks of the Boyle men, one who had shaggy eyebrows of his own, a roughhewn face, the rasping voice of a coal miner, an ability to express a concern for them. It was not within them to assail his motives, to interrogate his past, to question his conversion. It was enough that he had the courage to lead their resistance, to offer a different way of running their organization.

When Jock Yablonski was defeated and then murdered, the resistance movement inside the United Mine Workers of America almost came to an end. Some of its leaders who mourned at Yablonski's Pennsylvania graveside told lawyer Joe Rauh they could not go on. "Take my name off the lawsuit; I have a wife and children!" "I don't know what we can do now." Their talk was filled with fear; the tragedy obliterated their sensitivities. They needed a time of recuperation, of assessment of position.

One of the two surviving lawyer sons of Yablonski, the one they affectionately called "Chip," arose in sorrow and strength. He grieved for the father he had rejoined in the election campaign; his talks and his letters contained an expected note of bitterness. There were lines of sadness in his young face. His conversation would occasionally contain fleeting moments of silent meditation, their own unexpressed measurements of the burden he felt. Like an avenging son of legend, his work now was with coal miners who were willing to keep trying to reform the organization which had killed his father. He went before committees of the Congress to testify, he sent messages of progress and hope back to the coal fields, he had the strength to stand by his brother Kenneth when he stepped down from the witness stand in tears after he had told a Pennsylvania jury of finding the bullet-filled bodies of his father and the remarkable mother and sister who were also victimized.

But Chip Yablonski and the angered determination of the legal skill of Joe Rauh could not continue without leaders of men in the mining ranks. None of them had experienced the workings of command. None of them had been exposed to dealing with the higher lords of either the union or the companies. None of them had ever tested their capacity to stand in front of other men and persuade.

They had to be found and trained and allowed to emerge from the barest beginnings of their efforts in the 1969 election campaign.

There was Mike Trbovich, a frail, small man from western Pennsylvania, who began to give great amounts of his waking time when he was named president of the rebel group they called Miners for Democracy. Most of his productive years were behind him; his face too reflected the lines of toil and darkness and roughness that come with coal mining. There was short, stocky Louis Antal from the Pittsburgh fields, whose hoarseness bespoke decades of coal dust, looking even older than his fifty years. He would run for president of District 5 in 1970 against Boyle's man, Budzanoski, and tie the election into a new conflict of hope and desperation for all the contending forces.

It was Antal who expressed their aspirations of unionism. "We love our union," he said with evangelical fervor when he stood before the assembled reform groups in Ohio in late 1971. "We are miners inside the United Mine Workers of America. We want to make it a better union, not destroy it. Let us all never forget that as we work to get rid of the Tony Boyles and their crowd!" They cheered him for it; there was not one among them who doubted that their union was an absolute necessity for their welfare in the coal fields.

The Black Lung movement had produced its indigenous leaders, too. A quiet West Virginia miner named Arnold Miller emerged to work tirelessly for the benefit of the disabled and their women and their families. His face too carried the same vertical lines of travail that marked the countenances of his brothers. "I have black lung too," he said, almost apologetically, "but I didn't know it when I started all this." Like Trbovich and Antal, he had not been exposed to the polish of higher education or the opportunities for past union leadership, but his courage and willingness were so apparent that men readily followed his directions. There was an effusive black man named Robert Payne, whose outpouring of unlettered words expressed concerns of disabled miners, who would walk and picket and protest throughout the West Virginia mountains.

Miners for Democracy and the Black Lung Association and the widows' groups, led by some of the Farmington women whose husbands were still entombed, welded together and began to function almost like an opposition political party inside the United Mine Workers in the two years after the murder of Jock Yablonski. They gained steadily in strength. The Black Lung men went from coal town to coal town, forming new chapters. In March, 1971, more than three hundred miners came to a meeting in Harlan County to make the first important invasion of Boyle territory. Before that year was out, there was even one chapter inside District 19. They learned to use their combined efforts to protest the administration of the Health and Safety Act by the Social Security Administration. Other disabled miners in Kentucky with local lawyers to help them filed suit against the government to try to stop the sole reliance on X rays that were used to deny black-lung benefits. They published the *Black Lung Bulletin,* a monthly newsletter that went to their followers and supporters. It reported the developments of their struggles, it cried out for autonomy and democracy inside the union, it became their journal of resistance.

In District 12, in Illinois, the ancient Lewis battleground that had long ago succumbed to the will of the incumbent administration, men began to move away from the Boyle leadership toward the reform movement. Memories of their fathers were being resurrected. In Nova Scotia, where dissident forces had long been isolated, there were stirrings for new policies and new support for Miners for Democracy. The anthracite miners of northeast Pennsylvania, who had carried their district for Yablonski, increased their efforts. The Ohio rebels in District 6, who had also won their precincts for Yablonski, served as the host locals for most of the gatherings of the reform forces.

They came great distances in buses and cars to St. Clairsville, Ohio, in September, 1971, to hear Trbovich and Antal and Chip Yablonski report their progress. Women brought great pans of fried chicken and slices of ham and jars of baked beans and loaves of bread and urns of hot coffee to spread before the assembled miners.

The older men were still unwilling to utter a word against the memory of John L. Lewis. Few of them understood the legacies he had left, the methods he had bequeathed, the policies that had led to the disasters of their own days. Like the French soldier who revered the glories of Bonaparte, there was no need for them to inquire into the archives of the man who had once inspired them all. The considerable number of younger miners who joined with them had only the stories of their fathers to recall. Their bitterness was at Boyle; their belief was that he was responsible, in part or in whole, for the decay of the institution that still meant much to all of them.

The sacrifice of Jock Yablonski had begun to exert its influence upon them. His name had become an inspiration; martyrs of movements make their contributions from their graves.

There was also a foreboding influence upon Boyle and his supporters. The murder was a terrible stain; protests of their innocence could never quite remove the reality that Yablonski would not have been killed had he not opposed Boyle for president.

When news of the election-case ruling hit the mine fields in May, 1972, there was a relieved elation among all the dissident forces. What they had known from 1969 was now inscribed into finality after a court trial. There would be a new election in the United Mine Workers of America, free at last, like the words of the old spiritual hymn that moved civil-rights forces in the South in the early 1960's.

They came together under the banner of Miners for Democracy to hold their own convention, draft a platform, and nominate candidates for the offices of leadership in the union. They brought with them even another legal victory to add to their joys over the conviction of Boyle and the election ruling—the old trusteeship case that had wasted for so many years on the docket was also decided. The supervision and control over the district offices started by John L. Lewis by appointment of all the officers was declared illegal in all those districts that were before the court. Officers would now be elected, some of them for the first time in half a century.

They nominated soft-spoken Arnold Miller of the Black Lung Association as their candidate for president. Mike Trbovich was chosen to run for vice-president. Harry Patrick, one of the younger militant leaders, was picked to stand for secretary-treasurer. None of them had ever worked on a UMW payroll; they had acquired their status in leading rank-and-file miners in opposing the depradations of Tony Boyle, in battling for black-lung benefits, in trying to rebuild a new UMW.

Without awareness and even perhaps without intention, they had founded and built a new political party inside the institution. It was a rival force to the incumbent party. It had adopted a program and

chosen leaders, commandeered captains and lieutenants and sergeants and privates, raised money, and welded together a separate
and distinct political force that is necessary for any sustained opposition within any institution outside the formal structure of
government.

3·

After the national outrage over the murders, the Boyle party began
its own campaign of defensiveness, of effort for survival, of use of
the power and the money and the strength of incumbency. It was besieged on three fronts. There was a public opinion far more hostile
than even in the wartime strike periods of John L. Lewis. The
damning of Lewis then was tempered with grudging admiration; now
there was scorn and unmitigated distaste for the holders of the seat
of Lewis. It was like a public injunction, a massive restraint hanging
over them, a warning to proceed more carefully than in the past.
When John L. Lewis had annihilated the Save Our Union forces in
the 1920's and had used violence and miniature armies to combat
the rebellious Illinois miners in 1930, neither the law nor public
awareness interceded. Boyle had no such advantage.

The rebels on the second front were gaining in strength and power
month by month. The first counterattack by Boyle was to resurrect
the old cry of dual-unionism, as a device to combat their tormentors.
In September, 1970, Boyle and the executive board solemnly created
a commission to investigate dual-unionism in the United Mine Workers, like frightened committees of the Congress who make inquiries
into un-American activities. It was deputized to "investigate the fo-
menting, leading or encouraging of a dual union, or a dual movement
within the United Mine Workers of America." Are you now, or have
you ever been . . . ?

A few months later, another proclamation went out. The commission was given the authority to issue summonses to all members of the
union, like a court of law with its subpoena powers. "Any member
. . . summoned to appear . . . is required to so appear, and respond to all questions propounded by the members of such Commission. . . . The willful failure . . . to appear . . . and respond as
aforesaid, shall be an offense against the United Mine Workers of

America, subject to disciplinary action by the International Executive Board." The methods of bodies of government continue to have their similarities, as those who exercise control repeat the maneuvers that help maintain it.

This produced yet another court action, *Trbovich v. Boyle,* United States District Court for the District of Columbia, filed to seek to enjoin the summoning of leaders of Miners for Democracy to Washington to appear before the commission. The law provided more relief against private reprisals than it did against the depredations of a committee of the Congress. UMW counsel wisely agreed in court to postpone the proceedings of the commission, allowing the lawsuit itself to lie fallow to await some further movement at some more propitious time.

Their third area of involvement was with the toils of the law, which gave protection to the rebels and imposed its judgments on their past deeds. It absorbed the leadership. One irreverent staff man was even able to insert rare humor, when he quietly commented on the roses that daily adorned the lapel of Tony Boyle. "The roses generally wilt by about noon," he said, "there's not much sunlight in a courtroom."

The legal decisions of 1972 were devastating. All the strong defense in the election case, the corps of skilled lawyers, the explanation for every act could not counter the overwhelming evidence of the repeated violations of the law. Boyle would have to run again without the union treasury to draw upon, with his field lieutenants facing their own survival-elections in the districts, with a corps of government agents to insist upon honest conduct of an honest election.

Boyle would have to run carrying the burden of a federal conviction that could disqualify him even if he could somehow resurrect enough memories of the ways of Lewis to hold a majority of the votes. A Washington jury had found him guilty of every one of the thirteen counts on which he had been charged. His only hope was an appeal that might delay the eventual judgment for another two years.

The trial evidence was difficult to overcome. Robert Howe, who had directed the UMW political efforts for many years, was a major witness against Boyle. Under subpoena, he testified that he had personally warned Boyle about the illegality of using union money directly from the treasury for political contributions. There was a 1966 memorandum on this point from Howe to Boyle in the union's files; it became a critical exhibit at the trial. Howe's entreaties were ignored; none of the statutes meant much to Tony Boyle in his days of dominance when there was no one to question his word or challenge his will.

The indictment of Albert Pass followed soon after the conviction of Boyle and the election-case ruling. Tony Boyle was now aging and forlorn. He had changed from a youthful-appearing sixty-five years in 1970 to an old man of sixty-seven in 1972. He was in virtual hiding in headquarters in Washington, depending upon Suzanne Richards, his assistant, to run the daily affairs of the union and upon Edward L. Carey, his general counsel, to guide him through the almost impenetrable legal involvements.

There was no certainty that Tony Boyle could withstand an open campaign for the job that had been handed him by John L. Lewis. There was even talk in mid-1972 that lawyer Carey would run, claiming that his membership in the headquarters local union that was maintained for UMW employees made him eligible for office.

But ouster of the old regime was far from a certainty. Even with the restraints of the law, there was a body of experience and ability and loyalty to draw upon. Staff men had to save Boyle or the Boyle party to maintain their own jobs. They had the paid time to campaign, to visit all the mines, to draw upon every favor and every dollar that had found its way to the mountain precincts in the past. They had the rostrums and the abilities of skilled campaigners to turn facts upside down, to make black appear as white, to plumb the misjudgments that lie within any electorate.

There was the inherent weakness of the other party, the MFD, in that its candidates had never dealt with the moguls of industry, had never faced the responsibilities of bargaining for the welfare of coal miners over the nation, had never endured the demands of a serious campaign for office.

But even a de facto survival by the old regime, if it should somehow save a majority of the votes, cannot maintain its prerogatives of the past. Rules of law have finally made their impression. Proper records and proper accounts must now be kept. Officers in the districts will have to stand for election, rather than receive their commissions from the king. Coal miners have demanded the status of free men inside their institution and are now able, at least in the decade ahead, to retain it.

Tony Boyle stands as a tragic figure, convicted, scorned, debilitated by exposure. He learned about unrestrained power from a rare teacher, and in trying to emulate him, he opened the records of the past to an awareness of the inherent weakness of yielding all to great strength. He faces the possibility of prison, large fines and the discomfort of his last years of life in an unwanted isolation. Yet it was his destiny that he charted, and like most of us who cannot escape the episodes of our past, it is his to endure.

4·

The three forces of law, internal opposition and public opinion that assailed Tony Boyle and the UMW were weapons of correction. They came into play only after the decay of the institution had become a scandal. They sought to repair, to purge, to bring an end to the corruption of the past.

The law had been the primary corrective force. It had restructured the Welfare and Retirement Fund. It had removed the "neutral" trustee, Josephine Roche, who was rarely neutral. Her judgment usually deferred to that of John L. Lewis to form as he wished. Yet there was always a cloak of legality about it until litigation ended it, after a trial based upon evidence. She was no better able to resist John L. Lewis than the thousands of cheering miners who followed his will in convention after convention.

The Yablonski campaign could never have been maintained without lawyers and without court rulings. He and his successors had been forced to sue to preserve the most elementary of campaign decencies, which were denied John Brophy in his time. The autocratic control of the organization over its district officers, instituted by Lewis, could not be changed until 1972, when judges ruled in accordance with law. The nepotism, the waste of great sums on maintenance of power, the luxurious living, the self-aggrandizement could perhaps be ended by political change within the institution, but political change could never be possible without legal protection to enable dissenters to survive.

The law could also exert some force in the future to restrain a mammoth like Lewis or a charlatan like Boyle. But the law is hardly the panacea or the final wisdom room of Solomon or a dispenser of benign providence for all those who petition for its intervention. It has its human deficiencies—like the hesitancy of a Secretary of Labor to intervene in the 1969 election, when all reasonable evidence was that a massive tragedy was approaching; and like the bumbling of government lawyers in many of the Mine Workers cases; and like the absence of perception that dominates the conduct of so many judges who are unable to expand their awareness beyond what is obviously apparent. The penetration of a Judge Gesell is a rare occasion, just as a giant like Lewis is so unusual in human history.

The law is not always just or wise or comprehensible or immune from the frailties of its makers.

Its greatest protective failure is shown by the fact that the gross malfeasance inside the UMW occurred after the passage of a law that was supposedly designed to prevent it. The Landrum-Griffin Act was adopted in 1959 to set up a new code of federal behavior and fidelity for labor organizations and their officers. While it contained its own loopholes and deficiencies and irrationalities, it attempted to legislate a body of rules for unions not applicable to any other segment of society, as if there were some divine segregation of saints and sinners. Yet after it was enacted, Tony Boyle and his compatriots indulged in their plunder and their corruption as if its statutory presence were totally unknown.

For the forms of law to work, either in protection or correction, there must be a force of people behind them. They must gather the resources to use the courts and they, like aroused consumers, must be able to persuade that their cause is just.

The Miners for Democracy and the black-lung victims and the widows of old miners were able to put together all the corrective forces in the three years after the murder of Jock Yablonski to reform the institution. Their basic success has been assured, whether or not Arnold Miller, whose soul and personality are in polar contrast to John L. Lewis, is able to become the president.

The more serious inquiry is whether the successors to the corrupters will not in time repeat the mistakes of the old masters of the past. They face such dangers, not because they are evil men, but because the stresses of human personality, the complexities of organizational life, and the capacity of man to repeat his grossest errors are formidable realities.

One might ask, where is the future soul of the United Mine Workers of America? Where is its insulation from a depressing repetition of its misdeeds of the past? Would its leaders of the immediate future have successors in turn who would succumb to some charismatic genius of the future who would assume all authority and would generate another round of unfaithful malfeasance? Would it produce, as in so many political movements of the past, another affirmation of the insight that many of those who set out nobly to be their brother's keeper wind up by becoming his jailer?

5.

What, then, might be done?

The late philosopher and Socratic scholar Scott Buchanan often used to say that any question that could be answered was not worth asking. How do people structure their institutions to harness the grand ability of a Lewis without suffering the disadvantages of his darker side? How may they extract the finer qualities of both a Lewis and a Brophy without running afoul of the overpowering strength of one and the underpowering concepts of the other? How can outcomes be produced that will have in their wakes an extension of justice rather than adventures into corruption? Or, is the quest, never solved by the thinkers of the centuries, too demanding for mortal searchers—so human that it is inhuman?

One may only work at it.

Institutions of men have not yet learned an adequate lesson from the example of the political process of the nation. Labor unions, corporations, universities, churches, all of the quasi-public bodies, function primarily the same—without any countervailing strength to offset the leadership structure. The argument against it is all familiar: Unions are armies of dedication to a single interest, that of the workingman, needing, indeed requiring, the "efficiency" of a Lewis; corporations are in business to make a profit and ought not be deterred by luxuries of internal freedom; universities and churches too have a singularity of purpose that best functions with singularity of leadership. A case can be made that the system, for the most part, has functioned reasonably well. Deeper critics of the mammoth ills of our decades can make an impressive argument to the contrary.

Within these institutions of men, as in political government, there are constant, never-ending rivalries of opposing forces and contrary concepts. We find them in all the stories of human endeavor that fascinate us. The desire for colonial freedom of Adams and Paine and Jefferson was opposed by determined Tory supporters of the Crown, of the ties to mother England. The intensity of feeling over human slavery by both its defenders and its opponents rent the soul of a nation. The historian Henry Steele Commager has written of the ceaseless struggle between the quest for liberty and the desire for order. The pressing controls of management were opposed by workingmen, resulting in bloodshed, conflict and lawmaking that have occupied the nation's interest for a half century. Every political movement, every proposal for legislation, every plan of human action seems destined to find an opponent, some cache of contrariness that differs, that argues against, that desires to do otherwise. Its existence is the philosophical underpinning of our adversary system of law, a method whereby contending forces are provided an arena and a contest through advocacy for trying to produce a just result.

The draftsmen of our political constitution, and Madison primarily, understood this theory of opposing factions. They put together branches of government by function, and gave each of them powers and authorities and provided certain inhibitions. Madison's insight in the 51st *Federalist*—"If men were angels, no government would be necessary"—has been a guiding principle for mankind. The solution was to divide the king into pieces of wisdom, with one congregation able to check and balance against the other. Its success has been the stability of the republic.

The theory of opposing forces has produced political parties in political states. One association of men has formed to react against the other. These groups too struggle with human deficiencies of their own internal oppositions.

Outside of government, the fight for power within organizations of men almost always emerges out of a force that begins to resemble a political party, whether or not it intends that result. The process of the growth of opposition inside the UMW is a classic illustration.

When a governing authority inside any institution subdues its foes, a new cycle of difficulty often begins. The greatest peril comes from an inadequacy of restraint of individual power, as the histories of John L. Lewis and the United Mine Workers of America so incisively illustrate. The opposing difficulty, of course, is that small minds, restricted vision and rigid rules can deter man's creativity, hamper his efforts to expand, and pull him back into unimaginative bureaucracy. One may never be sure which of the two poles is the more harmful; the evidence seems to indicate that great power can lead to the greater abuses, can be more difficult to overcome, and can inflict the greater casualties. When thoughtful men break through the mediocrity barriers, as they inevitably do, far less devastation appears in their wakes.

When any strong man appears, unilateral strength is able to destroy the opposing-force concept in any organization without built-in safety devices. John L. Lewis was able to do it better than most, because he was more able than almost any of the dominant figures. It will occur again and again, generating eventual malfeasance, and in turn, unleashing new movements of resistance which may likely result in yet another depressing cycle with its wrongs and its casualties.

Institutions have made their efforts to cope with this ageless phenomenon. The wisdom of the ancient Church invented the concept of "devil's advocate." Armies throughout history have found it necessary to designate an inspector general. Our age has discovered the ombudsman. Corporations and universities thus far have been more responsive to its possibilities than have labor organizations, primarily because the demands upon them have been greater. The difficulty with all these devices is to endow the inspector general, the ombudsman, and the devil's advocate with enough freedom to allow inquiries into what may appear to be ultimate truth. No one of them has ever managed to cure the institutional ills of mankind. Yet they still have their uses and their potentialities.

It seems more important to win an argument.

In all cases, the constituency must be persuaded that its welfare lies with reason, not with power, that it was Daniel Weaver who was right, not John L. Lewis. This, of course, becomes one of nature's most difficult assignments, when Carlyle's hero appears and assumes overpowering authority. The skilled advocate's only chance of success is to join issue with each thrust of the strong leader's appeal, to deal directly with the terms that have meaning to the men who are swayed.

Red-mustached old John Hindmarsh, the perennial questioning delegate from District 12's Illinois rebels, lost all his arguments to John L. Lewis at UMW conventions when he yielded to the president on the issue of efficiency. When there is only theoretical democracy to offer in its place, "efficiency" will win every time with practical men. Someone had to show the assembled coal miners that true efficiency itself would suffer when they yielded all their authority to one man, even so gifted a creature as John L. Lewis. One might even say, especially so, when the leader is so supremely talented. Most men, bereft of projected vision, are seldom able to perceive this point in times of fear or in times of euphoria. These are the precise times when its qualities are most needed.

Therefore, it seems, in the tradition of a John Stuart Mill arguing the positive virtues of liberty, each quasi-public institution of man must have its advocates of efficiency through exercise of the will of many rather than the will of one. Until that case is made, demonstrably and effectively, over and over again, neither the law nor the ombudsman nor the inspector general can wholly save an organization from its own inner debilities. One of its most effective illustrations is the story of the great union of coal miners, founded in such poetic hope, with such noble aspirations, led so brilliantly by one of society's most gifted men, unable to prevent the great wrongs imposed upon it by the grant of total authority, and finally, drifting into indifference, abuse, corruption, and bloodshed, to the enormous harm of all its constituency.

In all of these, in every institution, in every government even, the contest continues between expediency and principle, as contending forces rise and fall like tides of the sea. Perhaps, like the questions that can never be answered, neither one nor the other will ever totally triumph. Meanwhile, the dreams of a Daniel Weaver continue to inspire men, just as recurrences of intuitive insights into reality fuel their accomplishments. Even as the universal lessons of the United Mine Workers of America are left with us, we know that men are not yet wise enough and not yet loving enough of their brothers, as the patterns of their histories go on and on and on.

Bibliography and Source Material

CHAPTER I

Evans, Chris, *History of the United Mine Workers of America.* Indianapolis: UMW, 1918.

Gluck, Elsie, *John Mitchell.* New York, 1929.

McDonald, David J., and Lynch, Edward, *Coal and Unionism.* Lynald Books, 1939.

Stone, Irving, *Clarence Darrow for the Defense.* Garden City, N.Y., 1943.

Storr, Anthony, *Human Aggression.* New York: Bantam Books, 1968.

Taft, Philip, *Organized Labor in American History.* New York: Harper & Row, 1964.

Warne, F. J., *Coal Mine Workers.* New York: Longman's, 1905.

Wieck, Edward A., *The American Miners Association.* New York: Russell Sage Foundation, 1944.

CHAPTER III

Alinsky, Saul, *John L. Lewis.* New York: Putnam, 1949.

Ameringer, Oscar, *If You Don't Weaken.* New York: Henry Holt, 1940.

Baratz, Morton S., *The Union and the Coal Industry.* New Haven: Yale University Press, 1955.

Bernstein, Irving, *The Lean Years.* Boston: Houghton Mifflin, 1960.

Brophy, John, *A Miner's Life.* Madison, Wisc.: University of Wisconsin, 1964.

Carlyle, Thomas, *On Heroes, Hero Worship and the Heroic in History.* Boston: Ginn, 1901.

Coleman, McAlister, *Men and Coal.* New York: Farrar & Rinehart, 1943.

Jennings, Eugene, *An Anatomy of Leadership.* New York: Harper & Row, 1964.

Mill, John Stuart, *On Liberty.*

Nation, The, March 18, 1925; April 25, 1928; March 26, 1930; August 24, 1932; November 20, 1935; March 26, 1936.

Taft, Philip, *Organized Labor in American History.* New York: Harper & Row, 1964.
United Mine Workers Convention Proceedings, 1924, 1927.
Wechsler, James, *Labor Baron.* New York: William Morrow, 1944.

CHAPTER IV

Alinsky, Saul, *John L. Lewis.* New York: Putnam, 1944.
Baratz, Morton S., *The Union and the Coal Industry.* New Haven: Yale University Press, 1955.
Bernstein, Irving, *The Turbulent Years.* Boston: Houghton Mifflin, 1970.
Coleman, McAlister, *Men and Coal.* New York: Farrar & Rinehart, 1943.
Galenson, Walter, *The CIO Challenge to the AFL.* Cambridge: Harvard University Press, 1960.
Hutchinson, John, "Captain of a Mighty Host, Notes on the Retirement of John L. Lewis." *Yale Review,* 50:42.
Levinson, E., *Labor on the March.* New York, 1938.
Nation, The, February 2, 1936; August 1, 1936.
Newsweek, February 7, 1938.
New York Times, October 5, 1952.
Sulzberger, Cyrus L., *Sit Down with John L. Lewis.* New York: Random House, 1938.
Taft, Philip, *Organized Labor in American History.* New York: Harper & Row, 1964.
United Mine Workers Convention Proceedings, 1936, 1938, 1952.
Wechsler, James, *Labor Baron.* New York: William Morrow, 1944.

CHAPTER V

Coleman, McAlister, *Men and Coal.* New York: Farrar & Rinehart, 1943.
Lane, Winthrop D., *Civil War in West Virginia.* New York: Huebsch, 1921.
Nation, The, May 8, 1937; October 5, 1921.
Newsweek, May 15, 1937.
New Republic, September 21, 1921; December 25, 1959.
Report, Senate Committee on Education and Labor, 74th Congress, No. 2046, "Violation of Free Speech and Rights of Labor."
Taft and Ross, "American Labor Violence: Its Causes, Character and Outcome, from The History of Violence in America." *The New York Times,* 1964.

CHAPTER VI

Business Week, Oct. 15, 1960; Feb. 14, 1969.
Coalfield Progress, Norton, Va., Feb. 28, 1952.
Flame Coal Co. v. United Mine Workers, 303 F. 2d 39 (6th Cir., 1962) (Federal Reports, Second Series).
Gilchrist v. United Mine Workers, 290 F. 2d 36 (6th Cir., 1961).
Meadow Creek Coal Co. v. United Mine Workers, 263 F. 2d 52 (6th Cir.).
National Labor Relations Board v. United Mine Workers, 74 Labor Relations Reference Manual 2938, U. S. Court of Appeals for the Third Circuit, 1970.
Nation, The, March 3, 1959; May 23, 1959.
New York Times, various issues throughout 1959; refer to Index.
Osborne Mining Co. v. United Mine Workers, 279 F. 2d 716 (6th Cir., 1960).
United Mine Workers, 92 NLRB 916 (1950).
Sunfire Coal Co. v. United Mine Workers, 313 F. 2d 108 (6th Cir.).
White Oak Coal Co. v. United Mine Workers, 318 F. 2d 591 (6th Cir.).

CHAPTER VII

Baratz, Morton S., *The Union and the Coal Industry.* New Haven: Yale University Press, 1955.
Caldwell and Graham, "John L. Lewis and Cyrus Eaton." *Harper's,* December, 1961.
Ramsey v. United Mine Workers, 265 F. Supp. 388 (United States District Court, Eastern District of Tennessee, 1967) (Federal Supplement Reports).
Raskin, A. H., "John L. Lewis and the United Mine Workers." *Atlantic,* May, 1967.
Tennessee Consolidated Coal Co. v. United Mine Workers, U. S. Court of Appeals for the Sixth Circuit, 1969.
United Mine Workers Journal, 1948, 1964.
U. S. News and World Report, March 1, 1957; November 9, 1959.
Wall Street Journal, October 29, 1968.

CHAPTER VIII

Blankenship v. Boyle, 77 Labor Relations Reference Manual 2140 (U. S. District Court, Dist. of Col., Apr. 28, 1971).
Charleston *Gazette,* April 7, 1969.

Congressional Record, April 14, 1969, H8869 et seq.; April 30, 1969, pp. 10860–61.

New York Times, June 16, 1971.

United Mine Workers Journal, 1946, 1947, 1948, 1949, 1950, 1951, 1960, 1961, 1971.

United Mine Workers v. United States, 177 F. 2d 29 (U.S. Ct. of App., Dist. of Col.).

United States v. United Mine Workers, 22 Labor Relations Reference Manual 2005 (U.S. Dist. Ct., Dist. of Col., Apr. 21, 1948).

Van Horn v. Lewis, 22 Labor Relations Reference Manual 2222 (U.S. Dist. Ct., Dist. of Col., June 23, 1948).

Wall Street Journal, March 15, 1963, May 2, 1963, December 26, 1968.

CHAPTER IX

Black Lung Bulletin, all issues, 1970, 1971.

Coal Age, February, 1971.

Coal Patrol (Appalachia Information, Washington, D.C.), all issues, 1970, 1971.

Congressional Record, February 8, 1971, E545 et seq.; June 11, 1971, E5760 et seq.

Health Rights News, October, 1971.

Nation, The, April 28, 1969.

New York Times, September 19, 1971.

Plaintiffs' Answers to Interrogatories, Yablonski v. Boyle, United States District Court, District of Columbia (1970–71).

United Mine Workers Journal, 1947, 1948, 1949, 1951, 1952, 1962, 1968, 1969.

Wall Street Journal, June 24, 1969, December 31, 1969, June 25, 1970.

Washington Post, June 11, 1971.

CHAPTER X

Business Week, October 15, 1960.

Congressional Record, December 1, 1969, H11529-30; March 9, 1970, H1581 et seq.; March 3, 1971, H3404.

Fortune Magazine, January, 1971.

Hodgson v. United Mine Workers, U. S. District Court, Dist. of Columbia, April 13, 1971.

Letter, Ralph Nader to Sen. Ralph Yarborough, April 26, 1969.

United Mine Workers Journal, 1969.

Wall Street Journal, Sept. 2, 10, 1964; Sept. 21, 23, 24, 1965; Feb. 2, 1966.

CHAPTER XI
Congressional Record, November 25, 1969, H11392 et seq.; January 19, 1970, H36 et seq.
Hechler, Ken, Letter, July 11, 1969, to George J. Titler.
National Observer, March 30, 1970.
New Republic, February 27, 1965.
Newsweek, December 25, 1969.
New York Times, through 1969 and 1970.
Rauh, Joseph L., Letters to Secretary of Labor George Schultz, with attachments, July 9, 18, 25, 30, 1969, August 13, 1969, December 1, 1969, January 13, 1970.
United Mine Workers Journal, 1969, 1970.
Shenandoah *Evening Herald,* June 30, 1969.
Titler, George J., Letter to Ken Hechler, June 20, 1969.

CHAPTER XII
Coal Patrol, 1970, 1971.
Congressional Record, June 2, 1971, H4574 et seq.
Miner's Voice, 1971.
New York Times, Sept. 2, 1969.
United Mine Workers Journal, 1968, 1969, 1970, 1971.

Index

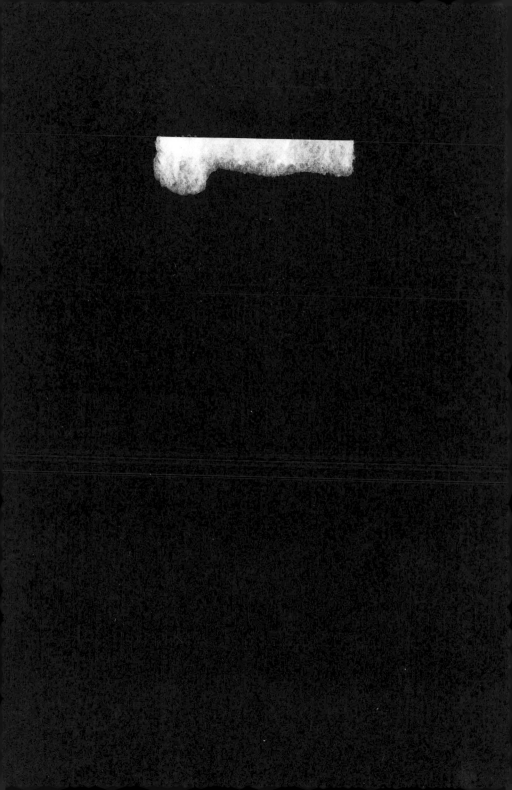